Demand the Impossible: Essays in History as Activism

DEMAND THE IMPOSSIBLE

ESSAYS IN HISTORY AS ACTIVISM

Nathan Wuertenberg & William Horne, eds.

Westphalia Press

An Imprint of the Policy Studies Organization
Washington, DC
2018

Westphalia Press
An imprint of Policy Studies Organization
1527 New Hampshire Ave., NW
Washington, D.C. 20036
info@ipsonet.org

ISBN-10: 1-63391-642-1
ISBN-13: 978-1-63391-642-5

Cover and interior design by Jeffrey Barnes
jbarnesbook.design

Daniel Gutierrez-Sandoval, Executive Director
PSO and Westphalia Press

Updated material and comments on this edition
can be found at the Westphalia Press website:
www.westphaliapress.org

CONTENTS

IV. JOBS AND THE ENVIRONMENT: MOVING BEYOND THE HERRENVOLK DEMOCRACY OF COAL

V. INSURING MENTAL HEALTH: TREATMENT AND ACCESS FOR THE MENTALLY ILL

VI. POVERTY AS POLICY: WAGELESSNESS AND AID

FOREWORD

TRANSFORM THE PROFESSION: ACTIVIST HISTORIANS AND THE AMERICAN PUBLIC

Keri Leigh Merritt
Independent Scholar

From W.E.B. DuBois and E.P. Thompson to Angela Davis and Eugene Genovese, some of history's best scholars have also been its most vocal activists. Perhaps more than academics in other fields of the humanities, historians frequently have taken the lead in active political dissent, often for leftist radical causes.

So why is this the case? Why are historians so attracted to current events, and so eager to respond to questions about the modern world? Does a deep understanding of history allow a person to better analyze the present?

The answers to these questions are quite simple. Historians are drawn to commenting on the current era because most of us are—at our cores—humanists. We studied history not simply for the love of knowledge or the love of subject, but instead because we believed (naively or not) that historical truths could, and should, help shape the future. We have realized that most human beings act in similar ways under similar circumstances, and we have been trained to realize the differences and nuances between situations. We attempt, at the most basic level, to discern the "how" and the "why" of certain events, drawing on the related fields of sociology, psychology, economics, political science, and even literature. Due to our rigorous training, we place people and actions within their proper context, and provide significant details that highlight their importance. In short, we provide a much-needed service to a nation that is currently engulfed in a political, economic, social, and even spiritual crisis. We offer to explain how we got here and what steps politically engaged people and coalitions have taken in the past to avoid catastrophe.

Whether demanding more from the Left, exploring the complicated historical relationship between African Americans and citizenship, or critiquing the racist relics of public memory, *Demand the Impossible: Essays in History as Activism* offers a fresh look at emerging issues for activist historians, and showcases the work of a newer generation of scholar-activists. A focus on coal and clean energy, an examination of the state of mental health care, and a study of America's (lack of a) social safety net all round out this provocative new volume. To be sure, these promising young historians are at the forefront of a larger movement that aims to reorient the entire profession. In short, rather than taking bold stances against prior iterations of inequality, we seek to address inequality in the present, and propose solutions for the future.

Although recently some very well-respected scholars have decried the rise of the "historian pundit," it is imperative that historians *do* continue to function as pundits. In fact, we need to continue to expand our opportunities to engage with the American people, in whatever form they are presented.

Whether we like it or not, sound bites, short-form pieces, and analogies sell. Historians cannot afford to sit idly by and allow pundits and journalists with no historical background to write them. Not only should we be writing op-eds, speaking in public and on podcasts, and reaching out and establishing personal connections to local journalists offering our expertise on stories, we should also be establishing political connections wherever possible. We need to be organizing local voter drives and attending town halls, lobbying our state and city level politicians, leading activist marches, and speaking at rallies. Finally, the most well-spoken scholars need to get out in front of the t.v. cameras and essentially become (vastly knowledgeable) talking-heads.

Perhaps more pressing than any other issue facing our profession is precisely this disconnect between scholars and the American people. Historians desperately need to figure out how to speak to the general public—the future of our profession depends upon it. Universities are facing an increasingly uncertain future, and history departments in particular are coming under fire. With the rapid increase of "adjunct" instructors and the coming demise of many smaller schools and community colleges, professional historians are necessarily going to have to adapt to the times. By better communicating with the public, we can show the value of history—and of a well-rounded higher education more generally. Still, as some of us withdraw from academe altogether, thus shifting our primary focus from educating college and graduate students to educating the public, we must keep several points in mind.

First, given the grave inequalities in education in this country, there are definite challenges in providing longer, more nuanced analyses of historical events. Many people do not receive a decent enough education to truly understand much more than basic historical explanations, and often we need to start with the assumption that the audience knows nothing.

Second, activist historians must come to terms with the fact that we live in a digital age where branding matters, particularly to the younger generations. Attention spans have undoubtedly shortened; desire to learn about our nation's past has declined. Historians are essentially left with two choices: we can complain and lament these societal changes, or we can adjust to modernity and attempt to reclaim our subject, speaking directly to the people, regardless of education level and in spite of a lack of interest.

Third, due to these potential barriers, it becomes important to "sell" our subject matter. This is often best accomplished through telling stories about people and local places, making some sort of connection to the reader. Analogy is often a useful hook, sparking people's interest and frequently leaving them wanting to learn more. Using plain language—speaking and writing simply—is key, and vibrant adjectives and adverbs are always helpful. Most importantly, we have to be able to distill very complex subjects down to two or three sentence ledes and "hooks." We must remain committed to staying in the public eye, whether it's in 140,000 words or 140 characters.

Historians *need* to be the ones on the front lines, speaking directly to the people. We should conduct ourselves as down-to-earth and easily approachable; we must do away with this Ivory Tower nonsense—we are simply everyday people who just happen to know a lot about the nation's history.

If scholars of the past fail to accomplish these objectives, not only do we slip back into obscurity, but we allow a politically-pointed media to essentially "teach" the American public, often incorrectly, and more often for propagandistic reasons—a terrifying prospect.

While this shift in our profession seems inevitable, in many ways this is a positive and needed change. Many of the problems that have plagued the

United States in the past—a horribly unequal economic system, a floundering democracy, deep inequities in education and housing, the ravages of racism, a grossly hyperactive carceral state, and even Constitutional crises —have continued to haunt us in the present.

As Martin Luther King, Jr. began planning his "Poor People's Campaign" in the late 1960s, he delineated the two Americas thesis, correctly observing that grave economic inequality led to multiple other forms of inequality. "One America is flowing with the milk of prosperity and the honey of equality," King preached. "That America is the habitat of millions of people who have food and material necessities for their bodies, culture and education for their minds, freedom and human dignity for their spirits." Yet, he continued, "each of us is painfully aware of the fact that there is another America, and that other America has a daily ugliness about it that transforms the buoyancy of hope into the fatigue of despair."

All the people who lived in that "other" America, of course, were burdened daily by "inadequate, substandard and often dilapidated housing conditions," as well as "substandard, inferior, quality-less schools." They were forced to choose between unemployment and jobs that did not pay living wages without an effective social safety net. Indeed, King correctly opined, the problem was ultimately structural: "This country has socialism for the rich, rugged individualism for the poor."[1]

Lamentably, nearly fifty years later King's speech still rings true. The notion of "two Americas" is clearly applicable today, perhaps more than ever. As persistent wealth and income inequality leads to serious inequities in other areas of life, it is incumbent upon scholars of the nation's history to explain to the American public why this is so, and how things may be changed. Indeed, the only way for academics to affect real change is precisely by taking our knowledge directly to the people, and explaining things in a way that is not only accessible, but also engaging.

It is clear that the time to act is now. With growing wealth and income inequalities, with the excesses and absurdities of the insatiable carceral system, with unwieldy and extremely expensive foreign policy, and with a federal government careening out of control, the time is now—undoubtedly and unequivocally—to become vocal dissidents. The time is now to reassess the nation's staggering wealth gap and the Thirteenth Amendment

1   Martin Luther King, Jr., speech to a union group in New York City, March 10, 1968, quoted in Eugene Robinson, "MLK's Call for Economic Justice," *Real Clear Politics*, Jan. 16, 2015."

slavery loophole. The time is now to act upon centuries of injustice, upon centuries of inequity, and upon the continuing legacies of slavery.

Indeed, we must ask ourselves: Why do we let the worst parts of our history continue to dictate the future? Historians have a solemn and morally righteous task ahead. Simply put, we must attempt to help lead the charge against the sins of the present, as they are so intricately and intimately bound to the past.

INTRODUCTION

DOING ACTIVIST HISTORY

William Horne and Nathan Wuertenberg
The George Washington University

In the months since we launched *The Activist History Review* on Inauguration Day 2017, one of the most frequent objections to our work has been that history is totally unrelated to the present. History, the story goes, is static—a predetermined set of facts that ground Americans in a common identity. Our current struggles, as depicted by pundits and politicians alike, are ahistorical—a temporary rupture with this ill-defined mass of great speeches, heated battles, and awe-inspiring innovations. The culprit in this American history-as-mythology may be our schools and textbooks which, laden with key terms and leading questions, often depict historical knowledge as complete rather than ongoing. Perhaps it is the timeline, with its deceptive beginning, middle, and end, which portrays history as linear and distant. It may even be our desire to view ourselves as unique, engaged in our own struggles wholly disconnected from those of prior generations. But whatever the cause, the mythological view of history is not only wrong; it is dangerous.

Donald Trump's campaign slogan "make America great again" epitomizes the misapplication of simplistic renderings of history. Whatever time the much-discussed phrase refers to, it misconstrues history as a greener pasture to which we can return. Nothing could be further from the truth. Prior generations experienced bitter struggles of their own. Many, like the Civil War, the Great Depression, or Jim Crow, were even more daunting than those we confront today. Moreover, not only are the issues we face produced historically—prior events, ideas, and systems of power created our world—but many are merely contemporary iterations of chronic problems faced by Americans. Expressions of exploitation rooted in race, class, and gender are hardly new. In many ways, they represent the foundation of American systems of power. This history is as complicated and messy as it is ever present. Americans are a living testament to its fruits and to the pressing need for rigorous and meaningful historical study.

The chapters of this volume serve several ends, all of which are meant to address problems generated by depictions of history-as-mythology, both within academia and more broadly outside it. First, they are intended to demonstrate the origins of contemporary public policy debates. Whether it is Kathleen Brian's analysis of the origins of the preexisting condition or Thomas Barber's inquiry into the roots of philanthropy's shortcomings, these works should help readers understand the foundations of contemporary political issues. Second, the essays are meant to show elements of historical continuity. Works like Kyla Sommers' on the longstanding racism inspiring Congressional Republicans to subvert D.C. statehood or Tom Foley's analysis of prior energy shifts reveal our chronic collective shortcomings. Identifying their persistence may help activists better articulate how we perpetuate crises through our cumulative failure to understand and address problems as ongoing. Engaging in dialogue with activists in this way represents the third purpose of this collection. The following investigations of monuments, racism, energy production, health care, poverty, and the nature of the Democratic Party draw from, and examine, issues important to contemporary dissidents. They are intended to inform activist struggles just as the ideas of engaged folk ought to drive scholarly inquiry. Finally, this body of work is meant to encourage academics to engage more fully in public discourse. While American scholars and universities have often been at the forefront of social struggles, many within the academy continue to depict this work as illegitimate. We hope this collection illustrates the utility and rigor of politically engaged scholarship and inspires others to take up the mantle, lest the profession make itself obsolete.

The collection is organized into thematic couplets. The volume opens with "Liberals, Leftists, and the Democratic Party," two analyses of the nature of the Democratic Party and its place in American politics. Where Ben Feldman sees the lack of any meaningful program of redistribution as a sign of conservative hegemony and Democratic failure, Nathan Wuertenberg views racism as the organizing principle behind Party initiatives and American politics more broadly. Wuertenberg asserts that, in Trump's victory, we see the response to the "fundamental needs of a white American national identity" ostensibly threatened by Barak Obama and Hillary Clinton. Feldman views the culprit as the corporate Democrat, expressed in Nancy Pelosi's famous remark that "We're capitalist. That's just the way it is." The two converge in the assertion, however, that the politics of the Democratic Party have failed to protect vulnerable Americans. The election of Donald

Trump, a boon to white nationalists and one percenters alike, lends credence to both critiques and makes a compelling case that activists must demand more of their political representatives.

The second couplet, "Racism and Rights: African Americans and Contested Citizenship(s)," works to unveil the complex mechanisms at play in the implementation and maintenance of racial hierarchies on both structural and individual levels. Kyla Sommers' "'Hands off DC': Race and Congressional Control of Washington, D.C." documents a long history of federal interference in the local politics of the national capital. Present-day efforts by Congressional leaders like Jason Chaffetz are rooted in that history, one that is characterized largely by the efforts of segregationist politicians to use the capital as a bulwark against the expansion of African American rights. Sarah Senette's "*Ferray vs. Pompeyo the Free Black:* Fear and Black Masculinity in the Era of the Haitian Revolution" observes similar processes at work in the trial of a black man accused of assaulting the white patron of a New Orleans tavern in 1795. For white judicial officials in colonial New Orleans, Pompeyo's alleged assault threatened the racial and gendered hierarchies that upheld their very livelihoods. As with later Congressional interferences in D.C. politics, the men prosecuting Pompeyo wielded the structural means at their disposal to quash the latest challenge to their social standing and preserve the status quo.

"Monuments and Power: Racism and Public Memory," the third section, examines the debates over monuments and public spaces that continue to provoke strong reactions from across the political spectrum. Douglas McRae's "Monuments, Urbanism, and Power in Urban Spaces: Looking at New Orleans, Louisiana from São Paulo, Brazil" explores transnational patterns of glorifying the exploitation of disadvantaged groups. David Rotenstein's "Producing and Protesting Invisibility in Silver Spring, Maryland," meanwhile, ties urban history to commemoration, observing the ways that local developers and politicians overlook the impact of white supremacy on the urban landscape. They demonstrate that Confederate monuments are part of a much larger tendency in the United States and abroad to whitewash histories of exploitation and abuse. Whether choosing to build statues of Confederates or gloss over segregation in public murals, local officials tend to erase the central role of racism in American history. Taken together, they show that altering monuments that glorify white supremacy does not destroy history, but rather preserves it.

The fourth couplet, "Jobs and the Environment: Moving Beyond the Herrenvolk Democracy of Coal," examines the intersection of the protests and movements surrounding climate change, energy production, and work. While Tom Foley examines an ongoing energy shift towards renewables, William Horne investigates the impact of mechanization facilitated by coal production in the early twentieth century. Foley and Horne argue that among the most significant pitfalls of energy transformations are the extent to which their benefits are realized unevenly. Working people, whether Horne's washerwomen of the 1930s or Foley's coal miners of the present day, find themselves all too easily discarded in favor of cheaper alternatives. Those of us advocating for clean energy policies may want to ensure that their financial benefits are spread more evenly if we hope to accelerate the shift to green technology and mitigate climate change.

"Insuring Mental Health: Treatment and Access for the Mentally Ill," the fifth section, explores the structures that prevent the adequate treatment of mental illness. Jade Shepherd examines a prior approach to mental illness in "Treating Mental Illness in Victorian Britain." She finds that although institutionalization could be difficult for patients, it provided a sense of community that many modern treatment methods lack. Kathleen Brian's "Inheriting Expulsions from the Insurance Industry" investigates early forms of the preexisting condition, created by life insurers to prevent those with mental illness from purchasing a policy. Shepherd's and Brian's essays illustrate the impact of monetized treatment on mental illness. Where deep cuts to public services undermined some of the communal aspects of treatment explored by Shepherd, the profit margins of corporations created systems that are still used to prevent those with mental illness from receiving benefits. Their work indicates that, if we hope to meaningfully improve mental health, we must encourage state and corporate actors alike to view patients as investments rather than expenses.

The final couplet, "Poverty as Policy: Wagelessness and Aid," takes a close look at the state and private charities as vehicles of social welfare. Tessa Davis's "Taxing Values: What Our Tax Code Says About Us" clarifies the logic behind the tax code and the ways policymakers use it to penalize or promote behavior. Part of what makes the tax system so complicated is also what makes it worthwhile, that "we allocate the shared responsibilities of government differently in the name of fairness." Thomas Barber examines the strings attached to charitable work in "From Moral to Political Economy: The Origins of Modern Philanthropy's Charitable Feedback Loop."

He argues that capitalism transformed charitable institutions into ways of encouraging growth rather than alleviating suffering. Davis and Barber suggest that much of our public discourse treats those receiving benefits, whether in tax relief or charitable services, as undeserving or burdensome. This view, they find, ignores the history of vulnerable groups and the public good accomplished by vigorously intervening to alleviate their suffering.

This collection of essays reveals much about us and our moment. It shows the substantive nature of the debates of the 2016 election. Rather than fading into obscurity, these issues continue to find expression from the streets of Charlottesville to the halls of Congress. They have deep historical roots and significant implications for our society—who we are and who we hope to become. Viewing them through a historical lens treats with respect those engaged in the political struggles of our day. Similarly, it illustrates the ways that we, as scholars, can use our work to contribute to ongoing debates. If we fail to contribute to these efforts, we risk convincing the public that our labor is obsolete and surrender the work of informing popular movements to those less aware of the roots of contemporary problems. Further, being unresponsive to the politics of our day validates depictions of scholars as elites who care little for the needs of working folks and marginalized communities. We can no longer restrict our work to boldly critiquing outdated forms of exploitation and inequality. The cost is simply too great.

I

LIBERALS, LEFTISTS, AND THE DEMOCRATIC PARTY

BE REALISTIC: DEMAND THE IMPOSSIBLE![1]

"We're capitalist. That's just the way it is."
— *Nancy Pelosi*

Ben Feldman
Georgetown University

On January 31, 2017, CNN hosted a Town Hall with Democratic Minority Leader Nancy Pelosi (D-CA). During the event, NYU-student Trevor Hill shifted from his prescreened question to a more substantive one.[2] Hill asked Pelosi whether she believed that the Democrats needed to embrace a left-Populism that could serve as a real alternative to the bigoted right-populism of Donald Trump and the Republican Party. Pelosi's response—which begins with the line quoted above—reveals a great deal about the limits of the Democratic imagination.

In her answer, Pelosi differentiated between the "shareholder" capitalism of the twenty-first century—the purpose of which is solely to generate wealth for investors, and the "stakeholder" capitalism that dominated the post-war boom. Referencing (it seems) an article written by Oil executive Frank Abrams in the *Harvard Business Review* in 1951, Pelosi noted, "no less a person in terms of capitalism than the chairman of the Standard Oil of New Jersey...said when we make decisions as managements and CEOs ... we take into consideration our shareholders, our management, our workers, our customers, and the community at large."[3]

Pelosi justified her position by noting the lower rates of income inequality under stakeholder capitalism. During this period, CEOs made "only" 40 times more than their employees, rather than the roughly 400:1 disparity of 2017. Herein lies the problem. Pelosi condemns the latter ratio as "an immorality," but Democrats—who have been suffering devastating electoral defeats at the local level for years before the 2016 election—cannot succeed in inspiring a generation who feel increasingly left out of American capitalism by harkening to its golden days. This rising generation of voters cannot accept a vision of a world where working people would be earning two-and-a-half cents for every dollar given to their employers, rather than a quarter for every one hundred dollars as one that is just and equitable.[4]

Real average income by percentile

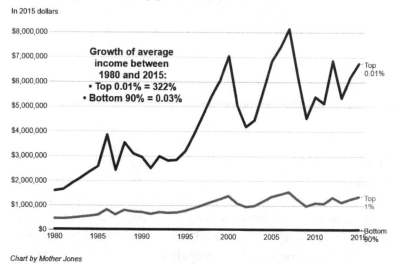

In 2015 dollars

Growth of average
income between
1980 and 2015:
• Top 0.01% = 322%
• Bottom 90% = 0.03%

Top 0.01%

Top 1%

Bottom 90%

Chart by Mother Jones

This chart from *Mother Jones* shows the extraordinary rise in income inequality over the last 35 years.[5]

Neither Pelosi nor many other politicians representing the Democratic establishment seem able to envision creating structures, or building institutions that might dramatically improve the lives of working people. They appear unwilling to address the fundamentally exploitative relationship between individuals, or between individuals and society. They reject the callousness of a Republican Party that seeks to deprive 24 million people of health care who are currently covered, but dismiss as utopian any plan to provide coverage for the *28 million people* who still do not have access under Obamacare. The vision of the corporate Democrat does not extend beyond applying bandaids to a welfare state crumbling under decades of vicious neoliberal assaults.[6]

Listening to Democrats try to craft messaging that will appeal to voters reveals this limited imagination. The mainstream of the Democratic Party is incapable of any utterance that does not sound like something you would say to try to sell a futon or whitening toothpaste. Responding to Donald Trump's claim that he would "make American great again," the Clinton campaign's insipid retort that "American is already great," was shockingly tone-deaf given the massive social and economic stratification of American society in the twenty-first century.[7] These sorts of focus-tested, banal faux-profundities—more fit for embroidering on a throw pillow than inspiring people to political action—are indicative of a Party either unwilling or incapable of accepting the degree to which they were in crisis *even before the election*. Democrats will continue to lose at the local and national levels if they cannot transcend their current politics: a bland, content-less multiculturalism that seeks to cure the ills of society by changing hearts and minds, without having to change structures and institutions.[8]

DEMOCRATIC LEGISLATIVE LOSSES UNDER OBAMA WHITE HOUSE
STATE LEGISLATIVE SEATS BY PARTY

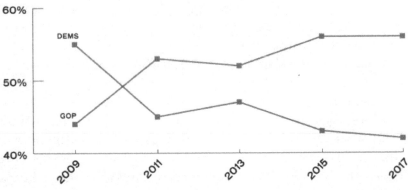

Source: National Conference of State Legislatures

This chart illustrates the extraordinary losses suffered by Democrats at the state level since Barack Obama took office in January 2009 (over 1,000 legislative seats gained by the GOP)[9]

At the time of this writing, the Democrats had just unveiled a slogan for the 2018 midterm elections: "A Better Deal: Better skills, Better jobs, Better wages."[10] While the platform itself does, in some significant ways, move toward a sort of economic populism, this catchphrase doubles down on a meritocratic vision of the economy—suggesting that wage and benefit inequalities should be addressed by skills training rather than by strengthening organized labor or massively expanding the social safety net. Additionally, it reinforces the idea that access to health care and education should be remuneration for hard work, rather than the basic rights of citizenship.[11] It is difficult to win if you allow your opponent to determine the rules, and this slogan suggests that the Democrats continue to accept the vision of the economy promoted by Republicans: that economic success is a zero-sum game, wherein individuals must acquire the skills necessary to defeat their competition, rather than finding some way to work together to the benefit of all.

The grassroots Left, and its handful of allies within the Democratic firmament, demand a bolder vision and a firmer commitment to addressing wealth and income inequality and expanding the social safety net. Rather than working to tamp down this emergent class-consciousness, the Democratic Party would do well to recall the critiques of American capitalism offered by Herbert Marcuse, Paul Baran and Paul Sweezy and other Western Marxian thinkers.[12] Their work in the early 1960s excoriated the limits of the liberal imagination during the period of post-war growth that Pelosi so fondly recalls.[13] Marcuse, Sweezy, and Baran argued that capitalism had been stabilized by providing a basic standard of living for (white) working people, and in doing so had limited the critical imagination of the industrial proletariat. Continuing segregation and a New Deal welfare state, whose benefits were given disproportionately to white men, had succeeded in dulling the nascent class-consciousness of the 1930s. This undermined the primary mobilizing force envisioned by Marx and Engles to counter a system whose foundation was one of exploitation. To Marcuse, the industrial labor force of post-war America was defined by "a pattern of *one-dimensional thought and behavior*," wherein political visions which "transcend the established universe of discourse and action are either repelled or reduced."[14] The increased material comfort available to working people, combined with a social safety net that disproportionately benefited white working men, led them to affirm a system premised on inequality. Rather than some perversion of the "stakeholder capitalism" lauded by Pelosi, today's "shareholder" capitalism is that system's logical culmination.

Baran, Sweezy, and Marcuse believed that the relatively widely distributed material growth of the post-war United States masked a sort of psychological impoverishment. To Marcuse, we were once able to envision a world outside of our own experience through artistic and cultural expression. As art has been increasingly commodified and absorbed into capitalist logic, "the oppositional, alien, and transcendent elements" in culture are destroyed. Easy access to aesthetic and sexual pleasure ultimately (to paraphrase Marcuse) "closes the universe of discourse" by robbing "man" of the ability to recognize, and thus to envision and articulate solutions to more fundamental, psychological needs. Without such articulations, dialectical logic (the basis of all philosophy and of social criticism) is impossible.

Baran and Sweezy shared Marcuse's critique of the limits of one-dimensional logic, but placed a greater emphasis on the need to connect what Baran referred to as the "psycho-struggle," with class struggle. As the foundation of capitalism is *material* (that is, that the system is at root a means of producing and distributing wealth predicated on extracting surplus value from labor and on the existence and defense of private property), a rational critique of capitalism must be a *materialist* critique. Detached from this material base, the "unhappy consciousness," of the American worker cannot "become a force against the prevailing irrationality" of the system, and the "psycho-struggle" would lead not to rational change, but to "cultural degradation" and the "aggressiveness ... [and] emptiness" characteristic of "fascist man."[15]

Baran and Sweezy argued that the natural tendency of capitalist economies was not growth, but stagnation. This was a belief they shared with many Keynesians (including Keynes himself), with one key distinction: they did not think that this trend—which would require massive investment on the part of the federal government—could be permanently forestalled or reversed under capitalism. This was not because sufficient spending was *theoretically* impossible, but rather—they argued—because the business interests in command of civilian government would never permit the necessary levels of spending on anything other than the military.[16] To many liberal economists in the 1950s and early 1960s, the assertion that the continuous growth experienced by Europe and the United States was ephemeral seemed like wishful thinking—a misguided attempt at "proving" the ultimate irrationality of the capitalist mode of production, and though the crises of the 1970s seemed to accord with predictions of secular stagnation, the boom-and bust economy of the 1980s–2000s did not. However, following the financial crisis of 2007–2008, the work of Thomas Piketty and others has led to a resurgent interest in stagnation as the natural state of developed economies, a state which was disrupted in the twentieth century by the massive destruction of inherited wealth during the First and Second World Wars.[17] Baran's prediction of the rise of "fascist man" in a politics devoid of class-content seems eerily prescient given the ascendance of Donald Trump following ten years of sluggish and inequitable recovery.

7

INCOME INEQUALITY IN THE UNITED STATES, 1910-2010

Reproduced in the *New Yorker*, this chart from Piketty's *Capital in the Twenty-First Century* illustrates that outside of the post-war decades, increasing income inequality has been the norm in the United States[18]

In analyzing the de-radicalization of the American working class, Baran, Marcuse, and Sweezy were pursuing a line of inquiry essential for any radical project: searching for revolutionary agency. Marx and Engels had seen the industrial working-class as the only potentially revolutionary force within capitalism. As Baran and Sweezy were quick to point out, this was not because of something essential to industrial labor, or to industrial laborers. Marx and Engels believed that it was the unique exploitation of the proletariat of the 1850s and 1860s—from whose labor the value that fueled capitalism's growth was extracted—that gave them their "world-historical" role.[19] Marcuse et al. suggested that, while the revolutionary potential of the (white) working class was extinguished, a fundamental transformation of society remained a possibility, and its agents could be found "underneath the conservative popular base." Those most exploited by twentieth-century Western capitalism were not white industrial workers within the imperial metropole, but African-Americans and the subjects of colonized nations in the developing world.[20] Only these groups—who existed within capitalism but "outside the democratic process"—retained the critical faculties necessary to conceive of, articulate, and fight for a rational and equitable society. Suppressing the revolutionary radicalism of these groups would drain the resources of the imperial powers. As "rot and breakdown" began to take hold in the West, a stagnant economy would lead to the increasing social (and economic) marginalization of those already on the margins.[21] The shrinking workforce would decrease opportunities for consumption and investment, and a new class-consciousness would spread up from the Third World, eventually reaching critical mass of working people within the imperial metropole.[22]

———————

While the economy of the United States in the twenty-first century is built on finance and service rather than on industrial production, a growing number of Americans have been pushed to the margins, unable to recognize the system as one that works for them. As is always this case, those on the margins are disproportionately people of color, women, and LGBTQ. Increasingly however, the economically marginalized are likely to share another demographic trait: age.

In looking back to the "youth revolt" of the 1960s, it is easy to neglect that while left politics were concentrated among the young, the young were not, by and large, active in left-politics. While those under 30 tended to be significantly to the left of their parents' generation on issues of culture (sexual expression, drug use, etc.), on many important issues associated with the Left, the youth of the 1960s were often *more* conservative.[23] Further, while many among the young Left were hostile to the cultural values of their parents, and to the racism, misogyny, and imperialism of the Cold War United States, that generation had no reason to see anything cloudy in their own financial futures.

This is not so for the young Left of today. Indeed, research undertaken by the Equality of Opportunity Project shows that the likelihood that children will earn more than their parents by age 30 has fallen from 90% to 50% over the last 50 years.[24]

As the first generation of Americans since the end of the Second World War who can expect to be *worse off* than their parents, those under the age of 35 may be the first generation since the Depression capable of joining together a cultural *and* an economic critique of capitalism, fulfilling Baran and Sweezy's vision of radical change as articulated in *Monopoly Capital*. Indeed, though faced with the grim reality of unified Republican rule under Donald Trump, and in spite of the best efforts of the Democratic Party, there are encouraging signs. Most notable is the tremendous

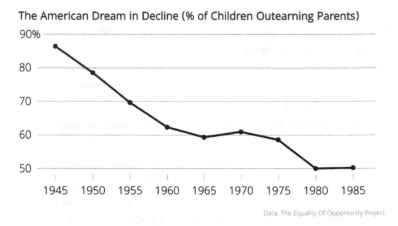

As this chart illustrates, the likelihood of out-earning one's parents has been in steady decline since Second World War.[25]

youth-support for Bernie Sanders: the Independent Vermont Senator whose "democratic socialism" was met with confusion and derision by the mainstream media and with hostility by the establishment wing of the Democratic Party. Despite low name-recognition and almost no institutional backing, the Sanders campaign received the votes of more young people than those Hillary Clinton and Donald Trump *combined*.[26]

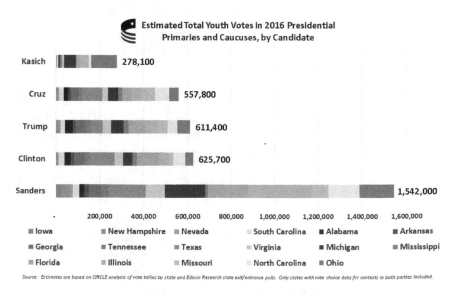

Sanders nearly tripled the total number of youth votes for Hillary Clinton.[27]

While the overwhelming majority of Sanders-supporters cast votes for Hillary Clinton in November, many did so joylessly, casting a vote *against* the vicious bigotry of Donald Trump and the Republican Party, rather than *for* the candidate who asserted that an America plagued by inequities of race, gender, and class was "already great." While we should avoid mono-causal explanations of the result of a national election, there is no question that a lack of enthusiasm for Clinton relative to that felt for Barack Obama in 2008 and 2012 played a key role in her defeat.[28] A campaign against so singularly a grotesque opponent as Donald Trump should not be close enough for external (and unpredictable) factors to swing the outcome. Most significant in skewing the results away from the Democrats has been the systematic disenfranchisement of people of color—though it can be argued that this too is the product of institutional failure on the part of the Democratic Party.[29]

Some Democrats have offered post-election critiques of Clinton's strategy—often sounding frustratingly similar to those put forward by Sanders and his supporters during the campaign. However, as the election of former Secretary of Labor (and Obama–Clinton partisan) Tom Perez over Congressman (and Sanders surrogate) Keith Ellison for Democratic National Committee Chair shows, many of the Party's power brokers have refused to learn from the mistakes of 2016.[30] Perhaps the most damning example of the ideological rigidity of the Democratic establishment was the special election for Georgia's sixth congressional district. In July 2016, now-Senate minority leader Chuck Schumer (D-NY) confidently opined that "for every blue-collar Democrat we lose in western Pennsylvania, we will pick up two moderate Republicans in the suburbs in Philadelphia, and you can repeat that in Ohio and Illinois and Wisconsin." National Democrats doubled down on this failed strategy when they spent a record sum of money on the race for Georgia-6, predicated on the belief that disgust with Trump's crass disregard for institutional norms would swing affluent suburbanites toward Democrats committed to good governance and fiscal rectitude. While there is no particular reason to believe that a bold Left-agenda would have won the votes of the "anti-Trump" Republican, there has not been any indication that adopting such an agenda would *hurt*, in large part because there has not been any evidence that a "moderate" Democrat can appeal to these communities.[31] A failure to recognize the intractability of these affluent white voters results in poor-resource allocation—trying to shift the choice of those already voting, rather than trying to mobilize those nominally on the side of the Left who are disinclined to vote (or who have been impeded from registering or casting a ballot).[32]

There is another, perhaps less obvious issue with Schumer's statement—that among too many politicos and journalists "working class" has ceased to refer to any material condition, and instead has become a signifier for rural, white, and socially conservative. Fulfilling Baran's warnings about the dangers of a politics denuded of class content, we find ourselves in a world where Kid Rock reads as authentically working class, while contingent university faculty do not. In asking college classrooms what it means to be working class, I have found that students mention race (white), religion (Christian), and music (Country). What they rarely think to mention, are wealth and income. As Gabriel Winant has written, identifying working class by these cultural signifiers or by conjuring up images of mid-century factories (one that is increasingly unrepresentative of the lives of working people in the twenty-first century), prevents the recognition of new class formations and potential political coalitions.[33]

Rather than emphasizing the shared precarity of working people across barriers of non-class identity, Democrats have helped to reinforce a false dichotomy between the interests of people of color and the interests of the white working class—a divide that has been weaponized by conservatives who seek to appeal to the cultural resentment of white voters. This is particularly true of a subset of pro-Clinton journalists and politicos who rallied behind the ahistorical belief that the universalism of social-democratic politics is *necessarily* a threat to issues of non-class identity.[34] While there are many white working men who will sacrifice their material interests at the altars of gender and racial hierarchy, the reification of this decision as something indelible or irreversible forecloses any possibility of a broad coalition of working people in the twenty-first century. Indeed, this sort of thinking has translated neutral observation—Bernie Sanders struggled to defeat Hillary Clinton among African American voters—into permanent electoral "reality"—the Left cannot appeal to Black voters. This in spite of Sanders' overwhelming favorability among African-Americans, and the fact that a left-economic agenda would have a disproportionately positive effect on people of color, who suffer the fullest brunt of capitalist exploitation.

As against the post hoc rationale that there is something fundamental to socialism to which people of color will be hostile, activists and scholars on the Black Left from W.E.B. Du Bois, to C.L.R. James, to Martin Luther

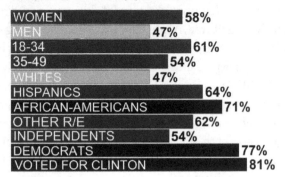

Approval ratings across demographics
Vermont Sen. Bernie Sanders (I) is the country's most popular
active politician, viewed favorably by 53% of voters.

WOMEN	58%
MEN	47%
18-34	61%
35-49	54%
WHITES	47%
HISPANICS	64%
AFRICAN-AMERICANS	71%
OTHER R/E	62%
INDEPENDENTS	54%
DEMOCRATS	77%
VOTED FOR CLINTON	81%

SOURCE: Harvard/Harris Survey
November 11-14, 2017

Media narrative to the contrary, Bernie Sanders is more popular with African-Americans and Hispanics than with Whites, and more popular among women than men.[35]

King Jr. have argued that the destruction of capitalism is the necessary (if insufficient) precondition for the eradication of other forms of systemic oppression.

Whether or not there is significant fallout from Center-Liberal intransigence remains to be seen. What is less open to debate is that, regardless of whether young Leftists organize within the Democratic Party, or outside of it (in organizations like Democratic Socialists of America), short-term success will be measured largely by the sort of pressure we are able to put on elected Democrats: a strategy that we have seen work in the early months of the Trump administration, as corporate Democrats like Cory Booker are forced to address their ties to pharmaceutical companies and for-profit schools.[36] The most viable long-term strategy almost certainly involves some combination of pressuring elected Democrats and working from the ground up to replace those Democrats who continue to resist that pressure.

During the 2016 primary, moderate liberals castigated Bernie Sanders's vision as utopian, and dismissed his theory of change—mobilizing the grassroots to demand that representatives prioritize their constituents over their corporate backers—as both unrealistic and undesirable.[37] Indeed, one of the singular moments of the 2016 Democratic Primary came in late January, when Hillary Clinton rejected pleas for universal health care by telling a crowd that those experiencing health crises cannot "wait for us to have a theoretical debate about some better idea that will never, ever come to pass." Representative of so many of the Party's failures over the past decade, Clinton seemed to be defining "the possible" in terms of what the Congress, as currently constituted, might support. Though verging dangerously close to tautology—i.e., my colleagues and I want this to pass, but it cannot pass because my colleagues and I will not vote for it—this was no doubt true of the 2015–2017 Congress, and is true of the 2017–2019 Congress as well. This is not lost on the Sanders-wing of the Party, which is why the crux of Bernie's "political revolution" is a massive activist and voter mobilization to reshape legislatures at the local and national level. Indeed, given that Republican legislatures will label even a center-right, pro-market bill like the Affordable Care Act as a sort of Bolshevism, mass mobilization seems to be *the most* pragmatic path to political change.

Since January 20, 2017, the Sanders strategy has—given the constraints of unified Republican governance—met with astounding success. Marches, rallies, and town halls have played a major role in pressuring Democrats, who, by instinct, tend to prioritize defending norms over winning power, to take a hard line against Trump nominees. Perhaps most encouragingly, Kirsten Gillibrand and other members of the Democratic caucus with presidential ambition have become increasingly vocal about the need to pivot to single payer after the fight to protect Obamacare ends.[38] Indeed in spite of the silicon-valley branding and self-defeating obsession with incentivization through tax credits, Schumer himself seems to be (slowly) moving beyond a glib dismissal of the working class vote, and toward a recognition that Democrats must stand *for* something, in addition to standing *against* Donald Trump.[39]

In addition to a defense of current modes of capital accumulation and the maintenance of existing structures of power and inherited wealth, key to understanding the failed policies and failed strategies of the Democratic Party is recognizing that they are undergirded by a failure of imagination: a closing off of the universe of discourse. One of the great successes of the Sanders campaign seems to be in having re-opened this discursive universe. Since January 2016, the number of Americans who believe the government is responsible for providing all citizens with health care has increased by 9%. Interestingly, this increase developed between January and November of 2016 and has remained steady since, suggesting that it is more of a response to the vision of the Sanders campaign, than to Republican attacks on the ACA since the election.[40]

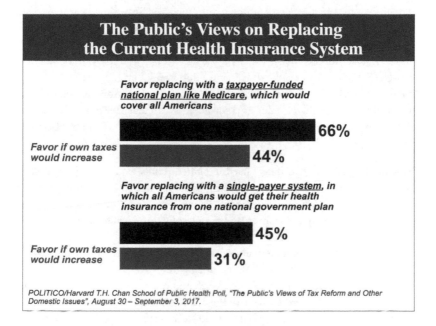

This Politico/Harvard T.H. Chan School of Public Health Poll shows that 66% of Americans prefer a government alternative to private health insurance, with a majority of those preferring a single-payer system.[41]

As Mike Konczal has written, "activism doesn't just reflect ideology. It can create it."[42] Throughout American history, change has come when liberal politicians have been dragged to the Left—sometimes willingly, sometimes not—by the direct action of a mobilized grassroots. From the abolition of slavery, to the passing of Social Security, to the legalization of same-sex marriage, major reorganizations of American political, social, and economic life often seem utopian until they become reality. If we want the sort of Party, or the sort of politics, that can both resist the Right *and* articulate a positive political vision, there is only one way forward: to demand the "impossible" until it is impossible no longer.

Notes

1   A popular slogan from the student demonstrations in Paris in May of 1968.

2   "Nancy Pelosi Town Hall." January 31, 2017. CNN. http://www.cnn.com/videos/politics/2017/02/01/nancy-pelosi-town-hall-capitalism-sot.cnn.

3   Abrams wrote that management needed to "maintain an equitable and workable balance among the claims of the various directly interested groups ... a harmonious balance among ... the stockholders, employees, customers, and the public at large." (Frank Abrams, quote in Elena Cabagnaro and George Curiel, *The Three Levels of Sustainability* (Sheffield: Greenleaf Publishing Limited, 2012). In a widely circulated 2014 article, economist Robert Reich referenced Abrams' speech, while also distinguishing shareholder and stakeholder capitalism. Robert Reich, "The Rebirth of Stakeholder Capitalism?," accessed March 23, 2017, http://robertreich. org/post/94260751620.

4   This is, of course, not to deny that the United States experienced tremendous economic growth *and* a significant compression of wealth and income between 1945 and 1973, During this period, social mobility—most noticeably for white men, but increasingly for women and people of color as well—was more easily achieved than at any other time in American history (both in spite of, and in some ways because of the fundamentally gendered and racialized construction of the New Deal Order). On this see (among others) Alice Kessler-Harris, *In Pursuit of Equity*: Women, Men, and the Quest for Economic Citizenship in 20th-Century America (Oxford: Oxford University Press, 2001) and Ira Katznelson, *Fear Itself: The New Deal and the Origins of Our Time* (New York: Liveright Publishing Corporation, A Division of W.W. Norton & Company, 2013). In pushing back against Pelosi and Schumer's vision of a race- and gender-inclusive mid-century capitalism we must not blithely dismiss the gains of the post-war welfare state. At the same time, defenders of "stakeholder capitalism" should recall that even at the height of American prosperity, nearly a quarter of all Americans lived below the poverty line, including over half of America's Black population.

5   Dave Gilson and Edwin Rios, "11 Charts That Show Income Inequality Isn't Getting Better Anytime Soon," Mother Jones, December 22, 2016, http://www. motherjones.com/politics/2016/12/america-income-inequality-wealth-net-worth-charts.

6   There has, of late, been considerable debate over the value of "neoliberal" as a term, and indeed, it has been employed as synonymous with Democrat, which, while not necessarily incorrect, has led to a dulling of the term's analytic value. Broadly considered, Neoliberalism is a philosophy based on the irrationality of individuals and the ultimate rationality of the market, which "makes decisions" based on the combined input of billions of economic actors. Each actor makes choices and the market values commodities based on these choices. Thus, the market is not only supremely rational, but is the promoter and the protector of individual agency; billions of choices made by self-interested individuals working neatly together to determine the precise value of all things. Neoliberalism is the belief that an unrestrained, unencumbered market, free from government intervention and oversight is, and always has been, the chief source of human liberty, and that the goal of government economic policy should be to create opportunity, rather than to provide

security. In pursuance of the goal of market liberalization, those operating under the neoliberal umbrella (including a number who eschew the label) follow a broad group of policies, including: destruction of artificial barriers to trade, deregulation of government, and lower taxes.

7   Due to quirks of the electoral map, the 2016 election was decided in the rust belt, leading to facile analyses that lay the blame for the Democrats' defeat *entirely* on the decline of good manufacturing jobs. While the Democrats' refusal to defend labor unions and manufacturing jobs in the Midwest may be responsible for Trump's victory over Clinton, it cannot explain gubernatorial defeats in deep-blue Maryland, or 1,000+ seats lost in state legislatures since 2008. There are a great many working people—and not just *white* working people—outside of the de-industrializing mid-west for whom America has not been "Great" in a very long time, if ever.

8   Alex Wagner, Chambers of Pain, *The Atlantic,* November 14, 2016, http://theatln. tc/2xg4xHn.

9   Reid Wilson, "Dems Hit New Low in State Legislatures," *The Hill,* November 18, 2016, http://thehill.com/homenews/campaign/306736-dems-hit-new-low-in-state-legislatures.

10 Chuck Schumer, "Chuck Schumer: A Better Deal for American Workers," New York Times, July 24, 2017, https://www.nytimes.com/2017/07/24/opinion/chuck-schumer-employment-democrats.html. That "better", is the ideal-value, rather than "sufficient," or "good", is telling.

11 Bernie Sanders frequently made the same error, saying that "no one who works 40 hours a week should be unable to afford healthcare."

12 Coined by the French philosopher Maurice Merleau-Ponty in 1955, the term "Western Marxism" gained currency following the publication of Perry Anderson, *Considerations on Western Marxism,* 1976. By Western Marxists, Anderson referred to Marxian theorists living in capitalist states to the West of the Soviet Union, who, in turning from politics to culture and aesthetics, had made fatal compromises with bourgeois theory. I argue that Anderson's taxonomization fails to consider scholars outside of Western Europe, and more importantly, the ways in which analyses of culture can inform real political praxis.

13 Herbert Marcuse, *One-Dimensional Man,* Paul Baran and Paul Sweezy, *Monopoly Capital.* On Western Marxism and its contested legacy, see (among others): Perry Anderson, *Considerations on Western Marxism* (London: Verso, 1976); Russell Jacoby, *Dialectic of Defeat: Contours of Western Marxism* (Cambridge: Cambridge University Press, 1981); and Martin Jay *Marxism & Totality: The Adventures of a Concept from Lukács to Habermas* (Berkeley: University of California Press, 1984).

14 Marcuse, 14.

15 Paul Baran to Paul Sweezy, February 3, 1957. There was of course, something problematic about the conception of "happiness" as an objective state—rather than an individually defined experience, and in his attempts to plumb the depths of cultural morass, Baran too often relied on the same moral assumptions as his capitalist interlocutors—seeing divorce, the consumption of narcotics, etc., as leading indicators of capitalism's degradations. Ben Feldman thanks Nicholas Baran for digitizing and sharing the Baran-Sweezy correspondence, a selection of which is now available form Monthly Review Press.

16 For Baran and Sweezy on stagnation, see Paul *Sweezy The Theory of Capitalist Development: Principles of Marxian Political Economy* (New York: Oxford University Press, 1942 and *Monopoly Capital*. On the neo-classical eclipse of institutional economics, see Theodore Rosenof, *Economics in the Long Run: New Deal Theorists and Their Legacies, 1933–1993* (Chapel Hill: University of North Carolina Press, 1997).

17 Thomas Piketty, *Capital in the Twenty-First Century* (Cambridge, MA: Harvard University Press, 2014).

18 John Cassidy, "Piketty's Inequality Story in Six Charts," *New Yorker,* March 26, 2014, http://www.newyorker.com/news/john-cassidy/pikettys-inequality-story-in-six-charts.

19 If one is true to Marx-as-method, rather than Marx-as-doctrine, the assumption that the working class must *necessarily* continue to be the locus of revolutionary subjectivity would be both an error of reification (one of Marx's chief critiques of Hegel) and fundamentally un-dialectic.

20 These thinkers only infrequently recognized the potential revolutionary power of women.

21 Sweezy to Baran (April 26, 1963).

22 Of course, this revolutionary wave barely reached the shores of the United States. The age of post-war growth had been presided over by Democrats (Truman, Kennedy, Johnson), and by Republicans (Eisenhower, Nixon) who were largely accepting the New Deal Order. When that order collapsed under the weight of stagnant growth, rising inflation, and high unemployment during the 1970s, the logic of market fundamentalism rushed in to fill the void. See (among others) Angus Burgin, *The Great Persuasion: Reinventing Free Markets Since the Depression* (Cambridge, MA: Harvard University Press, 2012); Kim Phillips-Fein, *Invisible Hands: The Making of the Conservative Movement from the New Deal to Reagan* (New York: W.W. Norton & Company, 2009); and Daniel T. Rodgers, *Age of Fracture.* (Cambridge, MA: Belknap Press of Harvard University Press, 2011 on the rise of the neoliberal economics since the 1970s.

23 Perhaps counter intuitively, in 22 Gallup polls on support for the War in Vietnam by Age (Under 30, 30–49, Over 49) taken between May 1965 and May 1971, *every single poll* showed support for the war *decreasing* with age. Support for the Vietnam War, Seanet, accessed March 25, 2017, https://www.seanet.com/~jimxc/Politics/Mistakes/Vietnam_support.html.

24 Lauren Gensler, "Only Half Of America's 30-Year-Olds Are Making More Than Their Parents Did," Forbes, December 9, 2016, https://www.forbes.com/sites/laurengensler/2016/12/09/american-dream-income-mobility-raj-chetty-study/#493601ef5cca.

25 Ibid.

26 Also encouraging is the significant increase in membership of America's largest socialist organization: Democratic Socialists of America (DSA). DSA has tripled in size over the past twelve months, and at just under 25,000 members, is now the nation's largest socialist party in generations.

27 "Estimated Total Youth Votes in 2016 Presidential Primaries and Caucuses, by Candidate," The Center for Information and Research on Civic Learning and Engagement, April 28, 2016, https://civicyouth.org/total-youth-votes-in-2016-primaries-and-caucuses/.

28 Trump received a lower share of the electorate (27.89%) than Romney in 2012 (28.33%). The Democrats saw their share of the electorate drop from 30.64% to 29.2%. The percentage of eligible voters who stayed home or otherwise rejected both major party candidates rose from 41.03% to 42.91% (a nearly 2-point drop since 2012, and a 4.51-point decline since 2008).

29 Ari Berman, *Give Us The Ballot: The Modern Struggle For Voting Rights in America* (New York: Farrar, Straus and Giroux, 2015). The failure to marshal opposition a powerful opposition at the state and local level has paved the way for radical assaults on the franchise by the Republican Party.

30 Glenn Greenwald, "Key Question About DNC Race: Why Did Obama White House Recruit Perez to Run Against Ellison?," *The Intercept,* February 24, 2017, https://theintercept.com/2017/02/24/key-question-about-dnc-race-why-did-white-house-recruit-perez-to-run-against-ellison/.

31 This objection that wealthy white voters will not vote for a socialist is reminiscent of critiques of Sanders' policies as politically impracticable. Given that a Republican-congress would reject *any* attempt at expanding the welfare state, there is not really a reason to prefer a "moderate" plan to a "Left" one. If either would be dead on arrival, it seems reasonable to at least take the opportunity to articulate a vision about which people can feel passionate.

32 Against protestations that the Democrats did attempt to appeal to the marginalized

and economically disenfranchised by running on "the most progressive platform ever": few voters develop an understanding of the issues by consulting alphabetized issues-lists on candidate web-sites. Campaigns run on rhetoric and emphasis as much, if not more, than on specific policy. As a study by the Wesleyan Media Project indicates, Hillary Clinton's campaign ads were disconnected from her policy proposals. "2016 Election Study Published," Wesleyan Media Project, March 6, 2017, http://mediaproject.wesleyan.edu/blog/2016-election-study-published/.

33 On new and potential working class formations beyond the industrial working class of the twentieth century, see Gabriel Winant, "The New Working Class," *Dissent*, June 27, 2017, https://www.dissentmagazine.org/online_articles/new-working-class-precarity-race-gender-democrats.

34 MSNBC's Joy Ann-Reid is particularly guilty of perpetuating this false narrative.

35 Jeremy Riddle, "One Poll Doesn't Equal 'Polls' & It Doesn't Make This Clintonite's Case Either," ExtraNewsfeed, November 28, 2017, https://extranewsfeed.com/one-poll-doesnt-equal-polls-it-doesn-t-make-this-clintonite-s-case-either-221ce96f707a. See also Jonathan Easley, "Poll: Bernie Sanders Country's Most Popular Active Politician," The Hill, April 18, 2017, http://thehill.com/homenews/campaign/329404-poll-bernie-sanders-countrys-most-popular-active-politician.

36 Herb Jackson, "Slammed by Left, Booker to Join Sanders on Drug Imports," NorthJersey.com, February 27, 2017, http://www.northjersey.com/story/news/new-jersey/2017/02/27/slammed-left-booker-join-sanders-drug-imports/98495840/.

37 Interviewed by *Vox*, former Obama speechwriter Jon Favreau wrote of Bernie's place "to build a mobilized grassroots that simply wrestles power away from those who have it," that "It's not just that Obama doesn't think that's feasible, it's that he doesn't think that's the right way to govern ..." http://www.vox.com/2016/2/11/10967374/obama-staffers-bernie-sanders also see Jonathan Chait's, "The Case Against Bernie Sanders," in *New York Magazine* http://nymag.com/daily/intelligencer/2016/01/case-against-bernie-sanders.html.

38 Suzy Khimm, "'Medicare for All' Isn't Sounding So Crazy Anymore," *New York Times*, July 15, 2017, https://www.nytimes.com/2017/07/15/opinion/sunday/medicare-for-all-isnt-sounding-so-crazy-anymore.html.

39 Chuck Schumer, "Chuck Schumer: A Better Deal for American Workers," *New York Times*, July 24, 2017, https://www.nytimes.com/2017/07/24/opinion/chuck-schumer-employment-democrats.html. While "A Better Deal" is embarrassing in presentation and insufficient in substance, it is certainly an improvement over the messaging of 2016.

40 Jocelyn Kiley, "Public Support for 'Single Payer' Health Coverage Grows, Driven

by Democrats," Pew Research Center, June 23, 2017, http://www.pewresearch.org/fact-tank/2017/06/23/public-support-for-single-payer-health-coverage-grows-driven-by-democrats/.

41 "Poll: On eve of Senate Vote, More Than Two-thirds of Republicans Want Congress to Enact an Alternative to the ACA," Harvard T.H. Chan School of Public Health, September 22, 2017, https://www.hsph.harvard.edu/news/press-releases/poll-republicans-aca-alternative/. See also Jocelyn Kiley, "Public Support for 'Single Payer' Health Coverage Grows, Driven by Democrats," Pew Research Center, June 23, 2017, http://www.pewresearch.org/fact-tank/2017/06/23/public-support-for-single-payer-health-coverage-grows-driven-by-democrats/.

42 Mike Konczal, "Who's Truly Rebuilding the Democratic Party? The Activists," August 9, 2017, https://www.vox.com/the-big-idea/2017/8/9/16115616/activism-democratic-party-health-care-free-college.

THIS REALLY IS YOUR AMERICA

Nathan Wuertenberg
The George Washington University

From the announcement of his candidacy in 2015 to his victory on election night a year later, many (particularly white liberals) viewed Donald Trump's ascent to the presidency with a sense of steadily growing disbelief. His infamous announcement speech on June 16, 2015 set the tone for the next eighteen months of his campaign, one plagued by revelations of sexual assault, racial discrimination, and the retweeting of white supremacist propaganda and conspiracy theories.[1] Only a month into that campaign, the *Huffington Post* dismissed Trump as a "sideshow," one that deserved to be covered in the Entertainment section rather than Politics.[2] *HuffPo* finally retracted its statement five months later, when Trump promised a "total and complete shutdown of Muslims entering the United States," declaring that it was "no longer entertained."[3] Two months after that, the outlet announced Trump's victory in the New Hampshire primary with the headline "A Racist, Sexist Demagogue Just Won the New Hampshire Primary," marveling in the subheading that "Donald Trump seriously did it."[4] By the time the votes were counted in November, *HuffPo* had become one of the loudest of many voices insisting that Trump's America was not their America.[5] I wish that were true. I also wish I had a million dollars.

If the exit polling is to be believed, by far the most reliable indicators of support for Trump were race, gender, and religious background.[6] Trump won white voters, men, and evangelical Protestants by double digits. Countless authors have written about the appeal of Trump's campaign to "Make America Great Again" among these groups.[7] They tie his success to a conviction within the white working class that the status of white Americans in the United States and, by extension, that of the United States in the world at large, is threatened by the gains made by other groups. Women, people of color, and immigrant communities over the past fifty years each appear to have experienced advances in equality and opportunity (advances symbolized by the election of the nation's first black president and nomination of the first female candidate by a major party). The root of the conviction that those advances represent a threat to white success, as the narrative goes, is the very real economic impact felt by the white working class, and especially white working class men, as the United States began to shift away from an industrialized economy in the late twentieth century. But, according to Nate Silver on *FiveThirtyEight*, the median household income of a Trump voter was $72,000, well above the national median of $56,000 and the $61,000 median for Clinton supporters.[8] On top of that, as the *New Republic* pointed out only a week after the election, the white working class was by no means the only white voting demographic to swing heavily for Trump.[9] In fact, as *Vice* noted shortly after the election as well, Trump won nearly every conceivable demographic of white voters, from white women to white college graduates.[10] By targeting those voters in swing districts in key states like Wisconsin, Michigan, and Pennsylvania with laser-like precision, Trump was able to patch together an electoral victory despite a record loss in the popular vote.[11]

Trump's electoral success sent many white liberals into a tailspin of anger and despair. Don't get me wrong. I'm angry too and I share your despair. But I'm also not surprised. Most of the pieces examining the roots of Trump's victory tend to focus on the last fifty years of American politics and social relations. These were years when the Republican Party came increasingly to rely on appeals to the racial fears of white conservative voters for electoral victories.[12] They were also years when the communities targeted by Trump achieved a series of halting and gradual advances in the direction of social progress. But if we look at Trump within the broader scope of American history, he's more the norm than the exception. He might be the first president to offer ill-informed, stream of consciousness policy "ideas" on Twitter every ninety minutes. But, he's not the first president to be accused of sexual assault.[13] He is not the first president to lash out against immigrant communities.[14] And he is certainly not the first president to rub elbows with white supremacists.[15] Like Trump, his predecessors in the Oval Office were not operating in a vacuum. They were behaving in ways that were not only tolerated but encouraged by their society at large. They rose to prominence in a nation that taught them that the key to American success was the exercise of political, social, and economic power by white, Protestant men, men like them, an exercise in the exclusion of groups without that power. It was a lesson that began before their nation existed and continues into the present, not as an outlier or undercurrent but as the very fabric of American national identity and power relations in the United States.

The roots of American identity can be found in that of Europeans in early colonial America, which was triangulated in terms of race, class, and gender.[16] By cementing their appropriation of capital, land, and labor through legislative acts and social rituals that placed white identity firmly at the top of the political, social, and economic hierarchies, elite colonial men were able to establish a racial coalition between themselves and white lower-class men.[17] This relationship enabled them to maintain their authority and gave white lower class men a stake in colonial power relations without allowing them to fully share in it.[18] This positioned white colonial men in opposition to women, enslaved Africans, and First Nations peoples, groups whose very existence threatened to upend the colonial power structures that benefited white men. These groups, in the eyes of those white men, needed to be feared, hated, and controlled for those power structures to remain in force. This system of racial and gendered exploitation provided white men with the motivation and justification to continue perpetrating acts of enslavement, imperial expansion, and sexual violence, acts that provided a series of self-replicating economic and social benefits.[19]

This pattern of exploitation continued right up to the point of the colonies' split from the British Empire. Indeed, a number of historians argue that racial fears of slave uprisings and attacks by native groups that developed during the colonial period were primary causes of the rebellion, fears that were specifically named in the Declaration of Independence as motivating factors.[20] Fueled by these fears, the American War for Independence became the jumping off point for a long future of native genocide and slavery that served as the genesis of U.S. imperialism. Conflict with British-allied native communities convinced rebel leaders to pour an increasing amount of resources into borderlands campaigns over the course of the war, in the process hastening the creation of bureaucratic state apparatuses in the West designed specifically to effect the destruction of native peoples. Perhaps most notably, delegates to the Continental Congress ordered an invasion of Haudenosaunee (Iroquois) lands in western New York in the summer of 1779, diverting precious men and resources away from the eastern campaigns under Commander-in-Chief George Washington in order to retaliate against particularly effective raids by British-allied Senecas. The campaign opened with a toast of "civilization or death to all savages," a presentiment Continental troops did their utmost to fulfill over the course of the invasion.[21] Their commander, General John Sullivan, was under strict orders from General Washington to bring about the "total destruction and devastation of [the Haudenosaunees'] settlements by "ruin[ing] their crops now in the ground and prevent[ing] their planting more."[22] It was, in essence, a total war, one intended to erase any evidence of native presence from the very earth itself with the cleansing power of fire. Thousands of indigenous refugees were forced to flee in the face of such attacks to the British fort at Niagara in search of food and shelter. Meanwhile Congressional leaders reveled in their victory, certain that their indigenous opponents had been reduced to nothing more than, in the words of one delegate, "Flees."[23] Claiming the status of conquerors, they demanded punitive land cessions from the Haudenosaunees in return for peace, cessions that opened the way to territories even further west and laid the foundation for the creation of transportation and trade infrastructures between the Atlantic Ocean and Great Lakes like the Erie Canal that ensured the United States' future success and continued expansion.[24] That success and the expansion that fueled it were rooted in acts of violence like the invasion against the Haudenosaunee, something that our founders not only perceived but encouraged. Indeed, they bet their nation on it.

The Sullivan Expedition was neither the first nor the last such campaign during the war, and such conflicts convinced many white Americans that native peoples had no place in the nation being built at their expense. This conviction fed into a growing conception of the United States as an exclusively white nation, one where opportunities would abound, but only for those that fit socially accepted and politically enforced definitions of belonging. This conception was likewise fed by the endemic presence of slavery, an institution that was central not only to the newly founded nation, but to the war that achieved its independence. Indeed, the perceived threat to the institution posed by Lord Dunmore's Proclamation in 1775 offering freedom to any slave of rebel masters that escaped to serve in the British military motivated many southern colonists to support independence. For most (if not all) rebel slaveholders, the defense of slavery against emancipatory overtures was the very reason their new nation was being formed. It is little surprise, then, that when independence was won, American slaveholders refused to participate in any political system that did not guarantee protections for the institution that defined every aspect of their lives. When some at the Constitutional Convention in 1787 suggested that the new federal government should have the power to regulate the slave trade, for example, John Rutledge of South Carolina declared that the Southern states would "not be parties to this union" and threatened to leave, a tactic repeated by other slaveholding delegates throughout the Convention and ultimately one that worked.[25] The document that emerged from the Constitutional Convention and was sent to the states for ratification contained numerous clauses protecting the institution of slavery and ensconcing the power of slaveholders. The Southern states would not have accepted the Constitution if it had been otherwise, and the United States would not have remained united without them. So, the U.S. was not just a collection of states, some slave states and some free. It was a nation that existed specifically because it protected slavery. It was a slave nation, built on notions of white racial superiority.

In the postwar period, the same elite white men whose fear had inspired the rebellion began to redefine themselves and newly define their nation. They worked to maintain the political, economic, and social benefits they enjoyed under the British Empire and bring together a group of (if the Constitutional debates were any indication) less than united states.[26] Perhaps more fueled by racial fears than ever before, they came more and more to embrace the notion that their new nation was one destined to preserve and defend the social hierarchies that had enabled their rise to power in the first place.[27] Several movements challenged elite white power in the decades that followed American independence and threatened to undermine the power relations enshrined by our nation's founders. Perhaps the most notable were the frequently overlapping anti-slavery and suffrage movements. Fueled by the idea that all were created equal, abolitionists and suffragists fought (sometimes together, sometimes apart) to roll back the growth of slavery and enfranchise women.[28] Their relationship was fraught with the power dynamics of the society they sought to reform. In fact, the suffrage movement was largely born from the frustrations of abolitionist women confronting the efforts of abolitionist men to limit their influence in the movement.[29] Even in moments when their interests did align, it was often to reify existing white gender norms. Abolitionists' charity work in Northern free black communities in particular was built on the precept that the key to black liberation was the elevation of black men over black women.[30] This indication of white anti-slavery activists' desire to assimilate free black communities under white cultural norms boded poorly for their commitment to black liberation after slavery. Indeed, abolitionists abandoned their commitments to black enfranchisement in the post-Civil War period in favor of reuniting white Americans in the North and South along the lines of race, a decision that allowed white capitalists throughout the nation to enrich themselves through the greater exploitation of former slaves.[31] A few decades later, white suffragists agreed to preclude black women from the vote in order to push through the Nineteenth Amendment.[32]

As with abolitionists and suffragists, other challenges to the authority of elite white men almost without fail were gradually undermined, fractured, and absorbed into the white American mainstream. Southern evangelicals that had once preached for the equality of all human beings in the eyes of God found that they gained more congregants by preaching against the spiritual liberation of slaves and women than for it.[33] Middle class voters that had fought in the early nineteenth century to gradually expand the electorate beyond wealthy elites eventually united with elites in their shared celebration of wealth and white racial identity.[34] Even recent European immigrant groups eventually came to benefit from this process, deliberately adopting white American cultural habits in order to become more ethnically palatable to native-born white Americans and benefit from the privileges of the social hierarchies that greeted them nationwide upon their arrival.

The result of the mainstream's success in assimilating these forces was the construction and growth of an aggressive American nationalism built along the lines of race, class, and gender to directly benefit rich, white men. Those benefits came at the expense of women, people of color, the lower classes, and the citizens of foreign nations. They bore the brunt of conflicts fought for "national glory" like the Spanish–American War and resultant Philippine–American War, military actions that combined left hundreds of thousands dead (the majority poor and not American). Millionaire publishers like Joseph Pulitzer and William Randolph Hearst promoted those wars to sell papers, while investors like Henry Cabot Lodge eager to eliminate Spanish restrictions on transoceanic trade pushed them through Congress.[35] Those groups also became the backbone of industrialized economic growth, which was celebrated as the key to the United States' global dominance. To feed starving families, they learned to live with the constant danger of hazardous working conditions imposed by rich employers looking to cut costs (conditions mirrored in the factories that rely upon immigrant labor today).[36] When they fought to improve those working conditions, they were brutally attacked and then replaced, actions actively supported or even perpetrated by the federal government.[37]

The unrest surrounding the Vietnam War in the twentieth century is a prime example of this process at work. Waged to expand US military power overseas at the expense of the Soviet Union's access to valuable natural resources in the Cold War arms race, the war was fought primarily by draftees selected under a system that offered deferments for those attending college or in essential civilian occupations. Because elite white men constructed American society to deliberately limit access to such opportunities to individuals like themselves, the burden of fighting the war fell disproportionately on poor men of color. Over three quarters of draftees were from lower middle class or working class backgrounds, and the state hit hardest by war casualties, West Virginia, was also one of the poorest.[38] Because military promotion structures favored college education and (despite military desegregation) featured rampant racial discrimination, the number of black soldiers placed into high-risk combat environments reserved for enlisted men was disproportionately high. In 1965, almost a quarter of the war's casualties were African American men.[39] Resistance at home to this state of affairs was met with overwhelming violence, as with the Jackson State killings in 1970, when police fired on a group of African American students protesting the war. Despite the event's equal gravity to the Kent State shootings the same year, it was largely ignored in favor of the latter shooting, which targeted middle class white students. Even more telling is the treatment of the Reverend Dr. Martin Luther King, Jr., who announced his opposition to the war in 1967 on the grounds of its disproportionate targeting of young black men.[40] President Lyndon Johnson (long a champion of black civil rights) responded with the question "what is that goddamned nigger preacher trying to do to me," an indication of the ease with which white allies could fall back on the racial power structures that favored their success when it became convenient.[41]

The events mentioned above were not the only times the U.S. government deliberately entangled itself in the strands of power at home and abroad. Many of America's most revered presidents won election specifically because of their commitment to white supremacy and its expansion. Thomas Jefferson and Andrew Jackson both rode to the White House on the coattails of voters informed by notions of white racial supremacy, and repaid that success by actively encouraging the expansion of slavery through wars of aggression against First Nations peoples.[42] Later, Woodrow Wilson sought to limit the increasingly effective activism of women and African Americans while deliberately stoking the flames of anti-immigrant sentiment, all in the name of protecting U.S. national security during an overseas war.[43] But, that's not all these three men have in common. They also happen to be the three presidents to which Donald Trump and his advisors have compared his electoral victory and administration.[44] That is not a co-incidence.

So why did Donald Trump win? It has at least something to do with the explanations offered by others before me. But, it also goes much deeper. His appeals to "Make America Great Again," his attacks against people of color and women, and his flirtations with white supremacy all tap into the fundamental needs of a white American national identity that has from Day 1 been taught to feel threatened by the rise of individuals like Barack Obama and Hillary Clinton. Donald Trump won the election because he won the white vote, and he won the white vote because he promised to maintain white power. Ignoring that fact and its historical origins does little to solve the problem. Being surprised enough by Trump's victory to declare that Trump's America is not your America does not prevent the return of overt white supremacy to American politics. Continuing to refuse to fully acknowledge the fundamental connection between Trump's message and the broader historical experience of the United States allows that message to continue to have power in American politics and society.

In the past fifty years, the United States has begun a slow and torturous movement in the direction of progress. In 1954, the landmark Supreme Court case *Brown v. Board of Education* allowed civil rights activists to chip away at Jim Crow laws in the South and begin the process of desegregation in public schools. In 1978, the Nixon Administration instituted the Philadelphia Plan, more commonly known as affirmative action, providing for more equitable hiring practices in the public sector. In 1969, Congress passed the American Indian Religious Freedom Act, protecting native rights to free worship and access to sacred objects and sites. But, at least some white liberals seem content to follow in the footsteps of their abolitionist and suffragist forebears. They pat themselves on the back for supporting minor advancements, declare themselves colorblind, and go home to ignore the issues that continue to face the allies they have abandoned.[45] Public schools have become increasingly segregated in the twenty-first century following anti-desegregation protests and white flight in the twentieth.[46] White women are affirmative action's largest beneficiaries and most vocal opponents.[47] Rock climbers continue to traipse about sacred indigenous sites like Devil's Tower during times of worship, despite court advisories to the contrary.[48]

Online, white Americans hashtag "notallwhitepeople" in response to activism, criticize protests by African Americans against a national anthem that objects to the freeing of slaves by British troops in the War of 1812, and accuse peaceful demonstrators of inciting riots.[49] These actions serve to salve a wounded sense of white racial security that is bolstered by an unquestioned pride in their nation and its place in the world. That white fragility enables the restriction of social progress, as it always has, and it has consequences for those that it does not protect. Now, with a growing number of white Americans embracing the form, if not the substance, of multiculturalism, they have begun to fear that a Trump presidency means experiencing for the first time the terror that those outside of their group have felt every moment for their entire lives. Fueled by that fear, they frantically Googled the term "white nationalism" after Trump's victory.[50] The reality is that they knew what it was their entire lives, just by another name. White nationalism is American nationalism rebranded. Until they realize that, their America will continue to be Trump's America.

Notes

1 TIME Staff, "Donald Trump's Presidential Announcement Speech," *Time*, June 16, 2015, Politics, http://time.com/3923128/donald-trump-announcement-speech/; The Cut, "Here Are All of the Accusations Women Have Made Against Donald Trump," *The Cut*, October 27, 2016, https://www.thecut.com/2016/10/all-the-women-accusing-trump-of-rape-sexual-assault.html; Jonathan Mahler and Steve Eder, "'No Vacancies' for Blacks: How Donald Trump Got His Start, and Was First Accused of Bias," *The New York Times*, August 27, 2016, Politics, https://www.nytimes.com/2016/08/28/us/politics/donald-trump-housing-race.html; Ben Kharakh and Dan Primack, "Donald Trump's Social Media Ties to White Supremacists," *Fortune*, March 22, 2016, http://fortune.com/donald-trump-white-supremacist-genocide/.

2 Ryan Grim and Danny Shea, "A Note About Our Coverage Of Donald Trump's 'Campaign,'" *The Huffington Post*, July 17, 2015, http://www.huffingtonpost.com/entry/a-note-about-our-coverage-of-donald-trumps-campaign_us_55a8fc9ce4b0896514d0fd66.

3 Jenna Johnson, "Trump Calls for 'Total and Complete Shutdown of Muslims Entering the United States,'" *The Washington Post*, December 7, 2015, https://www.washingtonpost.com/news/post-politics/wp/2015/12/07/donald-trump-calls-for-total-and-complete-shutdown-of-muslims-entering-the-united-states/?utm_

term=.45ace3f72c0b; Arianna Huffington, "A Note on Trump: We Are No Longer Entertained," *The Huffington Post*, December 7, 2015, The Blog, http://www. huffingtonpost.com/arianna-huffington/a-note-on-trump_b_8744476.html.

4   Ryan Grim and Igor Bobic, "A Racist, Sexist Demagogue Just Won The New Hampshire Primary," *The Huffington Post*, February 9, 2016, http://www.huffingtonpost. com/entry/donald-trump-new-hampshire_us_56b8fcc5e4b04f9b57dab13b.

5   The Wild Word Magazine, "Why Trump's America Is Not My Country Anymore," *The Huffington Post*, November 19, 2016, http://www.huffingtonpost.com/entry/why-trumps-america-is-not-my-country-anymore_us_582d7bfee4b0d28e55214abf.

6   *The Washington Post*, "2016 Election Exit Polls: How the Vote Has Shifted," *The Washington Post*, November 29, 2016, https://www.washingtonpost.com/graphics/politics/2016-election/exit-polls/.

7   George Packer, "Trump and American Despair," *The New Yorker*, June 18, 2017, http://www.newyorker.com/magazine/2016/05/16/how-donald-trump-appeals-to-the-white-working-class.

8   Nate Silver, "The Mythology Of Trump's 'Working Class' Support," FiveThirtyEight, May 3, 2016, https://fivethirtyeight.com/features/the-mythology-of-trumps-working-class-support/.

9   Eric Sasson, "Blame Trump's Victory on College-Educated Whites, Not the Working Class," *The New Republic*, November 15, 2016, https://newrepublic.com/article/138754/blame-trumps-victory-college-educated-whites-not-working-class.

10 Emma Fidel, "White People Voted to Elect Donald Trump," *Vice News*, November 9, 2016, https://news.vice.com/story/white-people-voted-to-elect-donald-trump.

11 Nate Cohn, "Why Trump Won: Working-Class Whites," *The New York Times*, November 9, 2016, https://www.nytimes.com/2016/11/10/upshot/why-trump-won-working-class-whites.html; Steven Bertoni, "Exclusive Interview: How Jared Kushner Won Trump The White House," *Forbes*, November 23, 2016, https://www. forbes.com/sites/stevenbertoni/2016/11/22/exclusive-interview-how-jared-kushner-won-trump-the-white-house/#1face1833af6; Nick Wing, "Final Popular Vote Total Shows Clinton Won Almost 3 Million More Ballots Than Trump," *The Huffington Post*, December 22, 2016, http://ww.huffingtonpost.com/entry/hillary-clinton-popular-vote_us_58599647e4b0eb58648446c6.

12 Jeet Heer, "How the Southern Strategy Made Donald Trump Possible," *The New Republic*, February 18, 2016, https://newrepublic.com/article/130039/southern-strategy-made-donald-trump-possible.

13 Thomas Jefferson's Monticello, "Thomas Jefferson and Sally Hemings: A Brief Account," Thomas Jefferson's Monticello, accessed July 25, 2017, https://www.

monticello.org/site/plantation-and-slavery/thomas-jefferson-and-sally-hemings-brief-account.

14 Steven Jones, "From Millard Fillmore to Donald Trump: Nativism and the GO," *The Greanville Post*, June 19, 2015, http://www.greanvillepost.com/2015/06/19/from-millard-fillmore-to-donald-trump-nativism-and-the-gop/.

15 "D.W. Griffith's *The Birth of a Nation* (1915)," PBS, accessed July 25, 2017, http://www.pbs.org/wnet/jimcrow/stories_events_birth.html.

16 See Kathleen M. Brown, *Good Wives, Nasty Wenches, and Anxious Patriarchs: Gender, Race, and Power in Colonial Virginia* (Chapel Hill: Published for the Institute of Early American History and Culture by the University of North Carolina Press, 1996).

17 See Rhys Isaac, *The Transformation of Virginia, 1740–1790* (Chapel Hill: University of North Carolina Press, 1983).

18 The idea that constructions of race fueled the creation of a coalition of white colonists and propped up elite power in colonial society (and underpinned later racial notions of freedom and political engagement in the United States) was suggested by Edmund Morgan in his 1975 book *American Slavery, American Freedom*. Morgan's volume, though flawed in terms of the author's arguments regarding the shift from indentured to enslaved labor in colonial Virginia, remains of some theoretical value in respect to the specific relation between race and politics in early America that it proposes. See Edmund S. Morgan, *American Slavery, American Freedom: The Ordeal of Colonial Virginia* (New York: Norton, 1975).

19 Robin Blackburn argues that the rise of colonial slavery is key to understanding the later rise of global capitalism and that the latter existed as a result of the former. See Robin Blackburn, *The Making of New World Slavery: From the Baroque to the Modern, 1492–1800* (London: Verso, 1997).

20 Historians point in particular to the white colonial reaction to British ministerial actions like the Royal Proclamation Line of 1763, which limited colonial expansion to the Appalachian Mountains to maintain peace with indigenous communities, and Dunmore's Proclamation of 1775, which offered freedom to the slaves of any white rebel colonist that joined the British military. Many white colonists viewed these actions as part of a larger plot by the British ministry to limit their perceived "rights" by aligning with their longtime social enemies. See Woody Holton, *Forced Founders: Indians, Debtors, Slaves, and the Making of the American Revolution in Virginia* (Chapel Hill: Published for the Omohundro Institute of Early American History and Culture, Williamsburg, Virginia, by the University of North Carolina Press, 1999); and Robert G. Parkinson, "Did a Fear of Slave Revolts Drive American Independence?" *The New York Times*, July 4, 2016, https://www.nytimes.com/2016/07/04/opinion/did-a-fear-of-slave-revolts-drive-american-independence.html?_r=0.

21 Frederick Cook and George S. Conover. *Journals of the Military Expedition of Major General John Sullivan against the Six Nations of Indians in 1779; with Records of Centennial Celebrations;* Prepared Pursuant to Chapter 361, Laws of the State of New York, of 1885. (Auburn, NY: Knapp, Peck & Thomson, Printers, 1887), Lieutenant Thomas Blake, 39.

22 George Washington to John Sullivan, May 31, 1779, accessed July 25, 2017, https://founders.archives.gov/documents/Washington/03-20-02-0661.

23 "Henry Marchant to Horatio Gates, August 24, 1779" in Paul H. Smith et al., eds. Letters of Delegates to Congress, 1774–1789. 25 volumes, Washington, D.C.: Library of Congress, 1976–2000). cited from HTML version at http://memory.loc.gov/ammem/amlaw/lwdglink.html.

24 See Alan Taylor, *William Cooper's Town: Power and Persuasion on the Frontier of the Early American Republic* (New York: Vingate Books, 1996).

25 "The Constitution and Slavery," The Gilder Lehrman Institute of American History,March 3, 2014, accessed July 25, 2017, https://www.gilderlehrman.org/history-by-era/creating-new-government/resources/constitution-and-slavery. See also David Waldstreicher, Slavery's Constitution: From Revolution to Ratification (New York: Hill and Wang, 2010).

26 For an overview of this process, see John M. Murrin, "Anglicizing an American Colony: The Transformation of Provincial Massachusetts" (PhD diss., Yale University, 1966). and T. H. Breen, *The Marketplace of Revolution: How Consumer Politics Shaped American Independence* (New York: Oxford University Press, 2004).

27 See David J. Silverman, "Racial Walls: Race and the Emergence of American White Nationalism," in Ignacio Gallup-Diaz, Andrew Shankman, and David J. Silverman, eds. *Anglicizing America: Empire, Revolution, Republic* (Philadelphia: University of Pennsylvania Press, 2015), 181–204.

28 See Daniel Walker Howe, *What Hath God Wrought: The Transformation of America, 1815–1848* (New York: Oxford University Press, 2007).

29 See Bruce Dorsey, *Reforming Men and Women: Gender in the Antebellum City* (Ithaca, NY: Cornell University Press, 2006).

30 See Dorsey, cited above.

31 See David W. Blight, *Race and Reunion: The Civil War in American Memory* (Cambridge, MA: Belknap Press of Harvard University Press, 2001).

32 See Louise Michele Newman, *White Women's Rights: The Racial Origins of Feminism in the United States* (New York: Oxford University Press, 1999).

33 See See Patricia U. Bonomi, *Under the Cope of Heaven: Religion, Society, and Politics in Colonial America* (New York: Oxford University Press, 1986); and Christine Leigh Heyrman, *Southern Cross: The Beginnings of the Bible Belt* (Chapel Hill: University of North Carolina Press, 1997).

34 See Sean Wilentz, *The Rise of American Democracy: Jefferson to Lincoln* (New York: Norton, 2005); and Howe, cited above.

35 See H. W. Brands, *American Colossus: The Triumph of Capitalism, 1865–1900* (New York, NY: Doubleday, 2010).

36 See Glenn Porter, *The Rise of Big Business, 1860–1920* (Hoboken, NJ: Wiley-Blackwell, 2014); and Eric Schlosser, *Fast Food Nation: The Dark Side of the All-American Meal* (Boston: Houghton Mifflin, 2001).

37 See David Ray Papke, *The Pullman Case: The Clash of Labor and Capital in Industrial America* (Lawrence: University Press of Kansas, 1999).

38 Jeffrey M. Leatherwood, "Vietnam War," *West Virginia Encyclopedia*, November 5, 2010, https://www.wvencyclopedia.org/articles/869.

39 James T. Patterson, *Grand Expectations: Postwar America, 1945–1974* (New York: Oxford University Press, 1995), 617.

40 Harvard Sitkoff. *Toward Freedom Land: The Long Struggle for Racial Equality in America* (University Press of Kentucky, 2010), 207.

41 See Sitkoff, cited above.

42 See Anthony F. C. Wallace, *Jefferson and the Indians: The Tragic Fate of the First Americans* (Cambridge, MA: Belknap Press of Harvard University Press, 1999); and Anthony F. C. Wallace and Eric Foner, *The Long, Bitter Trail: Andrew Jackson and the Indians* (New York: Hill and Wang, 1993).

43 See Katherine H. Adams and Michael L. Keene, *Alice Paul and the American Suffrage Campaign* (Urbana: University of Illinois Press, 2008).; Eric Steven Yellin, *Racism in the Nation's Service: Government Workers and the Color Line in Woodrow Wilson's America* (Chapel Hill: The University of North Carolina Press, 2013); and Arnold Krammer, *Undue Process: The Untold Story of America's German Alien Internees* (London: Rowman & Littlefield, 1997).

44 Will Drabold, "Trump Gave His Inauguration the Same Name That Woodrow Wilson Gave the Kickoff of the WWI Draft," *Mic*, January 24, 2017, https://mic.com/articles/166543/donald-trump-day-patriotic-devotion-draft-world-war-wilson-inauguration#.RPAcdpTWT; Hamilton Nolan, "A Full Transcript Of Donald Trump's Black History Month Remarks," *The Concourse*, February 1, 2017, Transcripts, http://theconcourse.deadspin.com/a-full-transcript-of-donald-

trumps-black-history-month-1791871370; Aaron Blake, "Reagan? Lincoln? Donald Trump Instead Embraces a Democratic Presidential Icon, Andrew Jackson," *The Washington Post*, January 21, 2017, The Fix, https://www.washingtonpost.com/news/the-fix/wp/2017/01/21/donald-trump-embraces-a-democratic-presidential-icon-and-the-controversy-that-comes-with-him/?utm_term=.82f81680eb09.

45 See Tim J. Wise, *Colorblind: The Rise of Post-Racial Politics and the Retreat from Racial Equity* (San Francisco, CA: City Lights Books, 2010).

46 Aris Folley and Brian Latimer, "Public Schools Becoming More Racially Segregated: Report," *NBCNews.com*, May 18, 2016, News–Latino, http://www.nbcnews.com/news/latino/public-schools-becoming-more-racially-segregated-report-n576121.

47 Victoria M. Massie, "White Women Benefit Most from Affirmative Action—and Are among Its Fiercest Opponents," *Vox*, May 25, 2016, https://www.vox.com/2016/5/25/11682950/fisher-supreme-court-white-women-affirmative-action.

48 Jason Blevins, "Tower Climber Plays Devil's Advocate," *The Denver Post*, May 7, 2016, News, http://www.denverpost.com/2008/07/31/tower-climber-plays-devils-advocate/.

49 Kat Blaque, "The Danger of Claiming 'Not All Men/White People/Privileged People' Are to Blame," Everyday Feminism, October 19, 2015, http://everydayfeminism.com/2015/10/notallcishets-internal-biases/; Christine Hauser, "Ruth Bader Ginsburg Calls Colin Kaepernick's National Anthem Protest 'Dumb,'" *The New York Times*, October 11, 2016, https://www.nytimes.com/2016/10/12/us/ruth-bader-ginsburg-calls-colin-kaepernicks-national-anthem-protest-dumb.html; A.J. Willingham, "Slavery and the National Anthem: The Surprising History behind Colin Kaepernick's Protest," *CNN*, August 31, 2016, http://edition.cnn.com/2016/08/29/sport/colin-kaepernick-flag-protest-has-history-trnd/; German Lopez, "Fox News Says Black Lives Matter Incites Violence. Critics Said the Same of MLK," *Vox*, September 2, 2015, https://www.vox.com/2015/9/2/9247901/black-lives-matter-mlk.

50 Amanda Taub, "'White Nationalism,' Explained," *The New York Times*, November 21, 2016, Americas, https://www.nytimes.com/2016/11/22/world/americas/white-nationalism-explained.html?_r=0.

II

RACISM AND RIGHTS: AFRICAN AMERICANS AND CONTESTED CITIZENSHIP(S)

"HANDS OFF D.C.":
RACE AND CONGRESSIONAL CONTROL OF WASHINGTON, D.C.

Kyla Sommers
The George Washington University

Outgoing Congressman Jason Chaffetz (R-Utah) made national head-lines and late-night punchlines when he suggested low income people should stop buying iPhones to afford health care.[1] In the District of Co-lumbia, however, Chaffetz is primarily known for his attempts to block D.C. legislation. Chaffetz served as the Chairman of the House Oversight Committee from 2014 to his resignation in June. The Committee over-sees the capital's budget, reviews its legislation, and can even overturn local laws. Chaffetz pledged to use this power to overturn a Washington law legalizing physician-assisted suicide. He also threatened to launch an investigation if D.C. used its tax dollars to defend undocumented immi-grants from deportation. After the city voted overwhelmingly to petition Congress to become a state, he suggested D.C. should instead retrocede to Maryland.[2]

District residents were determined to oppose the most recent meddler in District affairs. Activists formed the Americans for Self-Rule PAC to raise money to oppose Chaffetz in his next election, although the PAC's found-ing cause is now defunct.[3] City Council members sarcastically invited Chaffetz to local government hearings to mock his "interest in managing the affairs of the District of Columbia."[4] In February, after Chaffetz led the effort to overturn the District's legalization of assisted-suicide, so many Washingtonians called Chaffetz's office to voice complaints that the office switched to using a voice recording to answer phones.[5]

If Washingtonians are so active in their opposition to Congress members such as Chaffetz meddling in their affairs, why have residents been unable to stop Congress from wielding the power to override the D.C. government? It is impossible to answer this question without understanding the impact of anti-black racism in the governance of the nation's capital throughout its history.

Federal control of Washington began as a well-intentioned attempt to prevent Congress from being beholden to one state's interests, and when the federal government moved to D.C. in 1800, Congress controlled the District but allowed for some local autonomy such as mayoral and city council elections.[6] But D.C. policies quickly became a battle between Northern and Southern interests. With the defeat of the Confederacy, Radical Republicans sought to drastically increase black rights nationwide. Policy changes were easiest in Washington because Congressional reformers directly controlled the city's affairs. Some legislators even believed forging the capital in a radical, Northern image was "beautiful, poetic justice" that could serve to punish the former Confederacy. While most white residents opposed black enfranchisement (only 36 out of 7,339 whites supported it), over 2,500 black Washingtonians signed a petition to lobby Congress for suffrage. In 1867, Congress overrode President Andrew Johnson's veto and granted free black men the right to vote in D.C. years before the passage of the 15th amendment. In the 1868 mayoral election, nearly 50% of registered voters were black men and a coalition of African American and white Republicans elected Radical Republican Sayles Jenks Bowen as mayor over conservative former slave owner Richard Wallach. Recognizing the political power of black Washingtonians, the new Republican-run government pushed school integration, proposed anti-discrimination civil rights laws (several even passed), and ran black candidates in every ward in 1869 (several of whom won).[7]

The period of reform, however, was short lived. After a proposal to move the capital to a western city gained popularity, Mayor Bowen implemented an expensive public works project to improve Washington's infrastructure and image. Although much of the city's debt predated Bowen's administration, concern over government spending led to the election of Matthew Emery, a moderate Republican who promised to prioritize physical improvements over civil rights. During Emery's term Congress passed the Organic Act of 1871, which converted D.C. into a territorial state with mostly federally appointed leaders despite the opposition of Radical Republicans and African Americans who did not want to lose the franchise. President Ulysses S. Grant appointed Alexander "Boss" Shepard, a well-known business leader, as the governor of the new territorial government in 1873. After Shepard's ambitious municipal physical improvements incurred debt that was nearly twice the city's legal limit, an 1874 Congressional investigation recommended abolishing the territorial government and wholly submitting it to congressional control. Many white Washingtonians argued the plan would solve infrastructure and debt issues because Congress would fund 50% of D.C.'s budget. White Washingtonians also thought Congress, no longer controlled by Radical Republicans, was more favorable to their interests than democratic elections. Incredibly, they were willing to give up their right to vote to remove the ability of black people to have political power in Washington, D.C. In 1874, Congress dissolved the territorial government and created a Board of Commissioners, comprised of three appointed leaders, to run Washington's municipal government. The Organic Act of 1878, passed as part of the compromise that officially ended Reconstruction, made this structure permanent and Washington residents lost the franchise for nearly 100 years.[8]

Business leaders formed the Washington Board of Trade in 1889 and it quickly became the city's *de facto* oligarchical government. In the 50 years after the Board's founding, most in D.C. prioritized achieving Congressional representation over local self-rule. Home rule regained steam with the New Deal coalition, a group of mostly white liberals, Democratic Party officials, and labor activists who supported the idea of D.C. residents fully participating in the American tradition of democratic rule. This group found several important allies, including Eleanor Roosevelt and Hubert Humphrey, and in 1948 President Harry S. Truman included D.C. self-governance in the Democratic Party platform. From the late 1940s until the passage of the Home Rule Act in 1973, the idea of Washington self-rule received substantial bipartisan support.[9] From 1948 to 1966, the Senate passed home rule legislation six times but each time the House District of Columbia Committee blocked the bill from coming to a vote in the House of Representatives.

Southern segregationists had long controlled the House and Senate D.C. committees and used their power to ensure the capital's policies matched southern practices. Senator Theodore Bilbo (D-Mississippi) declared he wanted to be on the Senate Committee on the District of Columbia so he, "could keep Washington a segregated city."[10] The Southern-controlled House Committee on the District of Columbia encouraged segregation policies to the extent that a *Washington Evening Star* article opined "it must be observed as one of the ironies of history that the Confederacy, which was never able to capture Washington during the course of the war, now holds it as a helpless pawn." The report *Segregation in Washington*, commissioned by the American Council on Race Relations and authored by

Kenesaw M. Landis, concluded that these Southern segregationists kept D.C., "as the capital of white supremacy. Here they have demonstrated their racial theories to the world and gone home to brag about it."[11]

Unwilling to give up the power to cast the capital in a Southern image, the D.C. committees opposed home rule. Congress members and citizens also objected to self-governance, blatantly claiming that it would give black Washingtonians a major stake in the governance of the capital. The 1951 hearings on home rule before the Congressional Subcommittee on Home Rule and Reorganization illuminate the deep-seated opposition to black enfranchisement and governing. Several testifying acknowledged the role race played in opposition to Home Rule: "The most ridiculous, malicious, and odiferous complaint of all is the hatemongers' behind-the-hand remark, that, 'If we get home rule the Negroes will take over the city.'"[12] Another acknowledged, "one of the most persistent arguments against local suffrage in the past has been that so many residents of the District have voting rights elsewhere that minority groups would control local elections here."[13] Some in Congress also held this fear. "I remember there was a former Member of the Congress," Wilber S. Finch recalled, "who was reputed to have said that he would never vote for suffrage for the people of the District of Columbia as long as there was one Negro living in the District who would qualify as a voter."[14] Others admitted that while the objection was not discussed openly, "it is whispered about and is one of the silent obstacles to passage."[15] One Congressman reported that over 12 people told him "in private and not in confidence that they are opposed to this bill because of their fear it would give the Negro domination over the District of Columbia."[16] While D.C.'s black population rapidly grew, support for Home Rule within D.C. declined from over 80% in 1938 to 70% in 1946 with only 50% of white people supporting it. "Since 1946, more and more people are in opposition to Home Rule," Clifford Newell of the Arkansas Avenue Community Association testified. "There has been a big change in our population since 1946. Then, we had just gotten out of World War II, and thousands of war workers and soldiers were still in the city. Most of these have now either left the city and gone back home, or have bought homes and moved into suburban sections of Maryland and Virginia."[17] In other words, as the black population was more concentrated in D.C. and whites moved to the suburbs, fewer white residents supported home rule.

Following the *Brown v. Board of Education* ruling which overturned *Plessy v. Ferguson's* "separate but equal" doctrine, congressional power over D.C.

became an important component of the South's massive resistance to integration. President Eisenhower declared that D.C. integration would serve as a "model for the rest of the country" after the *Brown* ruling in May 1954. Unlike most school districts, the District integrated in the fall immediately following the decision.[18] Southern Congressmen on the House D.C. Committee contended that D.C.'s school integration only "modeled" that desegregation was bad for Washington and, therefore, would be bad for the nation. In 1957, a subcommittee appointed by John L. McMillan of the House D.C. Committee held hearings on the capital's school system as part of the South's blatant refusal to integrate. William Gerber, chief counsel for the subcommittee, asked school administrators and teachers leading questions to suggest integration destroyed Washington's schools because black students were inherently intellectually inferior, caused dangerous disciplinary problems, and could corrupt white children.[19]

The hearings, often called the Davis hearings after their chairman John C. Davis, were so reliant on distorted data and racist tropes that the NAACP called them "unhooded clan meetings" and the *Washington Post* slammed it as a "hatchet job."[20] Nevertheless, the Davis hearings achieved their intended purpose: the committee sent transcripts to schools in the South and used the information as an excuse to delay integration. In a speech following the hearings, Davis contended that Washington's example confirmed white people's main objections to integration: "health, the Negro's high crime rate and disrespect for the law, the lower mentality level, and the high rate of illegitimacy among Negroes." The District's schools' "sex problems" proved to Davis that "integrationalists and mongrelizers," as well as the "radical NAACP," wanted "intermarriage and complete mongrelization of the American people." Seizing upon the countless assertions that the capital should be "a model example of a nonsegregated city," Davis charged that the model had failed and D.C. was instead a cautionary tale:

> I have given you tonight, in brief, a picture of the deplorable situation in Washington. I have seen there the tragic results which come from the breakdown of segregation and substitution of an integrated public-school system. The same thing can happen, and will happen here, if the people meekly accept wrongful usurpation of power, and a Supreme Court dictatorship, as they did in Washington.[21]

Congressional opponents to self-governance also objected because they believed crime in the District justified *more* legislative control over the capital. Senator Olin Johnson and Representative Omar Burleson recommended that two companies of Marines patrol D.C. and Congressman Joel Broyhill introduced a bill to turn over control of the city police to Congress.[22] But, such attention to Washington crime also served another agenda: opposing civil rights. These congressmen argued that Supreme Court cases expanding civil liberties and the civil rights movement resulted in increased crime because, according to Senator Robert Byrd, "in such an atmosphere of permissiveness, civil disobedience and disrespect for civil law, the seeds of crime took deeper root, and the Nation is now reaping the harvest."[23] Washington was a prime target of such criticism because it had the largest proportional black population of any American city, was desegregated, and easily invoked national outrage as the capital. Politicians combined their opposition to liberal court rulings with sensationalized concern over D.C. crime to oppose civil rights reforms. Senator Olin Johnston made speeches in Congress almost daily connecting D.C.'s integration and crime because he believed newspapers failed to report the "chronic ailments that accompany forced integration."[24] Senator Allen Ellender asserted that D.C. crime proved "his contention that Negroes cannot govern themselves."[25] Congressman Davis said the capital was "noted for the great number of serious crimes committed in its limits" and bluntly stated, "Negroes are responsible for this high crime rate."[26]

Several "law and order" measures passed in the late 1960s characterized the desire to legislate greater control over District affairs in order to curtail civil rights. In 1966, the House and Senate passed a D.C. crime bill to limit the rights of the accused but Lyndon Johnson vetoed it believing it overly limited civil liberties. That same year, Johnson launched the President's Commission on Crime in the District of Columbia which, among other proposals, recommended restructuring the D.C. Police Department to alleviate accusations of racism and brutality. The Senate, however, blocked the recommendations.[27] Disregarding strong local opposition, "law and order" members of Congress scored a major victory with the passage of the 1970 D.C. Crime Bill under Richard Nixon (who ran on a heavily racialized "law and order" campaign in 1968). The bill, among other provisions, permitted "no-knock" warrants and preventative detention.

As Congress tightened its grip over the capital by peddling racism, activists in Washington increasingly organized to demand self-rule. In hearings on

Home Rule held in the early 1960s, D.C. civil rights groups like the Urban League and the Congress On Racial Equality testified in favor of home rule. After Johnson pledged his support for home rule in an address to Congress in 1965, the Association for a Democratic America, Washington Home Rule Committee, and D.C. Democratic Committee used traditional lobbying efforts to push legislation. With hearings in the mid-60s and a potential bill in 1965, many were optimistic that home rule would finally come to Washington. Their hopes were stymied when the House District Committee once again refused to bring the bill to a vote.[28]

After this failure, national and local black leaders and organizations intensified their protests and demands, making black rights the central issue in the fight for home rule. Prominent activist Julius Hobson filed a lawsuit alleging that District citizens' inability to vote violated the Constitution (particularly the 14th Amendment granting African Americans the right to vote) but the suit was rejected by the District court.[29] Free D.C., started by future mayor Marion Barry, lobbied businesses, especially members of the Board to Trade, to support the cause. In February 1966, Free D.C. distributed leaflets that showed long-time home rule opponents John McMillan and Robert Byrd holding black people as slaves with the help of "moneylord merchants." Martin Luther King, Jr. preached its importance and the D.C. Coalition of Conscience gathered signatures to show citizen support.[30] Over 4,000 people attended a 1966 rally for home rule held by Youth Organization United. In a *Washington Post* poll in 1966, black people nearly unanimously supported home rule.[31]

Despite such continued activism and support from many in D.C., home rule did not pass in the 1960s for three key reasons. First, the Senate and House District Committees could block any bill on the capital from coming to the floor. Byrd, head of the Senate District Committee, and McMillan, head of the House committee, were equally opposed to home rule.[32] Second, the business community, with many ties to Congress and considerable lobbying power, opposed it. Finally, many white people both inside the District and in the surrounding suburbs objected. Inside the capital, *Washington Post* polls showed that 40% of white people supported home rule, 40% opposed it, and 20% were unsure. Of the surrounding suburbs, all but Montgomery County (which had a larger black population than the rest) opposed it. The *Post* reported that "the arguments against home rule

45

center on higher taxes (feared by both Negroes and whites), corruption, less Federal aid and Negro control of the Capital." When asked about why they opposed home rule, white Washington residents clearly showed their racial resentment: "Lord, help us, if those n*****s ever get home rule;" "[I]t isn't right that the Nation's Capital be all colored;" "I'm opposed to it because it's going to be all colored;" "They don't have the right education to do the right job;" "Because a colored fellow would be mayor—no other reason."[33]

Joseph L. Rauh, Jr., founder of the Americans for Democratic Action and long-standing home rule advocate, released a statement in August 1966 warning that the continual denial of democracy would only increase the potential for racial violence. He remarked: "As discussion and peaceful protest fail to obtain results, alternative means of achieving recognition for a point of view will become ever more flamboyant, violent, and dangerous. What is in store for us without Home Rule is an ever-escalating guerilla warfare."[34] To quell such mounting tensions, President Johnson used executive powers to restructure the District's government in 1967. His executive order created a 9-person city council and a mayor-commissioner (all appointed by the executive branch) to govern the city and an elected school board to democratize education. Johnson appointed Walter E. Washington, an African American native Washingtonian who was the former head of the D.C. and New York City housing authorities, as mayor. The House and Senate District committees were not pleased and many refused to refer to Mayor-Commissioner Walter Washington as "mayor." In a shockingly racist gesture, John McMillan sent Washington a truck of watermelons to "welcome" him.[35]

Johnson's plan failed to solve the city's racial inequalities as vividly demonstrated by the explosion of protests and fires after the assassination of Martin Luther King, Jr. in 1968. Demonstrations for self-rule, often linked to black power, only grew. To quell such demands, Congress passed the District of Columbia Delegate Act in 1970 and granted D.C. a non-voting delegate in the House of Representatives. Reverend Walter Fauntroy, a well-known civil rights leader who helped organize the 1963 March on Washington, was elected and began serving in 1971.

Fauntroy harnessed the political power granted to African Americans by the 1965 Voting Rights Act to take down McMillan and finally bring self-government to Washington. Busloads of Washingtonians, organized by

Fauntroy, went to register black voters in South Carolina's 6th District, Mc-Millan's home district. Fauntroy wrote over 10,000 letters to contacts from the civil rights movement asking them to urge their Congress member to support home rule. Ron Dellums, a newly elected African-American Congressmen serving on the House District Committee, and Fauntroy lobbied their colleagues in the House to ensure that if self-government legislation came to a vote it would pass.[36] Their plan worked: in 1972, McMillan lost the Democratic primary to State Representative John Lenrette and in 1973, President Richard Nixon signed the District of Columbia Home Rule Act into law. Finally, after over 100 years of disenfranchisement, Washingtonians could elect their mayor, school board, and city council. But, even then, home rule came with restrictions and was heavily scrutinized. To this day, D.C.'s Congressional representative cannot vote and the city cannot impose a commuter tax or pass a budget that is not balanced. Despite such restrictions, D.C. rejoiced at home rule and the democratically elected administration made civil rights a cornerstone of governance.

In 1978, a coalition of wealthy white and working class black Washingtonians elected the now infamous Marion Barry as mayor. For those who had opposed home rule, Barry's tenure as mayor validated their belief that D.C., a city whose population was two-thirds black, could not govern itself. The capital was riddled with national and even international criticism for the countless accusations of government corruption, high crime rates, financial mismanagement, and Barry's arrest and eventual conviction for drug possession. But, for many, Barry was a champion who prioritized black Washingtonians and "symbolized an authentic version of black D.C."[37] Mere months after his release from jail, Barry was elected as Ward 8's City Council representative and was then reelected mayor in 1994.

Many Washingtonians believe to this day that Congressional hatred of Barry was part of the reason that less than a year after Barry's reelection, Congress created the District of Columbia Financial Control Board and took control of the city's finances. The Board forced drastic budget cuts and layoffs. While Barry initially requested help from Congress to deal with the city's growing debt and budget shortfalls, he did not expect their drastic approach and called it a "rape of democracy" and declared that D.C. could not survive as "half-slave, half-free."[38] The entire process was deeply intertwined with racial politics: many black Washingtonians were convinced the Control Board was all part of a Congressional plan to take the capital away from black control, while Congress selected black politicians to lead the process and ease accusations of racism. Kevin Chavous, then the City Council representative from Ward 7, explained that even moderate African Americans were skeptical of Congress because, "there is some built-in paranoia and distrust of Congress. It is the result of generations of congressional colonialism."[39]

In 1997, Congress further restricted D.C. autonomy when it voted to stop its federal payment to the city (a practice originating in 1878) and instead took control of the city's debts, its courts and prisons, and elements of its entitlement programs. The city is still barred from going into debt for any project that is not a capital or economic development program and all budgets must be certified as balanced by an appointed Chief Financial Officer. While the Financial Control Board is now dormant, it can be revived at any time. Former mayor Vincent Gray said the threat of the return of the Control Board was a "grim reaper at the door," and former City Council member Jack Evans claimed a Republican Congress would, "like nothing better than to take over this city again and say, 'We told you so.'"[40]

Indeed, Congress has stepped in multiple times to override legislation passed by the District government and public referendums over the years. Congress blocked a bill that allowed Medicaid funds to cover abortions in 1988, a measure to allow gay couples to register as domestic partners in 1992, the legalization of medical marijuana in 1988, and a clean needle exchange program the same year. Delegate Eleanor Holmes Norton, D.C.'s non-voting delegate since 1991, condemned the needle exchange ban in 2011 saying, "We have the highest AIDS rate in the United States only because the Congress of the United States has killed—I used these words advisedly—killed men, women and children in the District of Columbia by keeping the District for ten years from using needle exchange so that AIDS would spread throughout the city."[41] After the capital legalized same-sex marriage in 2009, several Congress members, including Jason Chaffetz, introduced legislation to once again ban gay marriage. More recently, Republicans used their control over D.C.'s budget and affairs to partially block marijuana legalization in 2014.[42] In July 2017, the House Appropriations Committee passed a measure that would repeal a D.C. law to legalize physician assisted-suicide.[43] The politicians who enforce their party platform over the democratic will of Washingtonians are partially capable of doing so because centuries of fear of black political power denied the nation's capital autonomy. Wielding this power is not benign. It is, rather, an act complicit with anti-black racism and the colonial rule of Washington, D.C.

Delegate Norton passionately rebuked those who denied D.C. full representation when she was interrupted during a speech in 2007 on the D.C. Voting Rights Act:

> I will not yield sir. The District of Columbia has spent 206 years yielding to people who would deny them the vote. I yield you no ground ... you have had your say and your say has been that you think the people who live in your capital are not entitled to a vote in their house. Shame on you.[44]

Studying Washington, D.C. and Congressional history reveals that a key reason Congress still has substantial control over the capital is rooted in racism. The very act that ended local elections in 1878 was in part intended to end black political power in the District. In response to the black freedom movement, segregationists made D.C. the posterchild for "massive resistance" and "law and order." Even after home rule, race continues to shape perceptions of the city. As activists push for D.C. Statehood and resist Congressional interference, the ugly racial history of the capital's governance must be an integral part of the movement for full independence. And, to quote Delegate Norton, "It's time that the District of Columbia told the Congress to go straight to hell."[45]

Notes

1   Tina Nguyen, "Jason Chaffetz: Can't Afford Trumpcare? Don't Buy an iPhone," *Vanity Fair*, March 7, 2017, http://www.vanityfair.com/news/2017/03/jason-chaffetz-healthcare-iphone.

2   Jenna Portnoy, "GOP House Chair: Maybe We Should Cut Off Part of D.C. and Send It Back to Maryland," *Washington Post*, January 31, 2017, https://www.washingtonpost.com/local/dc-politics/gop-house-chair-maybe-we-should-cut-off-part-of-dc-and-send-it-to-maryland/2017/01/31/2242753a-e7d0-11e6-80c2-30e57e57e05d_story.html?utm_term=.967fd7125059.

3   Paul Schwartzman, "Chaffetz Faces New Opponent: A D.C. PAC Created to Oust Him," *Washington Post*, February 28, 2017, https://www.washingtonpost.com/local/dc-politics/chaffetz-faces-new-opponent-a-dc-pac-created-to-oust-him/2017/02/27/2d6279f2-fd2d-11e6-99b4-9e613afeb09f_story.html?utm_term=.db75576a88e9.

4   Rachel Sadon, "D.C. Council Trolls Jason Chaffetz," DCist.com, February 9, 2017, http://dcist.com/2017/02/dc_council_trolls_jason_chaffetz.php.

5   Sadon, "D.C. Council Trolls Jason Chaffetz."

6   The history includes different levels of autonomy allowed at different times. D.C. was initially governed by a 3-person federally appointed Board of Commissioners, but this was disbanded in 1802 to allow for a six-person elected legislature and a Presidentially-appointed mayor. By 1820, the City of Washington was allowed to elect its mayor. Pushes to curtail D.C. autonomy began before the Reconstruction era but were always tied to disputes over political power and slavery.

7   Howard Gillette, Jr., *Between Justice and Beauty: Race, Planning, and the Failure of Urban Policy in Washington, D.C.* (Philadelphia: University of Pennsylvania Press, 1995), 50–56. Blaire Ruble, *Washington's U Street: A Biography* (Washington, DC: Woodrow Wilson Center Press, 2010), 28–29.

8   Gillette, *Between Justice and Beauty*, 57–68.

9   Gregory Borchardt, "Making D.C. Democracy's Capital: Local Activism, the 'Federal State', and the Struggle for Civil Rights in Washington, D.C." (PhD diss., George Washington University, 2013), 236–241.

10 Kenesaw Mountain Landis, *Segregation in Washington: A Report, November 1948* (Virginia: The University of Virginia, 1948), 88.

11 Landis, *Segregation in Washington*, 88.

12 "Statement of Kenneth Adams, President of the Young Republicans Club of the District of Columbia," "Statement of Clifford H. Newell, Representing the Arkansas Avenue Community Association," *Hearings Before the Subcommittee on Home Rule and Reorganization* (Washington: United States Government Printing Office, 1951), 70.

13 "Answers to the Board of Trade Pamphlet Entitled "Does the Kefauver Bill Really Provide for Home Rule," "Statement of Clifford H. Newell, Representing the Arkansas Avenue Community Association," *Hearings Before the Subcommittee on Home Rule and Reorganization*, 201.

14 "Statement of Wilbur S. Finch," "Statement of Clifford H. Newell, Representing the Arkansas Avenue Community Association," *Hearings Before the Subcommittee on Home Rule and Reorganization*, 75.

15 "Rebuttal of Board of Trade Arguments Against Home Rule for the District of Columbia," "Statement of Clifford H. Newell, Representing the Arkansas Avenue Community Association," *Hearings Before the Subcommittee on Home Rule and Reorganization*, 99.

16 "Statement of Marshall L. Shepard, Representing the Recorder of Deeds of the District of Columbia," "Statement of Clifford H. Newell, Representing the Arkansas Avenue Community Association," *Hearings Before the Subcommittee on Home Rule and Reorganization*, 221.

17 "Statement of Clifford H. Newell, Representing the Arkansas Avenue Community Association," *Hearings Before the Subcommittee on Home Rule and Reorganization*, 196–198.

18 David A. Nichols, "'The Showpiece of Our Nation': Dwight D. Eisenhower and the Desegregation of the District of Columbia," *Washington History* 16, No. 2 (Fall/Winter, 2004/2005): 44–65.

19 For more on the Davis hearings see *Hearings Before the Subcommittee to Investigate Public School Standards and Conditions and Juvenile Delinquency in the District of Columbia of the Committee on the District of Columbia House of Representatives* (Washington: United States Government Printing Office, 1956).

20 Borchardt, "Making D.C. Democracy's Capital," 97–100.

21 "Congressman James C. Davis Speaks to the State's Rights Council," November 28, 1956, University of Southern Mississippi Digital Collections, M393 McCain (William D.) Pamphlet Collection, Box 3, Folder 6, http://digilib.usm.edu/cdm/compoundobject/collection/manu/id/1521.

22 William Raspberry, "D.C. May Lose What Little Voice It Has on Police," December 24, 1967, *The Washington Post*, D1.

23 "Crime Rise Blamed on Supreme Court," *Washington Post*, August 1, 1962.

24 "Johnson Calls Press Lax on Integration," September 3, 1959, *The Washington Post*, A25. He further argued, "Police cannot solve 'evils caused by forced integration.'" In another speech, Johnston claimed that D.C. and New York had high crime rates because they were, "Two places where forced integration has been experimented with more than any other places in the United States."

25 "Ellender Calls District A 'Cesspool of Crime,'" June 17, 1963, *The Washington Post*, A6. He had recently been barred entry by three African nations for making similar comments. After listing figures of how much of D.C. was controlled by black people he argued, "you have the worst conditions in Washington where they are at the head than of any big city in the country ... To me, that just shows their inability to govern."

26 "Congressman James C. Davis Speaks to the State's Rights Council," November 28, 1956, University of Southern Mississippi Digital Collections, M393 McCain (William D.) Pamphlet Collection, Box 3, Folder 6, http://digilib.usm.edu/cdm/compoundobject/collection/manu/id/1521.

27 Jerry V. Wilson, *The War on Crime in the District of Columbia 1955–1975* (Washington: National Institute of Law Enforcement and Criminal Justice, Law Enforcement Administration, United States Department of Justice, 1978), 19–21.

28 Borchardt, "Making D.C. Democracy's Capital," 243–260.

29 Paul W. Valentine, "Suit by Hobson Asks Election of D.C. Heads," April 26, 1966, *The Washington Post*, B2. "U.S. Sees No D.C. right to Local Vote," January 28, 1967, *The Washington Post*, C4.

30 Borchardt, "Making D.C. Democracy's Capital," 259–272.

31 "Area Residents Support Home Rule, But They Don't Get Excited About It," October 4, 1966, *The Washington Post*, A1.

32 Borchardt, "Making D.C. Democracy's Capital," 241.

33 Area Residents Support Home Rule, But They Don't Get Excited About It," October 4, 1966, *The Washington Post*, A1.

34 Borchardt, "Making D.C. Democracy's Capital," 271–274.

35 Scott Berg, "Going Deep into the Nation's Capital," *Washington Post*, October 29, 2015, https://www.washingtonpost.com/opinions/going-deep-into-the-nations-capital/2015/10/29/1fac1392-5d72-11e5-b38e-06883aacba64_story.html?utm_term=.b32ba702338f.

36 Jacob Fenston, "How A Civil Rights Struggle In The South Helped D.C. Elect Its Own Leaders," January 9, 2015, http://wamu.org/story/15/01/09/how_a_civil_rights_struggle_in_the_south_helped_dc_elect_its_own_leaders/.

37 Credit to Daniel Robinson for this sentiment and phrase.

38 Mike DeBonis, "After 10 Years, D.C. Control Board is Gone But Not Forgotten," *Washington Post*, January 30, 2011, http://www.washingtonpost.com/wp-dyn/content/article/2011/01/30/AR2011013003901.html; Blaine Harden and David A. Vise, "Race and the Bottom Line in D.C.," *Washington Post*, March 19, 1995, https://www.washingtonpost.com/archive/politics/1995/03/19/race-and-the-bottom-line-in-dc/86564231-50f1-4b73-bb42-fbee7e62b89c/?utm_term=.d81b1b171a0f.

39 Harden and Vise, "Race and the Bottom Line in D.C.," 1995.

40 DeBonis, "After 10 Years, D.C. Control Board is Gone But Not Forgotten," 2011.

41 Pete Kasperowicz, "D.C. Delegate: Congress has 'Killed' with Needle Exchange Prohibition," April 5, 2011, http://thehill.com/blogs/floor-action/house/154047-holmes-norton-says-congress-has-killed-dc-residents-with-needle-exchange-policy.

42 D.C. now essentially has a legalized black market, far different than what D.C. residents voted to approve.

43 For more information on past actions to block D.C. laws see "Ending Congressional Interference," D.C. Vote, http://dcvote.org/ending-congressional-interference.

44 "Delegate Holmes Norton: D.C. Voting Rights Act," https://www.youtube.com/watch?v=VV3k8nERUOQ.

45 Paul Schwartzman, "Eleanor Holmes Norton Lacks a Vote But Not a (Withering) Voice," *The Washington Post*, October 22, 2012, https://www.washingtonpost.com/local/eleanor-holmes-norton-lacks-a-vote-but-not-a-withering-voice/2012/10/22/b9836b8e-188b-11e2-9855-71f2b202721b_story.html?utm_term=.e57bb9983f7d.

FERRAY VS. POMPEYO THE FREE BLACK: FEAR AND BLACK MASCULINITY IN THE ERA OF THE HAITIAN REVOLUTION

Sarah Senette
Tulane University

According to witness testimony, Pompeyo warned Don Ferray that he was "going to punch him in the face" just before he did so.[1] Ferray promptly returned the punch, but the fight was soon over. While a few blows traded in a tavern may seem to merit little attention, in the context of New Orleans' socio-racial hierarchy in the years surrounding the Haitian Revolution, Pompeyo's status as a free man of color meant that a barroom brawl quickly escalated into a legal battle. On August 7, 1795, both Pompeyo and black masculinity were on trial in *Ferray vs. Pompeyo the free black*. Rather than being judged as an individual, with individual relationships, the colonial New Orleans judiciary tried Pompeyo as a violent threat to their social order—one in which honor and manhood were for white men only.[2]

In 1791, four years prior to *Ferray vs. Pompeyo*, enslaved men and women on the French colony of Saint Domingue (now Haiti) rebelled against the brutal system of slavery on the wealthy sugar island. The only successful slave rebellion in history, the Haitian Revolution spread ideas of black liberty and equality throughout the Atlantic world and most especially the Caribbean.[3] Consequently, the New Orleans governmental body, called the Cabildo, began to conflate Caribbean blackness with revolutionary ideology.[4] For example, just one month after the Haitian Revolution, *síndico procurador general* Juan Bautista Poeyfarré reported to the Cabildo that "in the outskirts and within the city limits there [were] several bands of savage negroes disturbing the public tranquility." To assure that the Cabildo made the connection between these "negros" and those of Saint Domingue, Poeyfarré stressed that, *"such evil in the current state of affairs* might bring terrible consequences."[5] Raucous men of color might incite a revolt.

Similar fears of equality for people of African descent likewise resurfaced after the 1795 aborted uprising at Pointe Coupée, which was a mere six hours by horse to the northwest of New Orleans.[6] Unrest among enslaved people in Pointe Coupée started soon after the Haitian Revolution and continued to escalate. In response to a supposed 1791 plot by seven Pointe Coupée slaves, the Spanish Government issued a decree ordering better treatment of enslaved people in the area. Masters, however, ignored the decree and responded with increased brutality. The situation continued to worsen until 1795 when a second plot was uncovered. Afraid that leniency would only foment more unrest among Louisiana slaves, the governor ordered one white man and several free people of color implicated in the plot banished. He likewise ordered twenty-two people sentenced to ten years of hard labor and twenty-six people hanged. In the heat of summer, the commissioners had their severed heads displayed on pikes at various points—serving as warning to all people of color. Indeed, the commissioner placed two such heads in New Orleans and had many lining the river.[7] Aware that preventative as well as punitive action must be taken in order to maintain supremacy, the commissioners also got the backing of Governor Carondelet in 1796 and forbade "all commerce of slaves in this providence, coming direct from the Guinea Coast ... [and] the Americas, being neither Spanish nor foreign" to help them restrict the importation of enslaved Africans from the Caribbean.[8] In light of New Orleans's racial conflicts via the Haitian Revolution and the Pointe Coupée rebellion, which happened only a few months prior, the presiding judge's incredulous query to Pompeyo during the trial, "did [he] not *know* that it is a crime to raise a hand, especially from a man of color to a white and swear at him?" makes absolute sense.[9] From the judge's perspective, this was not a case about a barroom fight. Pompeyo's swing was a revolutionary act.[10]

According to Ferray, Pompeyo and his friends had been gambling in Ferray's tavern. When they finished, Pompeyo's friends left the building and Ferray ordered Pompeyo to pay the two and one half *reales* that he owed for the game of pool. Ferray then asserted that Pompeyo "told him some impudence and slanderous words and took off his jacket and became upset. He then said to the deponent 'I don't know what you are telling me I am going to give you a slap' and effectively hit him in the face."[11] By ordering that Pompeyo pay then and there, Ferray suggests that Pompeyo could not, or would not, agree to pay later. In the context of colonial New Orleans, credit functioned not only as a practical replacement for difficult to obtain gold and silver currency (specie), it also served a mechanism for demonstrating social standing and personal honor—two key elements in colonial manhood. Thus, when Ferray suggested that Pompeyo would not pay, he also slighted Pompeyo's public reputation and insulted his integrity. This interpretation of these events becomes more probable when, after Pompeyo promised to get the money, Ferray "did not wish to wait as he, [Pompeyo] had many tricks."[12] With his friends nearby and his honor in question, Pompeyo reasserted his manhood in the only way he could likely think of: he punched Ferray in the face.

As insulting as getting punched in the face probably was for Ferray, it appears that he was equally affronted by the "slanderous" insults Pompeyo "made reference [to] before his boys."[13] Far from an abstracted ideal, honor and credit helped structure community relationships and maintain social order.[14] Within Spanish New Orleans, issues of honor were frequently played out in court as men and women of all racial designations sought to negotiate their social standing.[15] Nor was it different in the case of *Ferray vs. Pompeyo*. When Pompeyo "mistreated [Ferray] and talked [to him] with words of inferiority," it was no longer a matter of interpersonal conflict, but a much larger issue wherein Pompeyo had stepped far outside the socially prescribed bounds.[16] In the service of law and order, the local government upheld the honor of people like Ferray at the expense of people like Pompeyo to buttress the position of New Orleans social elites—particularly in times of social unrest like New Orleans experienced during the Haitian Revolution.[17]

Besides crossing socioeconomic boundaries, the fight itself spread across social and racial lines. Sometime after the initial altercation, Ferray, Pompeyo, and "the Negro George" exited Ferray's establishment.[18] Once outside, the fight escalated. Pompeyo attempted to pay Ferray with currency deemed insufficient by Ferray, which quickly resulted in the two parties screaming at one another. Intervening, George offered "to go exchange the peso."[19] Likely hearing the yelling, a "white youth of the name of Bernardo" came out of his courtyard inquiring about the incident.[20] Pompeyo protested and said that he had only asked to exchange his money and that if given leave, he would go, exchange the money, and return. Bernardo, apparently unmoved by Pompeyo's assertion and wanting him to leave the vicinity immediately, "stood in anger asked for the penitent to leave."[21] Not moving quickly enough, "Bernardo grabbed him by the collar, gave [Pompeyo] a punch in the face and left with a cue of the billiard" after hitting Pompeyo with it two or three times on his head.[22] Then, "stained with blood, damaged and bleeding, they brought [Pompeyo] to the house of Don Francis Merieult superintendent of police" and had him arrested, despite the fact that Pompeyo denied any wrongdoing.[23] Within a very short time, the altercation between Pompeyo and Ferray multiplied to include other free people of color and whites. This violent escalation between various racial and social groups was exactly what the Cabildo sought to avoid in the wake of the Haitian Revolution. Racial violence once ignited, they feared, could spread rapidly.

This desire to control interracial and social mixing directly affected individuals like Pompeyo because the local government sought to prohibit, or at least regulate, zones of interracial contact, including the gambling hall where Pompeyo and Ferray fought. According to eighteenth-century philosophers of crime, the seriousness of an individual's transgression should be estimated by the injury done to society.[24] Thus, it was not the violation itself that posed problems, but the potential repercussions of the infraction. For example, in the issue of gambling, one New Orleans local argued to the Cabildo that the "risks of those who submit themselves to these disorders because of blind passion" should not be underestimated.[25] It was not a matter that could be isolated. Vice could spread and "the disorders of which this liberty of gaming can expose the ruin of all the citizens of the city."[26] Gamblers certainly risked "the peace of mind of [their] family," but more importantly, they were also "firing up the various classes of citizens as an epidemic which extends its havoc to every part."[27] Gambling was a "public school of vice and passions" wherein young men not only learned immoral behavior but mixed with their social inferiors, including people of color and slaves. By being in a gambling hall, Pompeyo's morals were already in question, in the eyes of the court, and even though Pompeyo's infractions were relatively minor, their potential impact on society was not. The court judged Pompeyo not as an individual who made some mistakes, but as an enemy of the state and a threat to society writ large.[28]

Pompeyo also appeared threatening to the court in another way: he lived with a white woman named Polly Lee. Little is known about Lee, other than that she was white, born in England, and a maid. The particulars about Lee, however, would not have concerned the court; they would have only cared that she was white and lived with a black man during a period when that was becoming increasingly taboo. Despite the frequency of interracial relationships between white men and women of color, white women rarely had publicly sanctioned relationships with men of color in the latter part of the eighteenth century. Yet, Pompeyo "had in his possession a white English maid" and "lived gracelessly" with Lee for "his happiness."[29] The use of the word "graceless" could mean one of two things in this context. It could connote the social awkwardness of a white woman living with a black man, or it could suggest that they lived without God's grace—or in sin. The word "possession" also implies that Lee was with Pompeyo against her will. Regardless, neither interpretation suggests that the court approved of his relationship and the fact that it happened for "his happiness" indicates that they blamed Pompeyo, once again, for transgressing social mores.[30]

Pompeyo's relationship with Lee negatively affected his case for several reasons. First, it threatened the court officials' own manhood. According to Laurence Powell, white men demonstrated a preference for women of color even after New Orleans' demography balanced because they had more freedom by entering into relationships with a woman of color than they had when they married, especially if they were already propertied enough not to need the social prestige of "legitimate" marriage.[31] Sex across the color line was a sign of status and was supposed to be the purveyance of affluent white men. Yet, it was also the duty of white men to protect the chastity of white women in their care. As officials of the city, Polly Lee was technically under the protection of the Cabildo. Thus, Pompeyo threatened their manhood on two fronts. In having an interracial relationship, he must have appeared to parody the sexual privileges enjoyed by his social superiors: white men. Furthermore, he demonstrated the court's inability to protect the sexual virtue of white women in their care. More generally, systems of patriarchy, such as those that ordered Spanish New Orleans, necessitated the participation of social inferiors to uphold the power of white men. In his relationship with Lee, Pompeyo fundamentally refused to endorse the system that validated the court's own white manhood.[32]

In the late eighteenth century, Spanish American social order was inextricably tied to an elaborate racial and gendered structure in which, ideally, white Spanish men stood at the zenith. Spanish American systems of social order revolved around both *limpieza de sangre* or "purity of blood" and a *sistema de casta* or a "caste system." These two features of Spanish American social ordering bound together ideas of race, gender, and social position through intimate relationships or marriage. With the advent of Enlightenment ideas about science, increasingly elaborate taxonomic classifications of socio-racial hierarchies emerged in Spanish America that "made the gen-

Figure 1. Casta Painting, 1777,
Ignacio María Barreda.
Real Academia Española, Madrid, Spain

dering of race and the racing of gender, as well as social hierarchies, ordained by nature."[33] These ideas of gendered, racial, and social hierarchy resulted in the widespread popularity of *casta* paintings in Spanish America. Generally, *castas* were arranged in a series of sixteen panels that each depicted a racial union and the product of that union.[34] For instance, in the first panel of Ignacio María Barreda's 1777 *casta* painting, he depicted a Spanish man, an Indian woman and their *mestizo*, or mixed race, child (Figure 1). As each couple moved further away from having "pure" Spanish blood, the apparel of each couple and background in each panel indicated less wealth and social prestige. For example, in the first panel, the couple was indoors and appeared well dressed. However, in the final panel, the couple was in far less expensive clothes and out of doors. It is easier to see this distinction in the 1763 *casta* series by Miguel Cabrera. The first image in the series depicted a Spanish man, a *Mestiza* woman, and their *Castiza* child. All were dressed in fine clothes and surrounded by a plethora of material goods, indicating their wealth, high social position, and nearly pure Spanish-ness (Figure 2). The second image, which appeared toward the end of the series, depicted a *Lobo*, a word that literally means wolf, but in this use connotes a "mixed breed" man and an Indian woman, whose child was classified as *Albarazado* (Figure 3). Their clothes are of poor quality, particularly the father's clothes because he would have been lower on the racial hierarchy. They are also depicted as working, which indicates a lower social position. Thus, when the court refers to Pompeyo as "the Negro" or "said Negro" and not by name, it extends beyond a mere racial classification.[35] Pompeyo's race also indicated his social standing and who would have been an appropriate mate. While not an inflexible standard, racial classification in Spanish America had social, gendered, and scientific connotations. To the court, Pompeyo was not only defying social and racial conventions in his relationship with Lee, he had stepped outside of the "natural" order at a time when that very order was under siege in the Caribbean.[36]

With the growing international tensions in the 1790s surrounding the Haitian Revolution, local officials saw the maintenance of racial and social order as critically

Figure 2. 1763 Casta Painting,
Series by Miguel Cabrera
De Español y Mestiza, Castiza
Real Academia Española, Madrid, Spain.

Figure 3. 1763 Casta Painting,
Series by Miguel Cabrera
De Lobo y d'India, Albarazado
Real Academia Española, Madrid, Spain.

important to the future of the colony and attempted to decrease interracial mixing. This was no easy task. First, as the *casta* paintings evidence, phenotypic appearance was not a true indicator of race. Each of the images of mixed race couples was labeled because the image itself in no way made clear whether this was a *Lobo*, a *mestizo*, a *blanco*, a *negro*, or any other "racial" permutation. Furthermore, the fact that this elaborate system of classification existed whatsoever also indicates the racial fluidity of Spanish American society—despite the histrionic attempts of the government to order intimate relationships. Likewise, the large population of free people of color itself suggests that interracial relationships were quite common in Spanish New Orleans as some free women of color (although not all) gained their wealth and independence "from *blanco* consorts and fathers."[37] Racial and social fluidity abounded in Spanish New Orleans. Spanish Laws prohibiting interracial and socially asymmetric marriages, while largely successful, did not prohibit intimate relationships, as they were beyond their control. To the court, Pompeyo's case was an opportunity to assert their authority over these relationships while simultaneously buttressing their own manhood and dictating their version of the proper social and racial order.[38]

Pompeyo's relationship with Lee went beyond flouting the social, racial, and natural order of Spanish New Orleans. It also evoked whites' fears of slave rebellion and virile black masculinity in the era of the Haitian Revolution because it questioned their ability to protect the chastity of white women from the assault of black men.[39] According to trial testimony, Pompeyo "mistreated" Lee and "punished her" during their time together.[40] Whether or not Pompeyo actually mistreated Lee is not knowable. What is significant, however, is that in mistreating Lee, Pompeyo represented the ostensibly bestial nature of black men—especially in relationship to white womanhood.[41] Ideas of black masculinity as fundamentally animalistic may have been influenced by the sheer preponderance of enslaved men in Spanish New Orleans in 1795. However, news concerning the Haitian Revolution almost certainly skewed the court's perception of Pompeyo. Gruesome accounts detailing the revolution circulated throughout the Atlantic and Caribbean after 1791 and many highlighted the mutilation of helpless white women and children by black men. In *Incendie du Cap, Révolte générale des Nègre, Massacre des Blancs*, a frontispiece from a book on the Haitian Revolution, African male violence played a pivotal role in creating social chaos and summarized white male fears about the spread of social disruption (Figure 4). In the center of the image an African man chased a white family with his saber bared. The exposed breast of the white female and the phallic symbolism of the saber indicated the sexual underpinnings in this scene of social chaos. The implication being that social disorder will lead to the sexual "disorder" of procreation far outside of the natural socio-racial caste. Furthermore, in an account by Joseph Francois Lacroix, he asserted that "girls with their breast torn asunder looked as if they were begging for their mothers; mothers, with their pierced arms held the slaughtered children at their bosom."[42] The threat to white women in this passage is clearly sexual because of the repetition and description of women's breasts. The women themselves also echo the stereotypes of white female asexuality as they are described either as "girls" or "mothers." Accounts such as these directly challenged white manhood. They demonstrated that in the face of black violence, white men were unable to protect the honor of white women and would have influenced the court's treatment of Pompeyo upon learning that he lived with, and potentially mistreated, a white woman.[43]

Figure 4. *Incendie du Cap. Révolte générale des Nègres. Massacre des Blancs.* Lithograph, Frontispiece from the book *Saint-Domingue, ou Histoire de Ses Révolutions,* 1815, Paris: Chez Tiger.

In this climate of hostility toward assertive black men, the court would have viewed all of Pompeyo's actions as crimes against the natural order of society, rather than merely a dispute between two individuals. Unsurprisingly, they found Pompeyo guilty of assaulting a white man and slander, and deported him to Havana. The court claimed "[Pompeyo] must not remain in this city because of ... his arrogant temper and insolence to white people in general."[44] The distinction that Pompeyo's temper is a threat to whites "in general," and not to any specific white person suggests they treated

Pompeyo, not as an individual, but a symbol of black masculinity. In addition to his "insolence" Pompeyo was deported "also because of the inappropriate and scandalous life that he held."[45] Given the number of taverns and pool halls in New Orleans during the late eighteenth century, it is probable that the court was more scandalized by Pompeyo's cohabitation with Polly Lee than by his gambling.[46] Unfortunately for Pompeyo, he embodied an almost perfect confluence of social, racial, and sexual offenses in the eyes of the court. Charged with the difficult task of maintaining their social order in the era of the Haitian Revolution, the Court attempted to remove the threat by removing Pompeyo.

Although it is easy to see Pompeyo as the embodiment of white fears in an age of unrest, he should not be stripped of his humanity or agency. Despite being railroaded by influential white men, Pompeyo never admitted to criminal activity and would not sign the confession. In his last documented statement during the trial, Pompeyo affirmed that he understood the charges, but said "*he did not do it* and ... declared [his] truth under oath."[47] With the benefit of historical hindsight, Pompeyo's verdict seems to foretell Louisiana's continued fear of black men. Yet to his friends and relatives, Pompeyo's place within revolutionary currents likely mattered far less than the fact that they would almost certainly never see him again.

Notes

1   Louis Listau translator for *Ferray vs. Pompeyo,* August, 1795, pg 7, trans. Sarah Senette and Alix Rivere, Judiciary Court Records, Louisiana Historical Center, Old US Mint, New Orleans, Louisiana.

2   I am using the term manhood despite the fact that this study is about masculinity to draw a distinction between colonial ideas of whiteness and manhood, and blackness and masculinity. The latter would have more animalistic connotations. In this I lean heavily on Gail Bergman's *Manliness and Civilization.*

3   Laurent Dubois, *Avengers of the New World* (Harvard University Press, 2005), 6.

4   The Cabildo was composed of two levels of judicial officers called regidors and alcaldes. The alcaldes covered the general jurisdiction in New Orleans and were

selected by the regidors. The latter of whom obtained their offices by purchase. If the case was considered minor, the alcaldes issued the final judgments. Conversely, a three-judge court of two regidors and the trial alcalde hear appeals. Outside of New Orleans, each parish had military judges, aided by syndics (formerly French commandant) who held general trial powers. The final authority, however, was held by the Governor-Intendant. For a brief description on the transition from the French Superior Council to the Cabildo, see: H. Ward Fontenot, "The Louisiana Judicial System and the Fusion of Cultures," *Louisiana Law Review* 63, no. 4 (2003): 1053–1055.

5 Don Francisco de Riaño to Cabildo, May 27, 1791, in Acts and Deliberations of the Cabildo (English translations), Public Library, New Orleans, Louisiana. With racial tensions already high, the attempted slave revolt at Pointe Coupee, Louisiana, 1795, made a volatile situation worse.

6 Pointe Coupee is located approximately 110 miles northwest of New Orleans. The average horse can gallop at about 20–35 miles per hour. Allowing for rest, the distance could easily be traveled in under six hours.

7 Jack D. L. Holmes, "The Abortive Slave Revolt at Pointe Coupée, Louisiana, 1795" *Louisiana History* 11, no. 4 (Autumn 1970): 342–344, 352–353.

8 Minutes of the Cabildo, February 19, 1796, Acts and Deliberations of the Cabildo (English translation), City Archives, New Orleans, Louisiana.

9 *Ferray vs. Pompeyo*, October 1, 1795, pg 23 Judiciary Court Records, Louisiana. [italics added for emphasis]

10 While any direct effect of the rebellion on the trial is not knowable, it nonetheless serves as an example of planter's and white leader's fear of revolutionary blackness. Moreover, the abortive uprising occurred amidst a general milieu of black revolutionary currents emerging from both the Caribbean and from the French 1794 proclamation freeing slaves in the colonies. As the extreme response to a rebellion that did not actually take place indicates, in 1795 whites would have been seeing black revolution at every turn and would have punished any racial transgression harshly.

11 *Ferray vs. Pompeyo*, October 1, 1795, pg 7 Judiciary Court Records, Louisiana. It should likewise be noted that this line is unclear and could also be translated as "he threw his beer at him." This idea of escalating conflict and insult to manhood, though, remains the same.

12 Ibid., 10.

13 Ibid.

14 Scott K. Taylor, *Honor and Violence in Golden Age Spain* (New Haven, CT: Yale University Press, 2008), 7.

15 Derek Noel Kerr, *Petty felony, Slave Defiance, and Frontier Villainy: Crime and Criminal Justice in Spanish Louisiana, 1770–1803* (New York: Garland Publishing, 1993), 235–260.

16 *Ferray v. Pompeyo*, October 1, 1795, pg 15 Judiciary Court Records, Louisiana.

17 Lyman L. Johnson and Sonya Lipsett-Rivera, eds. *The Faces of Honor: Sex, Shame, and Violence in Colonial Latin America* (University of New Mexico Press, 1998), 3–5, 9.

18 *Ferray vs. Pompeyo*, October 1, 1795, pg 21, Judiciary Court Records, Louisiana.

19 Ibid.

20 Ibid.

21 Ibid.

22 Ibid.

23 Ibid., 22.

24 Cesare Beccaria, *Of Crimes and Punishments*. trans. Aaron Thomas and Jeremy Panzen, (University of Toronto Press, 2009), 19.

25 Don Perdo Dulcido Barran. pg 23. of Petitions, Letters, and Decrees of the Cabildo, 1770–1803. February 7, 1800. City Archives, New Orleans Public Library.

26 Ibid., 23.

27 Ibid.

28 Ibid.

29 *Ferray vs. Pompeyo*, October 1, 1795, pg 17, Judiciary Court Records, Louisiana.

30 Owens and Mangan, *Women of the Iberian Atlantic*, 40–42; Lawrence N. Powell, *The Accidental City: Improvising New Orleans* (Cambridge: Harvard University Press, 2012), 287, 288, 290, 291, 294–295; Kenneth R. Aslakson, *Making Race in the Courtroom: The Legal Construction of Three Races in Early New Orleans* (New York University Press, 2014), 6.

31 Powell, *The Accidental City*, 288.

32 I am also using Laura Edwards "Enslaved Women and the Law: Paradoxes of Subordination in the Post-Revolutionary Carolinas," *Slavery & Abolition* 26, no. 2 (August 1, 2005): 305–323, for the idea that patriarchy occurs in levels that must be supported by social inferiors.

33 María Elena Martínez, *Genealogical Fictions: Limpieza de Sangre, Religion, and Gender in Colonial Mexico* (Stanford University Press, 2008), 4–5.

34 Casta paintings in the latter part of the eighteenth century became increasingly elaborate, including one casta painting that had forty-nine different racial categories. For a brief discussion on castas in New Orleans, see Emily Clark, *The Strange History of the American Quadroon*, 4–7.

35 *Ferray vs. Pompeyo*, October 1, 1795, pg 10, 12, 13 Judiciary Court Records, Louisiana.

36 Martínez, *Genealogical Fictions*, 4–5; Ilona Katzew, *Casta Painting: Images of Race in Eighteenth-century Mexico* (Yale University Press, 2004), 1–2, 111–113.

37 Jennifer Spears, *Race, Sex, and Social Order in Early New Orleans* (Baltimore: Johns Hopkins University Press, 2009), 130.

38 Ibid.; Shannon Lee Dawdy, *Building the Devil's Empire: French Colonial New Orleans* (University of Chicago Press, 2008), 9, 141–144.

39 In contrast to the idea of manhood, I am using the term masculinity to convey a sense of physical power and not necessarily social dominance. Again, I am extrapolating this idea from Gail Bergman's *Manliness and Civilization*.

40 *Ferray vs. Pompeyo*, October 1, 1795, pg 17, Judiciary Court Records, Louisiana.

41 It should be noted that nowhere in the trial transcript does the court use this exact language. I am making this argument assuming that discourse would have some effect on their perception of Pompeyo.

42 Joseph Francois Pamphile vicomte de Lacroix, trans., Sarah Senette, *La Révolution de Haïti* (Paris 1819, reprint Karthla ed., 1995), 328.

43 The horrible irony in this argument is that the converse would have been true for men of color. Women of color, particularly enslaved women of color, were frequently the victims of sexual assault and black men would have had little recourse and certainly not expectation to protect their sexual honor.

44 *Ferray vs. Pompeyo*, October 1, 1795, pg 24, Judiciary Court Records, Louisiana.

45 Ibid.

46 Jack Holmes, "The Spanish Regulation of Taverns and the Liquor Trade in the Mississippi Valley," in *The Spanish in the Mississippi Valley 1762–1803*, ed. John McDermont (Urbana: University of Illinois Press, 1974), 158–159; Gilbert C. Din and John Harkins, *The New Orleans Cabildo: Colonial Louisiana's First City Government 1763–1803* (Baton Rouge: Louisiana State University Press, 1996), 16.

47 *Ferray vs. Pompeyo*, October 1, 1795, pg 23, Judiciary Court Records, Louisiana; I have also chosen to add the italics to emphasize the adamancy that I believe Pompeyo would have used due to his frequent denial of the charges.

III

MONUMENTS AND POWER:
RACISM AND PUBLIC MEMORY

MONUMENTS, URBANISM, AND POWER IN URBAN SPACES: LOOKING AT NEW ORLEANS, LOUISIANA FROM SÃO PAULO, BRAZIL

Douglas McRae
Georgetown University

In May 2017, the planned removal of monuments in New Orleans captured national attention, with reports of tempers flaring and tensions rising among protestors and counter-protestors in one of the United States' most historically and culturally significant cities.[1] The city of New Orleans eventually removed four monuments, three of which depicted Confederate leaders and another commemorating an 1874 uprising by a white paramilitary organization, the Crescent City White League, against the multiracial Reconstruction-era state government of Louisiana. Similar monuments are scattered across the Deep South; by one count, in 2016 approximately 700 Confederate statues and monuments could be found in public spaces in the United States, the overwhelming majority in the former Confederacy.[2]

After New Orleans, cities including Richmond, Lexington (Kentucky), and St. Louis made motions toward following New Orleans's example, either to remove or otherwise seriously rethink the place of monuments to the Confederate cause in public spaces. State politicians elsewhere have dug in further, preparing for inevitable struggles on their home turf. One Mississippi state legislator, in a show of incredibly poor judgment, called for the lynching of those who authorized the removals in New Orleans, pledging on social media to do "all in my power to prevent this from happening in my state."[3]

Then, in August, violence broke out in Charlottesville. Since May, far-right organizers had led a series of rallies in the Virginia college town, ostensibly against the removal of a statue of Robert E. Lee, maintained in a public park also named for the Confederate general. In August, one day before new student move-in at the University of Virginia, a much more coordinated event by white supremacist organizers shocked the nation in both its imagery and aftermath. Again, demonstrators initially cited the status of the Lee monument as the motive behind this "Unite the Right" rally, but it became increasingly clear that much more was at stake than a statue. The violence of that day (namely the death of a protestor and the injury of nineteen others at the hands of a domestic terrorist) tipped the scales toward an awakening: city officials in Baltimore removed almost immediately four Confederate monuments that they had previously mulled removing. Meanwhile, protestors in Durham, North Carolina tore down a statue of a Confederate soldier in front of the county courthouse.[4] The surreal image of the downed statue, seemingly deflated on the courthouse lawn, powerfully recalled the Haitian aphorism "an empty sack does not stand," or Langston Hughes's poetic observation on dreams deferred: "maybe it just sags like a heavy load. Or does it explode?"

Despite this sudden sea change in attitudes, the end has not yet been written on Confederate monuments or for the communities facing struggle and conflict. Media reports throughout the events leading up to Charlottesville often attempted to portray two sides to the monuments saga, at times grasping to demonstrate the old assertion that one person's hate is another person's heritage—though in light of the neo-Nazi presence at Charlottesville, this stance has become increasingly hard for many to uphold. Searching for a middle ground, however, has always threatened to muddle certain basic truths about the Confederacy, namely the rebel government's declared commitment to slavery and its expansion, as well as the entrenching of the white supremacist ideology that justified the subjugation of African Americans. While furor over the monuments may seem like a recent concern, activists and officials that advocate for removal recognize that the struggle over the city's public spaces stretches much further back than often recognized. The 2015 massacre at Emanuel AME Church in Charleston and the emboldening of the far right (repackaged as the "alt-right") in the wake of the recent presidential election have only heightened the urgency of efforts to confront symbols of the Confederacy across the South.[5]

I watched these events unfold from a physical remove, while living in the sprawling Brazilian megacity of São Paulo. As a native of Jackson, Mississippi, three hours north of New Orleans and in the heart of the Deep South, my heart was as close as my opinion was unequivocal: Confederate monuments must come down as part of the long, contentious and necessary process of dismantling structures of white supremacy in the United States. My own interests as a historian of Brazil and Latin America, however, also led me to reflect on the meanings of historical monuments in urban spaces beyond sites in the United States. The events of the summer of 2017 have provided ample examples of how power and narrative operate in urban spaces, examples that have a more universal application.

Commentators in the U.S. have also occasionally made the point that removal misses possibilities to contextualize, trying to straddle a line between appeasing monument defenders and their critics.[6] This viewpoint implies that removal by public authorities misses an opportunity for deeper historical understanding. Monuments and other pieces of the built environment that make up cities become flashpoints for controversy precisely because they are points of encounter for what French historian Pierre Nora recognized as the "fundamental opposition" between memory and history.[7] A comparative reflection on the meaning of monuments and commemoration allows us to unravel the arguments for Confederate monuments having an unquestioned place in our society by looking at precisely how history contests memory adapted as the dominant narrative.

Monumental structures make up part of the built environment of any urban landscape—sometimes their purpose is primarily symbolic, like a statue. At times, however, architecture and infrastructure too assume monumental aspects: elite figures or political circumstances that facilitated the construction of a park, building, or road become implicated in the finished structure's identity.[8] Whether functional or figurative, monuments reflect more than urbanism; that is, the art and study of city planning and design. They also reflect relations of power, embodying the ideologies of their creators and boosters. Contesting these monuments stands to unsettle assumptions about place and hierarchy in urban societies; rather than rendering historical memory as a static outgrowth of the past, monuments are places where memory is cast as history, and where relations of power are made tangible. In what follows, I will give some examples from São Paulo of contesting historical meanings in the urban landscape of memory, connecting how activist efforts have countered the accepted narratives undergirding the city's history, thus far with mixed results. These struggles take place in countless forms on the local level in cities everywhere; the purpose, however, of comparing cities as different as New Orleans and São Paulo is to emphasize how struggles over representation and power take place in landscapes of memory, reflecting broader societal conflict.

Looking at Another America:
Myths of Brazilian Frontiersmen in São Paulo

Scholars frequently compare the United States and Brazil—in addition to vast geographical and natural resource endowments, both nations have historical legacies of slavery and violence toward Afro-descendants and indigenous peoples. The U.S. South and Brazil were two of the most important players in the wider circum-Atlantic expansion of slaveholding economies in the early nineteenth century, a period that some historians have started to recognize as an era of "second slavery"—an expansion of enslaved labor that allowed for soaring agricultural exports including cotton, coffee, and sugar for the global industrial economy.[9] Among many divergences, however, Brazil notably lacks a major domestic conflict comparable to the U.S. Civil War. In fact, a basic contrast to draw between the United States and Brazil is the latter's gradual trajectory of emancipation, versus the violent armed conflict in the former that finally broke the back of Southern slaveholders in 1865. The fact that a wave of disaffected ex-Confederates migrated to Brazil after the Civil War speaks to the perceived similarities in the minds of planters seeking to restart their lives in another America.[10]

In Brazil, on the other hand, a series of gradual abolition measures over several decades prolonged slavery until 1888. Regional differences on the question of abolition certainly existed in Brazil, with greater abolitionist fervor in the economically declining Northeast, versus in the burgeoning coffee-producing Southeast, encompassing much of the province of São Paulo and absorbing a good portion of Brazil's nineteenth century enslaved population—a parallel movement to the domestic "Second Middle Passage" that took place in the U.S., as planters transferred an estimated one million slaves to the Deep South.[11] Post-abolition romanticizing of the slaveholding past certainly occurred into Brazil's republican period, often in service to propping up the myth of Brazilian racial democracy, yet nothing resembling the pro-Confederate "Lost Cause" ideology—a nostalgic cult to militarized honor and chivalry, often with open ties to white supremacy—emerged in Brazil. Indeed, white supremacy manifested in other nefarious ways, namely through eugenicist ideologies of racial improvement through "whitening," which sought to address Brazil's comparative economic underdevelopment.[12]

Despite these divergent trajectories between Brazil and the U.S., a point of comparison to the monuments under scrutiny throughout the South exists in São Paulo in the form of the *bandeirantes*.[13] While today São Paulo is the most cosmopolitan city in Brazil's most economically dynamic region, it started as a humble frontier outpost in 1554. Over the next century and a half, it became a launching point for the *bandeiras*—expeditions which set forth into the continental interior in search of mineral riches and native peoples to enslave, named for the flags they carried aloft as they advanced. In addition to capturing and enslaving Brazil's native peoples, bandeirantes (as the leaders of such expeditions were known, also translatable as "pathfinders") also waged war against autonomous communities of ex-slaves, known as *quilombos* in Brazil. The most celebrated quilombo of the seventeenth century, known as Palmares, was eventually brought down by a detachment of Paulista bandeirantes in 1695, after nearly a century of existence at the fringe of colonial sugar plantations its inhabitants once worked.[14]

The legacy of the bandeiras is, thus, easily linked to colonialism, violence, and slavery.[15] Yet the historical bandeirante underwent a significant image makeover as Brazil transitioned from Portuguese colony to independent nation in the nineteenth century, and as São Paulo (the historic base of the bandeiras) transformed from a backwater provincial capital into the industrial center of South America at the turn of twentieth century. As the city expanded and its industrial economy flourished, city builders plowed much of its historical architecture and natural landscape under concrete, metal, and pavement in the name of material progress and cultural modernity. Parallel with the melting away of the material past, the city's intellectuals sought inspiration in mythical adventurers of earlier centuries.

Conflict with the Brazilian federal government in the first half of the twentieth century culminated in a failed 1932 Paulista "Constitutionalist" uprising to reclaim regional autonomy from the government of Getúlio Vargas, who had taken power in a coup two years earlier. The aftermath of the revolt aided in solidifying an enduring Paulista identity, founded on modernity and progress, that had its origins in the path-finding ways of Brazil's first explorers, the bandeirantes.[16] Part of this new valorization involved the construction of commemorations that cast bandeirantes less as mixed-race slave raiders that they were (whose dialect and even dress purportedly resembled that of the native Tupi) and more as white, entrepreneurial European explorers, always looking toward the distant horizon, with hardly a weapon in sight.

One such representation of the bandeirantes has recently served as a flashpoint for controversy. A well-known icon of São Paulo's south zone, the Monument to the Bandeiras looms over the northernmost entrance of Ibirapuera Park. This imposing stone sculpture, composed of multiple muscular figures dragging a small boat in their wake, appears to be marching northwest up Avenida Brazil, the thoroughfare that bisects São Paulo's affluent Jardins neighborhoods. Brazilian modernists conceived of the sculpture in the 1920s as a way to revalorize Brazil's colonial history, yet the project only acquired momentum (and funding) after the aforementioned 1932 regional revolt. State governor Armando de Sales praised the statue's proposed design in 1936, claiming that the gradually diminishing height of the monument's figures represented "hierarchy, inseparable from discipline and one of the most beautiful principals of social organization."[17]

Since its inauguration in 1953, the completed Monument to the Bandeiras has persisted as an interpretation of such themes. Its multiple meanings, however, have recently faced challenges from below. In 2016, in tandem with protests for indigenous rights and recognition, the monument was doused with paint under cover of night. The blood-red splatter marks left on the monument served as reminders of the murderous acts of the historical bandeirantes as well as contemporary echoes of the continued threats of violence faced by indigenous peoples and Afro-Brazilians in the present.[18] In a city where graffiti and street art often overlap with political meanings, the purposeful defacing of the monument can make a statement about the historical narratives represented in public spaces.[19] Despite the often observed fact that the Monument to the Bandeiras appears to depict Brazil's historical racial groups among its figures, seemingly representing the ideal of racial democracy, the veneration of social hierarchy and the directive of colonial conquest generate discomfort and tension.

Graffiti and defacement have also been a first line of contesting the meanings of monuments in places like Marion Square in Charleston, South Carolina. The base of the statue of nineteenth century politician and native son John C. Calhoun at Marion Square was purposefully defaced in the wake of the massacre at the AME Emmanuel Baptist Church in 2015. Calhoun, perhaps South Carolina's most well-known statesman, was also a progenitor of states' rights and Southern secession, all in the name of preserving and expanding slavery. Though conventional historical accounts have placed Calhoun in a great triumvirate "part of the furniture of American memory" alongside fellow Congressmen Daniel Webster and Henry Clay, the making of a Calhoun monument in a central public space of Charleston has invited engagement, including criticism, for those who come into contact with it.[20] The tagging of statues with graffiti, independent of historical patrimony laws that such an act violates, serves as a way to confront directly received narratives, and indeed became increasingly visible in the summer of 2017.

In an essay discussing the challenges of collecting oral histories, sociologist Karen E. Fields revisits an anecdote told by her grandmother regarding black Charlestonians' perspectives on the Calhoun statue, recounting the memory of adults and children alike deliberately defacing the statue around the turn of the twentieth century, necessitating that the statue's keepers elevate it onto a high pedestal. Fields concludes that parts of her grandmother's story are ultimately unverifiable, and perhaps are deliberate "misrememberings" intended to spur a younger generation to resist racism as their forbearers bravely did. The story that Fields uncovers in the archives "opened out instead of pinning down" the story: the unveiling of the first Calhoun statue in 1879 evidently provoked scandal, in part because of its proximity to an allegorical statue of a semi-nude female figure. Newspapers reported that the statues came to be known as "Calhoun and he wife" a phrase rendered in Gullah syntax that suggests that those that laughed the loudest at the statue were Charleston's black residents.[21] The statue of Calhoun was eventually replaced and repositioned on a pillar, while no mention is made in the archival records about resistance or public vandalism. Despite uncovering no corroborating evidence for her grandmother's original story, Fields's anecdote nonetheless speaks to the histories and memories that monuments generate. Recounting this example does not seek to idealize such types of furtive resistance, however they took place, but rather to emphasize the longstanding contestation that occurs when representations of power and hierarchy are erected in public spaces.

The name and image of pro-slavery figures like Calhoun are pervasive in the South, and in similar fashion, the name and image of the bandeirantes are also unavoidable throughout São Paulo's urban landscape. Yet it has been the visual depictions of the bandeirantes in sculpture and in paintings that have come under the most scrutiny and occasionally, revision. Another statue in São Paulo's Santo Amaro region of the bandeirante Borba Gato has been covered in graffiti and was convicted in a mock "people's trial" that highlighted the crimes of the bandeirantes. In addition to performative acts of protests, public institutions like the Museu Paulista, one of the region's largest historical collections, have begun to reevaluate their collection's bandeirante iconography. A modest outdoor exhibit in front of the museum in one of São Paulo's public parks breaks down the various problematic portrayals in works created primarily between 1903 and 1935, emphasizing that the history of any society is made through choices: what to emphasize and what to hide. In this case, the violence and war that accompanied the advance of Portuguese colonial society is absent from monumental depictions. While the reflection falls short of outright removal, in this instance it is also the work of activists that has led to a deeper engagement with these century-old pieces.

The monuments to the bandeirantes in São Paulo city are products of a self-conscious crafting of Paulista identity, whitewashing historical figures twice: once figuratively by muting their violent impact on those they enslaved, and second literally by depicting them as of primarily European descent in appearance. These choices of depiction emerged from a time when Paulista elites, emboldened by their region's economic successes, chose to promote their whiteness as evidence of their recourse to modernity, juxtaposing themselves not just with black Paulistas whom they systematically excluded, but also with the rest of Brazil that trailed behind São Paulo's economic lead.

Generally, we may view these and other monuments as simultaneously reflecting two historical times: the moment or era they commemorate, and the context in which they were created. The second meaning is often less evident when compared with the first, but both interact with the present moment. Returning to the monuments commemorating Lee, Beauregard, and Davis, we have depictions that emphasize leaders and warriors, often with their own weapons sheathed and holstered, divorced completely from any notion of the cause for which they ordered men into battle. The context in which they were built is also relevant. Most Confederate monuments across the South came up in the era after Reconstruction, a period that produced a new political alignment between the defeated planter class and rising Redeemer industrialists. It was not quite a restoration of the antebellum elite, but the subsequent "New South" alliance sought to maintain tight control over black Southerners and poorer white working folk.[22] Postwar white elites oversaw this wave of monument construction, which buttressed the "Lost Cause" mythology and tacitly condoned the wave of violence carried out against African Americans in this period. These two historical times came together in present-day commemorations found in public squares, along thoroughfares, and in traffic circles.

Taming the Minhocão and the Road to Reclaiming Urban Spaces

While statues and obelisks are among the recognizable references for monuments, sometimes the built environment of the city itself can assume monumental dimensions. In other words, the commemorative power of the built environment often parallels such structures' functional purpose in the city. Though a building or thoroughfare may officially commemorate a person or event, its actual physical presence evokes the moment and circumstances in which it came to be.

Due west of São Paulo's historic center, there rises an imposing elevated highway, popularly known popularly as the *Minhocão*, or giant worm, after a mythical Amazonian beast of gargantuan proportions. The municipality of São Paulo conceived of the Minhocão during the first mayoral administration of Paulo Maluf, one of Brazil's most notorious politicians. With little regard for the impact on the quality of life for the neighborhoods and families in the vicinity that the monstrous thoroughfare invaded, the elevated way stood as a monument to pharaonic public works and a commitment to an automobile-centric transportation system.[23] Here was another monument of sorts to Paulista modernity: while the rest of Brazil at the end of the 1970s languished in economic crisis brought by debt-fueled double-digit growth, São Paulo sought to reassert its place as South America's economic and financial center.

The Minhocão's first official name, General Artur da Costa e Silva Elevated Highway, was a tribute to Brazil's president from 1968 to 1973. Costa e Silva had appointed Maluf, his close friend and political ally, as mayor of São Paulo in the midst of Brazil's 21 years of military dictatorship from 1964 to 1985. The Brazilian military had seized power in a 1964 coup and gradually tightened its grip on dissidence and political expression. By the time Costa e Silva assumed the presidency, the hardline of the military had taken control and dispensed with any veneer of constitutionalism in favor of authoritarian rule. The Minhocão, completed in 1970, came to symbolize, both through its official name and its imposing physical presence, the long reach of military rule. As Brazil slowly transitioned to civilian rule during the 1980s, São Paulo was simultaneously becoming synonymous with violent crime and extreme social segregation, an image that dogged its claim to modernity. (Incidentally, the codename of the police operation in São Paulo state implemented in 1969 to hunt down, detain, and torture dissidents and leftist guerrillas was Operation Bandeirante). The two miles of elevated road careening through the city's core did little to ameliorate traffic and much to aggravate living conditions in the vicinity.

Recent efforts by community activists as well as progressive city administrations have sought to reimagine this paean to authoritarian government and municipal malfeasance. The intrusion of the Minhocão contributed to the decline of the quality of life for the residents of surrounding areas of Vila Buarque and Santa Cecilia, neighborhoods that had been wealthy suburbs in the late nineteenth century but by the 1930s had begun to decline—a tendency exacerbated by the construction of the elevated highway. Recently, efforts have been made to transform this urban landscape again. One act was symbolic: in 2014, the Municipal Secretary of Human Rights and Citizenship established a coordinating committee on "the right to memory and truth" with the stated purpose of "rescuing the memory and the truth about grave human rights violations practiced in the city of São Paulo during the dictatorship that controlled the country from 1964 to 1985."[24] An initiative of the municipal office also sought to rename forty streets and roads in São Paulo named for figures associated with the military dictatorship, including Costa e Silva Elevated Highway. In 2016, the municipality officially renamed the Minhocão for João Goulart, the president deposed in the 1964 coup.

Costa e Silva's name has been wiped from the elevated highway, though in local imagination the highway remains the Minhocão—its physical presence holds sway over all. As mentioned, the highway has the worst impact on nearby residences, yet efforts have been made to tame the beast. Noise from weekday traffic on the Minhocão reverberates off third-story windows at the level of the expressway, while the smell and imprint of automobile pollution sears the environment. Meanwhile, the Minhocão's concrete underbelly rose over the original two-way thoroughfare below, blocking sunlight from above and heightening a sense of insecurity in its shadow.

Recently, city councilmembers and activists have pushed to remake the entire structure into a public park. In the windows of some neighbors, banners reading "Minhocão Park" visible on Sundays speak to this vision. In fact, every Sunday the Minhocão is closed to automobile traffic and transforms into a pedestrian park. Dog walking couples, teenage skateboarders, and weekend joggers traverse the road, while coconut water vendors and makeshift used clothes vendors ply their wares. Walking on an elevated four-lane overpass past mid-level stories of apartment buildings has an almost post-apocalyptic quality, as if some disaster had emptied the city of its ubiquitous automobiles. Further plans to transform the Minhocão into an elevated park have been floated—though Brazil's current economic and political crisis may delay that eventuality. In a city council meeting, a longtime resident who favored dismantlement of the highway piece by piece testified to the "43 years of suffering" that the Minhocão had brought. Others expressed suspicion about the putative benefits of a public park, worrying that spontaneous partying and soccer games were just as much a nuisance. The impact of an eventual repurposing or deconstruction of the Minhocão always invites concerns of "real estate speculation" (in other words, gentrification) if the area becomes overly desirable for more well-off Paulistanos.[25]

The trajectory of the Minhocão resembles that of similar intrusive overpasses and elevated highways also found in cities across the United States.[26] Roads are not monuments in the same sense that statue depictions of Jefferson Davis or Robert E. Lee are; yet their physical presence shapes the surrounding landscape of memory. Such exercises of power have been associated with Robert Moses, the influential New York City park commissioner, accused of remaking New York City with complete and deliberate disregard of its African American residents. The projects conceived under Moses, from swimming pools to bypasses, have a similar impact to that of monuments: they reflect a specific vision for a city (in this case, New York), grounded less in historical remembering but rather in deliberately remaking the city over rather than around those that live in it.

In the example of monumental pieces of infrastructure, the issue is often less for who they are named, but rather for the urbanist ideals that they embody. Anyone who has approached New Orleans along eastbound Interstate 10 (the Claiborne Expressway, named for the first U.S. governor of the Louisiana territory) has noticed how the elevated road passes over a wide stretch of low-lying neighborhoods, including the historically African-American Tremé neighborhood. As told by residents, the Claiborne Highway went up in the 1960s with little regard for the surrounding residential and business community, aggravating the inequalities of the city's racial geography.[27]

Reclaiming spaces invaded by bypasses and elevated highways is not specific to New Orleans, and in other urban areas such development overwhelmingly affects working-class communities, populations that often have the least amount of say regarding urbanist interventions into their neighborhoods. Expressway projects were never inevitable; in fact, preservationists successfully deterred the building of a six-lane elevated expressway adjacent to the French Quarter around the same time the elevated Claiborne expressway came into existence.[28] Activist efforts to prevent as well as decommission and even remove elevated highways seek to reclaim a former glory, repurposing a space captured in the name of a progress and modernity that forgot the very residents that would live in its shadow.

Monuments in their various forms play an important part in shaping our perceptions of cities and the societies that inhabit them. The ways in which parts of the urban environment are critiqued and contested are important aspects of transforming urban life and creating historical narratives that address a broader spectrum of historical memory. As with statues commemorating Confederate figures, two historical times shape the present landscape of memory that surrounds structures like elevated highways. In the case of Confederate monuments, the commemoration of the Confederacy is already questionable due to the historical fact of that government's cornerstone of slavery. The origins of the commissioning of the Confederate monuments in the post-Reconstruction era have equal, though frequently obscured, relevance for understanding why such monuments have persisted in public spaces. In a similar sense, monumental structures are also imbued with historical values and ideologies, and opposition to their persistence by activists reflects many of the dynamics present in the contestation of more conventional monuments. Their removal is more difficult if not impossible—even idealistic repurposing or redevelopment schemes threaten to be handed over to the whims of the real estate market, inviting creeping gentrification and neighborhood displacement.

At the same time, it is precisely activism and organizing that build community, creating networks and memories that span generations and continuously counter attempts to naturalize inequality in the city—in the case of New Orleans, such a genealogy of organizing with all its successes and setbacks can be traced back at least to *Plessy v. Ferguson*, the court case that originated in New Orleans and legally sanctioned separate but equal institutions.[29] At the same time, urban renewal projects that took place in the decades before and after the end of Jim Crow in the South often sought to replicate those inequalities and continue to make money from the rents and poverty of cities' poorer, often non-white residents. As historian N.D.B. Connolly points out from the perspective of Miami, racial apartheid in the name of profit may be identified in cities throughout the Americas.[30] While not as pronounced in racial terms in São Paulo (a product of the historical narrative of racial democracy), top-down urbanism threatens to exacerbate social inequality and literally pave over older historical cityscapes. This physical and visual concretization of inequality also has symbolic meaning in the urban landscape of memory. The struggle to reclaim urban space and remove archaic monuments is thus linked in important ways.

I began writing this essay as a response to a heightening public interest in the fate of the Confederate monuments in New Orleans. At this stage, further removals are in motion riding the wave generated by confrontations between white supremacist groups and counter-protestors in Charlottesville. It is essential to emphasize for Americans trying to make sense of what has taken place that actions taken regarding monuments, up to and including removing them, do not constitute an erasure of history. Rather, they represent a direct engagement with dominant historical narratives, the multiple meanings behind these monuments and the ideologies that justified their construction and continuance in public spaces. Defenders of the monuments who cast them as neutral, apolitical, eminently historical or otherwise unquestionable elements of urban spaces are the ones who are erasing historical memory.

Notes

1   Richard Fausset "Tempers Flare Over Removal of Confederate Statues in New Orleans" *New York Times,* May 7, 2017, https://www.nytimes.com/2017/05/07/us/new-orleans-monuments.html; Janell Ross, "Tensions Rise as New Orleans Prepares to Topple Confederate Monuments," *Washington Post,* May 7, 2017, https://www.washingtonpost.com/news/post-nation/wp/2017/05/07/tensions-rise-as-new-orleans-prepares-to-topple-confederate-monuments/. This essay is a revised and expanded version of an piece published as "Monuments and Urban Power: Looking at New Orleans, Louisiana from São Paulo, Brazil," May 26, 2017, https://activisthistory.com/2017/05/26/monuments-and-power-in-urban-spaces-looking-at-new-orleans-louisiana-from-sao-paulo-brazil/.

2   Southern Poverty Law Center, *Whose Heritage? Public Symbols of the Confederacy*

(April 2016), 8, https://www.splcenter.org/20160421/whose-heritage-public-symbols-confederacy. This publication also includes a Community Action Guide for local activism aimed at removing Confederate symbols in public spaces.

3   Donna Ladd, "Rep. Karl Oliver's Lynching Call Tursn Spotlight to Mississippi Statues," Jackson Free Press, May 22, 2017, http://www.jacksonfreepress.com/news/2017/may/22/rep-karl-olivers-lynching-call-turns-spotlight-mis/.

4   An updated list of proposals and actions for removal may be found here: "Confederate Monuments Are Coming Down across the United States. Here's a List," *New York Times*, https://nyti.ms/2v2Qznb, accessed August 17, 2017.

5   Jelani Cobb, New Yorker "The Battle Over Confederate Monuments in New Orleans," *The New Yorker*, May 12, 2017, http://www.newyorker.com/news/daily-comment/the-battle-over-confederate-monuments-in-new-orleans/; "Why It Matters," #TakeEmDownNola, http://takeemdownnola.org/why-it-matters/,accessed July 18, 2017.

6   See for example: Gary Shapiro, "The Meaning of our Confederate 'Monuments'," *New York Times*, May 15, 2017, https://www.nytimes.com/2017/05/15/opinion/the-meaning-of-our-confederate-monuments.html. While Shapiro arguably makes a useful distinction between the intentions of monuments and memorials, his "contextualist" position seemingly ignores the actual post-Civil War context in which many monuments in question were conceived and created, as will be argued below.

7   Pierre Nora, "Between Memory and History: *Les Lieux de Mémoire*" trans. by Marc Roudebush, *Representations*, No. 26 (January 1989), 8. For other non-U.S. examples of contemporary disputes over historical monuments and memory, see Elke Zuern, "Nambia's Monuments to Genocide," *Dissent*, https://www.dissentmagazine.org/blog/namibia-genocide-monuments-reparations-germany; William Neuman, "A Hammer Comes Down in Colombia on an Honor for Britain," *New York Times*, November 19, 2014, https://www.nytimes.com/2014/11/20/world/americas/a-hammer-comes-down-on-an-honor-for-britain.html; Michel-Rolph Trouillot, *Silencing the Past: Power and the Production of History* (Boston: Beacon Press, 2015[1995]), 154–156 and passim; Sabine Marschall, *Landscape of Memory: Commemorative Monuments, Memorials and Public Statuary in Post-Apartheid South Africa* (Boston: Brill, 2010).

8   See the illuminating case of underexpressway parks in Miami, Florida, in N.D.B. Connolly, *A World More Concrete: Real Estate and the Remaking of Jim Crow South Florida* (Chicago: University of Chicago Press, 2016), 1–16.

9   Sven Beckert and Seth Rockman, "Introduction: Slavery's Capitalism," in Sven Beckert and Seth Rockman, *Slavery's Capitalism: A New History of American Economic Development* (University of Pennsylvania Press, 2016), 11–12. Also, see

the collected articles in *Review: A Journal of the Fernand Braudel Center* 31, No. 2 (2008). Also, see Sven Beckert, *Empire of Cotton: A Global History* (New York: Knopf, 2014) for an account of the relationship between the British-centered global textile industry and the violent expansion of slavery in nineteenth century North America.

10 The transnational significance of Brazilian *confederados*—as this cultural group, confined mostly to two towns in western São Paulo state, is known—is beyond the scope of this piece, though it does speak to wider sense of shared hemispheric identity and belonging experienced by Southern slaveholders in the mid-late nineteenth century. See: Cyrus B. and James M. Dawsey, eds. *The Confederados: Old South Immigrants in Brazil* (Tuscaloosa: University of Alabama Press, 1988); Laura Jarnagin, *A Confluence of Transatlantic Networks: Elites, Capitalism, and Confederate Migration to Brazil* (Tuscaloosa: University of Alabama Press, 2008); Matthew Pratt Guterl, *American Mediterranean: Southern Slaveholders in the Age of Emancipation* (Cambridge, MA: Harvard University Press, 2008).

11 Beckert and Rockman, "Introduction: Slavery's Capitalism," 22; Edward Baptist, *The Half Has Never Been Told* (New York: Basic Books, 2014), Ch 1.

12 The comparative literature on race in the U.S. and Brazil is vast and spans decades as well as disciplines. One of the most important recent interventions that synthesizes debates and contributes new insights is Edward E. Telles, *Race in Another America: The Significance of Skin Color in Brazil* (Princeton: Princeton University Press, 2006).

13 Historian Micol Seigel has argued that comparative studies of the U.S. and Brazil flatten the transnational dimension and mutual constitution of cultural and social discourses. See *Uneven Encounters: Making Race and Nation in the U.S. and Brazil* (Durham, NC: Duke University Press, 2009). There is certainly a transnational dimension to the image of the bandeirantes, Brazilian and North American scholars alike have compared with pioneers or frontiersmen. While this transnational aspect is important, in this instance I am specifically interested in the comparative role that monuments play in urban spaces versus the transnational encounters that may have contributed to those monuments' ultimate forms.

14 Palmares, its legendary leader Zumbi, and historical quilombos (from which many rural Afro-Brazilian communities trace their ancestry) continue to inspire activism as well as scholarship. See João José Reis and Flavio dos Santos Gomes, "Quilombo: Brazilian Maroons During Slavery," *Cultural Survival Quarterly* 25, No. 4 (January 2002): 16; Robert Nelson Anderson, "The Quilombo of Palmares: A New Overview of a Maroon State in Seventeenth-Century Brazil," *Journal of Latin American Studies* 28, No. 3 (October 1996): 545–566.

15 For a timely comparison between monuments in New Orleans and monuments commemorating violent conquest in the U.S. West, see Rebecca Solnit, "The Mon-

ument Wars," *Harper's Magazine* (January 2017), https://harpers.org/archive/2017/01/the-monument-wars/.

16 Barbara Weinstein, *The Color of Modernity: São Paulo and the Making of Race and Nation in Brazil* (Durham, NC: Duke University Press, 2015), Ch. 2.

17 Quoted in Roberto Pompeu de Toledo. *O capital de vertigem: uma história de São Paulo, 1900–1954* (São Paulo: Companhia de Letras, 2015), 362 (All translations from Portuguese are my own).

18 See John Hemming, *Die if You Must: Brazilian Indians in the Twentieth Century* (London: Macmillan, 2003), the third in a trilogy on a history of Brazilian indigenous peoples since European contact. The news website Rioonwatch (<http://www.rioonwatch.org/>) has become a vocal source of information on police brutality against Afro-Brazilians, especially in Rio de Janeiro, during and in the wake of the 2014 World Cup and 2016 Olympics. Its community-based coverage has served as a productive intersection for scholarship and activism.

19 Nate Millington, "The Aesthetic Politics of Graffiti Removal in Contemporary São Paulo," *Situated Urban Political Ecology Collective*, February 28, 2017, http://www.situatedupe.net/the-aesthetic-politics-of-graffiti-removal-in-contemporary-sao-paulo/; Russell White, "Brazil: Pixação, São Paulo's Urban Calligraphy," *Latin American Bureau*, May 17, 2016, https://lab.org.uk/brazil-pixacao-sao-paulo%E2%80%99s-urban-calligraphy/.

20 Merrill D. Peterson, *The Great Triumvirate: Webster, Clay, and Calhoun* (New York: Oxford University Press, 1987), 6.

21 Karen E. and Barbara J. Fields, *Racecraft: The Soul of Inequality in American Life* (New York: Verso, 2014), 181–186.

22 C. Vann Woodward, *Origins of the New South, 1877–1913* (Baton Rouge: Louisiana State University Press, 1971[1951]), 21–22.

23 The impact of the military dictatorship's obsession with "automobility" was part of a longer Brazilian and global trend, described in Joel Wolfe, *Autos and Progress: The Brazilian Search for Modernity* (New York: Oxford University Press, 2014), 158–160; For a recent account of the origins of Maluf's malfeasances and the Minhocão, see Alex Cuadros, *Brazillionaires: Wealth, Power, Decadence, and Hope in an American Country* (New York: Random House, 2016), Ch. 2.

24 "Coordenação," Available in Portuguese at: <http://www.prefeitura.sp.gov.br/cidade/secretarias/direitos_humanos/direito_a_memoria_e_a_verdade/coordenacao/index.php?p=152459>.

25 Marcelo Mora, "Criação de parquet gera 'racha' em audiência sobre pública o Minhocão," *G1*, September 10, 2014, http://g1.globo.com/sao-paulo/noticia/

2014/09/criacao-de-parque-gera-racha-em-audiencia-publica-sobre-o-minhocao.html; O Estado de S. Paulo, "2024. Adeus, Minhocão ... até nunca mais," *O Estado de S. Paulo*, January 24, 2014, http://sao-paulo.estadao.com.br/noticias/geral,2024-adeus-minhocao-ate-nunca-mais,1122538.

26 Laura Bliss, "In Divided Denver, a Highway Promises Reconnection," *CityLab*, January 12, 2017, https://www.citylab.com/equity/2017/01/in-divided-denver-a-highway-promises-reconnection/512660/.

27 Michael E. Crutcher, *Tremé: Race and Place in a New Orleans Neighborhood* (Athens: University of Georgia Press, 2010), Ch. 4; Laine Kaplan-Levenson "'The Monster': Claiborne Avenue Before and After the Highway," *New Orleans Public Radio*, May 5, 2016, http://wwno.org/post/monster-claiborne-avenue-and-after-interstate.

28 Richard O. Baumbach Jr., and William E. Borah, *The Second Battle of New Orleans: A History of the Vieux Carre Riverfront Expressway Controversy* (University: University of Alabama Press, 1981).

29 Donald E Devore, *Defying Jim Crow: African American Community Development and the Struggle for Racial Equality in New Orleans, 1900–1960* (Baton Rouge: Louisiana State University Press, 2015).

30 Connolly, *A World More Concrete*, 6–8.

PRODUCING AND PROTESTING INVISIBILITY IN SILVER SPRING, MARYLAND

David S. Rotenstein
Independent Scholar

Introduction

Silver Spring, Maryland, developed during the early twentieth century as a sundown suburb: an area covering more than ten square miles where racial restrictive deed covenants prevented African Americans from owning or renting homes.[1] Located in Montgomery County about 6 miles north of downtown Washington, D.C., Silver Spring did not begin desegregating its businesses until the late 1950s and housing discrimination remained legal there until 1968, when the county's open housing law went into effect. Despite dramatic changes in Silver Spring's demographics and politics, the community's history and historic preservation efforts remain as segregated as its earlier public culture. New residents with no diachronic attachments to the community and a historically white and wealthy power regime complicate local efforts to make history and historic preservation more inclusive. African Americans, the Jim Crow era, and the civil rights actions that helped break down racial barriers in Silver Spring in the 1960s remain invisible in published histories and in the commemorative landscape.

I live in Silver Spring and I make my living in public history. In recent years, my work has focused on suburban gentrification and how people of color are displaced from communities and erased from the historical record.[2] In 2011, my family moved from Silver Spring to an Atlanta, Georgia, suburb where African Americans were being displaced by aggressive real estate practices that were converting the city into a new wealthier and whiter suburban enclave. As Decatur was emerging as an Atlanta-area destination for new residents and as a hipster-friendly playground for Atlanta's burgeoning middle class, its history was being rewritten and imagineered to fit the city's new image—its brand. In the 1980s, when Decatur officials sponsored citywide historic resource surveys, those products included African American historic places and stories about the black experience in Decatur.[3] By the first decade of the twenty-first century, newer historic preservation efforts covering the same spaces and time periods omitted African American history and historic sites.[4] It is as if Decatur had always been a wealthy white Atlanta suburb. When we returned to Silver Spring in 2014, I found the same erasures in Silver Spring's official histories. My work at the intersection of history, historic preservation, race, and gentrification began exposing how the processes that led to the displacement of residents of color are tied to the production of histories and historic preservation programs that render them invisible by omission.

Since the turn of the twenty-first century, Silver Spring has experienced a substantial amount of reinvestment from the public and private sectors resulting in community rebranding efforts and large-scale redevelopment projects. At the same time that capital began flowing back into the community, a historic preservation advocacy organization formed to preserve old buildings and to "create and promote awareness and appreciation of downtown Silver Spring, Maryland's heritage."[5] Though the organization has been unsuccessful in its preservation of the community's bricks and mortar, it has become a highly visible presence in Silver Spring through its quixotic and adversarial historic preservation advocacy efforts, the publication of books and articles about Silver Spring's history, its walking tours in the central business district, and the design and placement of heritage trail signs throughout the downtown.[6] Cumulatively, these efforts have produced a nostalgic and racially biased version of Silver Spring's history that excludes people of color and mutes their experiences in the community.[7] These histories have influenced official county planning documents, statements by elected and appointed officials about the community's history, and the general population's understanding of Silver Spring's past.

During the summer of 2016, I began asking my neighbors, people in the Saturday farmer's market, and Montgomery County's elected and appointed officials if they could tell me where to find sites associated with African American and civil rights history in downtown Silver Spring. Scott Whipple, the supervisor in the county's historic preservation office since 2007, could not identify any. Gwen Wright, the county's planning director and Whipple's predecessor in the historic preservation office, replied that the only one she could think of was a historical marker recounting an episode involving an enslaved person during the Civil War.[8]

Despite the lack of sites identified in my informal survey, in my research on the black experience in Silver Spring, I was able to identify about 20 stops in the central business district. The locations included sites of oppression (businesses that discriminated whose buildings are preserved and celebrated as part of Silver Spring's nostalgic past) and sites of resistance. I then began conducting Black History Tours in Silver Spring's central business district to help raise awareness of the community's missing African American history. After one of the tours in June 2017, there was an event in one of Silver Spring's historical parks where residents shared stories of discrimination and participants could submit comments to Montgomery County agencies undertaking renovations in the park. The event invited people to "protest invisibility and help make Acorn Park more inclusive."

This chapter examines twentieth century history in Silver Spring and how history and historic preservation are produced there. Using documentary research and interviews with residents, county officials, and others done between 2014 and 2017, I explore the intersection of race, history, historic preservation, and the commemorative landscape in a community undergoing rapid change. The essay ends with the June 2017 event in Silver Spring's Acorn Urban Park. It was an experiment combining activism and history in an attempt to reframe how history and historic preservation are produced in Silver Spring. Though unresolved as of this writing, the event may be used as a model for similar grassroots efforts to make community history and commemorative landscapes more inclusive and accurate.

A Little Silver Spring History

Silver Spring is an unincorporated community that shares a boundary with the District of Columbia. The community's origin legend is that Francis Preston Blair (1791–1876), a Washington journalist, was riding his horse through the area in 1840 when he discovered a mica-flecked spring. Blair subsequently bought 289 acres and named his new plantation Silver Spring. By the time the Civil War broke out, Blair was one of the largest landholders and enslavers in Montgomery County (twelve slaves in 1860).[9] Though Blair became a prominent advisor to President Abraham Lincoln and his son, Montgomery Blair, served as Lincoln's postmaster-general, the family quickly abandoned the Republican Party during Reconstruction. They rejoined the Democratic Party and became supporters of a movement to relocate formerly enslaved people to Africa.[10]

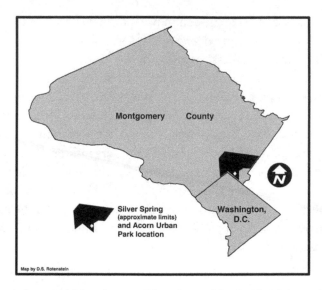

Figure 1: Location Map showing Silver Spring Maryland and Acorn Urban Park.

By the end of the nineteenth century, the Blairs had substantial real estate holdings in Montgomery County bordering the District of Columbia. During the first quarter of the twentieth century, Edward Brooke Lee (1892–1984), Montgomery Blair's great-nephew, expanded his family's real estate investments by buying up and consolidating large farm tracts to develop "restricted" and "exclusive" residential subdivisions. In the 1920s, Lee founded the North Washington Realty Company, which developed most of his properties through the 1940s.

In 1925, Lee was one of several real estate entrepreneurs who founded the Silver Spring Chamber of Commerce.[11] Two years later, in 1927, they embarked on a branding and marketing campaign that included display advertisements in Washington newspapers touting "Maryland North of Washington" as a prime investment opportunity: "the logical place in which to build for posterity."[12] Maps published in these ads illustrated new and proposed residential subdivisions, proposed parks, major roads leading to downtown Washington, and the area's two country clubs.

Despite Lee's planning and branding efforts, Silver Spring never became anything more than a collection of geographically contiguous nineteenth century hamlets and twentieth century residential subdivisions. In speculating on regional toponymy, contemporary writers have ignored the 1920s efforts to create a sprawling Washington suburb and the 1955 Montgomery County legislation that fixed the unincorporated area's boundaries as a county-regulated "suburban district."[13] Twenty-first century bloggers and journalists have written that the sprawling Silver Spring area is the product of United States Postal Service ZIP Code assignments.[14] However, the area is generally coterminous with the extent of racially restricted residential subdivisions platted between 1904 and 1948.[15] Race, not postage, informed the creation of Silver Spring.

As he was acquiring substantial real estate holdings, Lee also was consolidating political power in Montgomery County and heavily Democratic Maryland. Lee had enlisted in the Maryland Infantry in 1912 was a founder of Silver Spring's National Guard armory. After World War I, Lee returned to Montgomery County a decorated officer and became Comptroller of the State of Maryland (1919–1922) and he served as Maryland's Secretary of State (1923–1925) before being elected in 1927 to the Maryland House of Delegates. Lee was a founder in 1925 of the Maryland-National Capital Park and Planning Commission and he provided influential support for the creation of the Montgomery County Civic Federation.[16]

Lee was Montgomery County's uncontested political boss through World War II. He frequently is described as Montgomery County's political boss and the "father of modern Silver Spring." Though his political power waned after a new Montgomery County home rule charter was enacted in 1948, Lee remained fierce defender of the segregated suburbs he helped to create.[17] Even as late as 1967 as civil rights laws were being debated and enacted by the U.S. Congress, state legislatures, and local jurisdictions like Montgomery County, Lee was railing against legislation that he believed would dismantle the suburbs that he had helped create.[18] "Since law-enforced opening of homes and home communities is only aimed at White owned homes and White occupied communities, the law-enforced open housing statutes are Anti-White laws," Lee wrote in the Bethesda-Chevy Chase Advertiser in March 1967.[19]

Although Lee became the best-known among Silver Spring's early land speculators, there were earlier efforts to establish residential subdivisions there. Some of these were classic streetcar suburbs platted in the 1880s. Most, however, began appearing during the first two decades of the twentieth century. The automobile and the demand for housing in an expanding Washington metropolitan area in suburban Maryland and Virginia accelerated development during 1920s.[20] That decade kicked off a real estate boom in suburban Montgomery County that continues through the present.

Real estate development in Silver Spring, in many respects, reflected national trends. In an era before zoning and in which segregated housing was the rule throughout the United States, restrictive covenants attached to residential subdivisions used minimum house costs and explicit language excluding African Americans, Jews, and others as barriers to entry in many neighborhoods. Subdividers and community builders touted these exclusions as a means for protecting their investments and the investments of the white middle-class homeowners they were courting.[21]

The first restrictive covenants attached to properties in Silver Spring were included in deeds executed by Virginia attorney and real estate speculator Robert Holt Easley (1856–1941). In 1902, Easley bought 67 acres near Silver Spring's B&O Railroad station; two years later, he filed a plat of "Building Sites for Sale at Silver Spring" in Montgomery County land records with 156 lots.[22] Easley's deeds prohibited the people buying his lots and all subsequent owners from selling or renting the properties, "the whole or any part of any dwelling or structure thereon, to any person of African descent."[23]

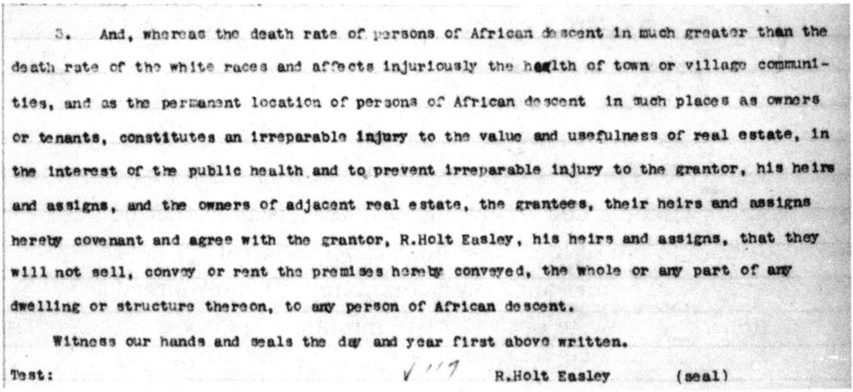

3. And, whereas the death rate of persons of African descent in much greater than the death rate of the white races and affects injuriously the health of town or village communities, and as the permanent location of persons of African descent in such places as owners or tenants, constitutes an irreparable injury to the value and usefulness of real estate, in the interest of the public health and to prevent irreparable injury to the grantor, his heirs and assigns, and the owners of adjacent real estate, the grantees, their heirs and assigns hereby covenant and agree with the grantor, R.Holt Easley, his heirs and assigns, that they will not sell, convey or rent the premises hereby conveyed, the whole or any part of any dwelling or structure thereon, to any person of African descent.

Witness our hands and seals the day and year first above written.

Test: R.Holt Easley   (seal)

Figure 2: Earliest known racial restrictive deed covenant filed in Silver Spring. R. Holt Easley to William and Hannah Jouvenal, April 7, 1904. Montgomery County Land Records Liber 178, folio 88.

Easley's subdivision was the first of more than 50 racially restricted residential subdivisions that were platted and developed between 1904 and 1948 in an area roughly bounded by the District of Columbia, Rock Creek

Park, the Prince Georges County line, and the unincorporated community of White Oak. This area, which Lee and his real estate cohort called "Maryland North of Washington," came to be known during the remainder of the twentieth century as "Greater Silver Spring."

In 1948, the United States Supreme Court ruled in *Shelley v. Kraemer* that racial restrictive covenants were unenforceable.[24] For the next 20 years, however, redlining, steering, and discrimination in multi-family housing kept Silver Spring almost exclusively white.[25] Though there were pockets of African American households on the margins of Silver Spring's historic core (e.g., Lyttonsville and Chestnut Ridge), these nineteenth century unincorporated hamlets occupied areas where real estate speculators were unable to consolidate sufficient lands to create twentieth-century subdivisions. Many of these areas were also so sufficiently stigmatized because of their African American residents that they were unattractive real estate investments.

As late as 1967, *Washingtonian* magazine was reporting on the appeal Silver Spring had for whites moving away from Washington: "They love it because it's easy to commute to Washington," Judith Viorst wrote. "And, they love it because Negroes, so far, have been safely left behind at the District line. Virtually everybody says so, one way or another."[26]

Only after interventions by civil rights activists in the late 1950s; the relocation of about 200 African American Department of Labor employees to Silver Spring in 1961 and the subsequent enactment of an open accommodations law in 1962; and the passage of an open housing law in 1968 (just before federal legislation) did Jim Crow's racial barriers finally begin falling in Silver Spring. The civil rights era in Silver Spring was incredibly tumultuous and exacerbated by the community's proximity to the nation's capital with its massive demonstrations, white flight, and Cold War policies dispersing federal offices into the suburbs and exurbs.[27]

Producing Silver Spring History

The ways in which history and historic preservation are produced in Silver Spring effectively *reproduce* the exclusion of people of color from earlier periods by rendering them invisible in published histories, designated historic properties, and heritage-themed place-making. Historians researching housing, businesses, and commercial architecture omit the African American experience from Silver Spring's narratives. These books, articles, historic preservation documents, documentary videos, and heritage trail signs privilege and celebrate stories of segregationists like Lee, his Blair kin, and other early community boosters.[28]

Some of the erasures are easily identifiable. In 2005, Jerry McCoy and the Silver Spring Historical Society published a book titled *Historic Silver Spring* in Arcadia Publishing's Images of America series. That book did not mention African Americans, 1960s civil rights protests held in downtown Silver Spring, and it did not include the historically black Lyttonsville community, which abuts Silver Spring's historic core.[29]

Earlier examples include *Silver Spring Success: an Interactive History of Silver Spring, Maryland*, a book first published in 1995, and a comprehensive historic resources survey of Silver Spring's central business district that was completed in 2002.[30] Neither of these works addressed Jim Crow policies and housing segregation, neither contained the words "black" or "African American," and neither discussed the sites in Silver Spring's central business district where substantial civil rights actions occurred. These include Crivella's Wayside Inn where, in 1962, African American Department of Labor employees were declined service, touching off nearly four years of highly publicized complaints with Montgomery County's Human Relations Commission and litigation in state court.[31] Civil rights activists also demonstrated at apartment communities in downtown Silver Spring and in streets where segregationist developers and apartment community owners and managers had their offices.[32]

More academic studies of Silver Spring's history include several articles on the community's commercial architecture and planning by The George Washington University architectural historian Richard Longstreth. These works analyze suburbanization in the Washington metropolitan area by focusing on development in Silver Spring during the middle part of the twentieth century. Longstreth's work omits African Americans and the role Jim Crow segregation played in Silver Spring's formative years.[33] Like other writers on Silver Spring's history, Longstreth ignores the white supremacist policies of Silver Spring's early community builders that were crucial to its development.[34]

Though Longstreth's work has focused on Silver Spring's commercial properties and multi-family housing, his students have drilled down in into Silver Spring's residential subdivisions. A 1994 George Washington University master's thesis in American Studies examined Silver Spring's development between 1920 and 1955. The thesis included a chronological history of Silver Spring's development as a Washington suburb and a substantial appendix with every residential subdivision recorded in Montgomery County. The author fails to address racial restrictive covenants, African Americans, or the stark demographic reality (virtually all white, except for domestic servants) of the area in which the subdivisions were developed.[35]

Figure 3: Silver Spring Heritage Tour sign, 8200 block Georgia Avenue, commemorating the Little Tavern hamburger stand. Photo by David S. Rotenstein.

Other erasures are less accessible. These include the many racial micro-aggressions people of color experience when walking through downtown Silver Spring, i.e., heritage tour signs that omit segregation from celebratory narratives about local businesses during Silver Spring's "heyday" and narratives that minimize the role Jim Crow segregation played in that period.[36] One example is embedded in a heritage trail sign in the 8200 block of

Georgia Avenue. The sign marks the location of the Little Tavern, a popular hamburger stand that had opened in the 1930s. When the Silver Spring Historical Society sought to have the building designated in the Montgomery County Master Plan for Historic Preservation, longtime African American residents questioned the proposal because of the restaurant's well-known (among African Americans in Washington and Montgomery County) practices prior to 1962 of refusing service to blacks.[37]

After failing to secure designation and protection, the building was demolished and the heritage tour sign was placed in 2010. The sign makes a concession to the history of Jim Crow policies first introduced to the Silver Spring Historical Society during the 2003 historic preservation campaign, but it does so in ways that minimize the restaurant chain's white supremacy. The sign reads:

> In 1957, the Montgomery County branch of the National Association for the Advancement of Colored People conducted a survey of 18 cafes—nine in Silver Spring, nine in Bethesda. Six were cited for refusing sit-down service to African-Americans, including the Little Taverns in each community (*they only offered carry-out*).[38]

The heritage tour sign misrepresents the NAACP efforts to identify and eliminate segregation in Montgomery County businesses. The 1957 survey described in the sign text was one of several done by the NAACP and Montgomery County organizations between 1955 and 1962. The parenthetical statement that the Little Tavern only offered carry-out suggests to readers that the discrimination there wasn't so bad because no one could get a seat at the hamburger stand. According to the *Washington Post* account of the 1957 survey, African American testers "were refused all but carry-out service" in the chain's Silver Spring and Bethesda locations.[39] The Little Tavern was the only Silver Spring establishment tested that year; by December 1961, Silver Spring's Little Tavern was one of 19 establishments surveyed that did not discriminate based on race, whereas another 10 continued to discriminate.[40]

Throughout Silver Spring, the erasures and misrepresentation of the community's contested racial history create a hostile environment for longtime African American residents and for newcomers. It is an environment where, by ignoring African American experience, locals and developers celebrate white supremacy. If a community's monuments and commemorations are a window into its social values—its soul—then Silver Spring's commemorative landscape conveys troubling messages connoting inclusion for its white residents and exclusion for people of color.[41]

The Silver Spring Memory Wall: Erasure by Insertion

A very public example of erasure is embedded in one of five murals comprising a public artwork installed in the 1990s. The Silver Spring "Memory Wall" is a series of murals in Acorn Urban Park depicting five important elements of Silver Spring's history: Francis Preston Blair's 1840s mansion; the Civil War; Silver Spring's first armory on the eve of World War I; the B&O Railroad station in 1941; and, the rehabilitated 1938 Silver Shopping Center.

Figure 4: Acorn Urban Park and the Silver Spring Memory Wall, May 2017. Photo by David S. Rotenstein.

Installed on the façade of a commercial building, the Memory Wall was conceived as mitigation for exceeding zoned development standards. Baltimore-based Caldor, Inc. had proposed building a new three-story department store in a disinvested industrial area in the Silver Spring central business district. The vacant site where Caldor wanted to build its new store once had been a printing plant and was located adjacent to Acorn

Urban Park, a historic site regulated by the Montgomery County Historic Preservation Commission. Under Montgomery County's "optional method of development," applicants could get additional density by providing on- and off-site amenities. The Caldor improvements also enabled Montgomery County parks officials to renovate Acorn Park. Cumulatively, the Caldor proposal would offer shopping alternatives then unavailable in Silver Spring and it would "provide significant improvements to an historic resource."[42]

The Silver Spring Memory Wall was created, in part, to proclaim that Silver Spring was alive and again open for business.[43] A Washington mural artist was contracted to paint five panels "depicting historical images or moments from Silver Spring's past."[44] The Maryland-National Capital Planning Commission and a Silver Spring art advisory group had control over the mural contents and the property owner granted a perpetual easement to Montgomery County for "periodic maintenance."[45]

The murals' content was developed by the artist Mame Cohalan, a Silver Spring residents' arts advisory board, and officials in Montgomery County's Planning Department. Planning Department memoranda note that the murals were the "first attempt to realistically depict Silver Spring's history in a representational public art form."[46] Planners memorialized Cohalan's observations that the historical photographs she was using to design the murals failed to show people of color: "The artist would like to explore having more cultural diversity in the 20th century images."

Cohalan confirmed this in an interview I did with her in April 2017. In our conversation, Cohalan explained to me how she used photographs as the basis for the three scenes depicting Silver Spring in the twentieth century. And then she added some artistic license. "I felt that at a train station there should be some diversity because everybody takes a train," she said. "There was just a little part of my doing, my participation in this, where I knew I was manipulating, sticking myself and my opinions into the picture."[47]

Cohalan recalled working with an engaged community interested in celebrating Silver Spring's history while also cultivating a carefully crafted image. The artist described the Memory Wall project as a marketing campaign for Silver Spring: a branding tool for the community that, by the 1990s, had become increasingly ethnically diverse. By the first decade of the twenty-first century, Silver Spring could boast of a large African American population in addition to a substantial immigrant community that included

Latinos and a large enough Ethiopian population to be dubbed Washington's "Little Ethiopia."[48]

Figure 5: Silver Spring Memory Wall mural illustrating the B&O Railroad platform c. 1941. Photo by David S. Rotenstein.

The Silver Spring Memory Wall, with its insertion of black bodies into spaces and in a time where they never would have been found establishes erasure by creating an imaginary visual narrative. African Americans who see the murals recognize that African Americans could not have stood alongside whites on the train platform in 1941. Or 1951. Or even 1961. Charlotte Coffield, a lifelong resident of Silver Spring's historically black Lyttonsville community recalls growing up in a segregated Silver Spring. In 2017, she told an interviewer what she thought about the Memory Wall's images: "I noticed that they had black people there and white people standing in line to catch the train but in 1941 that would not have happened."[49]

To look at Silver Spring today and the many representations of Silver Spring's past, it would be easy for a newcomer to assume that the community had always been diverse and that it never was a sundown suburb that excluded people of color. Public art like the Silver Spring Memory Wall reinforces that false sense of history. The timing of the inception of my black history tours, collaborations among Silver Spring nonprofits that address social justice issues, and the renovations in Acorn Urban Park created a space for confronting the racialized ways in which history and historic preservation are produced in Silver Spring.

Protesting Invisibility in Acorn Park

In early 2017, the Maryland-National Capital Park and Planning Commission began soliciting public input for proposed renovations in Acorn Park. A pair of local nonprofit organizations, IMPACT Silver Spring (IMPACT) and Montgomery County chapter of Showing Up for Racial Justice Montgomery County (SURJ), and I collaborated to organize an event to protest the invisibility of African Americans in the ways history is presented in the park and to take direct action with Montgomery County officials. We dubbed our small collaboration "Invisible Montgomery" and our efforts culminated in an event on Saturday June 10, 2017, in Acorn Park.

Figure 6: Participants in the Protesting Invisibility event June 10, 2017. Photo by David S. Rotenstein.

The Acorn Park protesting invisibility event was inspired by an account in architectural historian Dell Upton's 2015 book, *What Can and Can't be Said: Race, Uplift, and Monument Building in the Contemporary South*.[50] Upton recounted efforts by residents of Savannah, Georgia, who protested against invisibility in Savannah's commemorative landscape by demanding an official African American monument.[51] Silver Spring's African American residents had much in common with their Savannah counterparts: both communities celebrated their white supremacist histories in public monuments and historical representations while omitting official commemorations dedicated to people of color.

Representatives from IMPACT, SURJ, and I met several times in the weeks leading up to the June 10 event. We drafted publicity flyers and shared them via social media and in businesses near Acorn Park. We also drafted a petition letter addressed to county officials, which participants could sign, and a postcard with a brief excerpt from the petition letter and space for individualized comments.

In addition to inviting the community at large, we also asked a couple of lifelong residents of Lyttonsville to share their memories of life in Jim Crow Silver Spring and about how they think history and historic preservation are produced in the community. They recalled being excluded from Silver Spring's businesses and living in a neighborhood that lacked running water and paved roads until well into the Cold War. And, they described the marginalization they felt by being excluded from published histories and Silver Spring's commemorative landscape.

After the dialogue in Acorn Park concluded, participants were invited to move to Bump 'N Grind, a popular coffee shop in the next block. The store's owners helped to publicize the event and they allowed us to set up several laptops connected to the store's Wi-Fi where participants could file their comments on Acorn Park directly to the Montgomery County Department of Parks via the agency's open town hall web portal. Conversations begun in the park continued inside the store and seven people filed comments electronically.

Suggestions for making Acorn Park's history more inclusive included adding another bank of murals above the existing ones in the Memory Wall and commissioning a sculpture of a local civil rights leader. Participants also contemplated replacing the existing signage that celebrates Silver Spring's white supremacist founders with signs that also discuss slavery, Reconstruction, Jim Crow, and the civil rights actions (demonstrations, litigation, etc.) that occurred in Silver Spring during the 1960s.[52] Discussions among IMPACT and SURJ staff and volunteers also identified a need for a county recognized advisory body to participate producing a more inclusive history in the park and beyond.

Figure 7: Participants in the Protesting Invisibility event file comments electronically. Photo by David S. Rotenstein.

The Long Road to Visibility

In scheduling the yearlong effort to renovate the park, the Montgomery County Department of Parks announced plans to hold one meeting with stakeholders in the summer of 2017 to present the results of the agency's outreach efforts. Parks agency officials expect to deliver finalized plans to the Montgomery County Planning Board for approval in early 2018. Nearly a month after the Protesting Invisibility event, Montgomery County Parks' Director Michael Riley acknowledged receiving our petition letter and comments. Riley's letter thanked us for our comments and welcomed our participation in future public meetings. The letter also underscored the privileged role that the Silver Spring Historical Society has among Montgomery County officials as an authority on Silver Spring history and historic preservation. "The Silver Spring Historical Society also shares an interest in interpreting the history and resources of the park," Riley wrote.[53]

The loose coalition formed under the "Invisible Montgomery" umbrella to produce the protesting invisibility event in Acorn Park will be following future releases by county officials and we plan to attend all additional public meetings. We hope that the example set in Acorn Park will be a model for additional efforts in Silver Spring and elsewhere in Montgomery

County to reframe how history and historic preservation are produced to make them more inclusive and accurate. Silver Spring's downtown privileges white experiences at the expense of African Americans, presenting a whitewashed history that overlooks the ways white residents accumulated capital and influence by excluding African Americans. Future efforts may be directed at replacing existing heritage trail markers and creating public art that engages and strives to tell the story of all of Silver Spring's residents, including the many new immigrants who have moved here since the turn of the twenty-first century. One step I plan to take is to work with a Spanish language interpreter to adapt my existing Black History Tour to create a bilingual tour that helps create attachments to the community for new residents.

Silver Spring, like many communities throughout the nation, has invested heavily in promoting its diversity as part of its brand.[54] That diversity is of recent vintage and it was not easily achieved. By protesting invisibility in Acorn Park, we took the first steps towards reframing Silver Spring's history and opening public spaces for a more honest and inclusive history for all of our residents and visitors.

Acknowledgments

The Protesting Invisibility project would not have been possible without the organizing expertise of IMPACT Silver Spring and SURJ. IMPACT's executive director Jayne Park and staff members Carolyn Lowry, Lanita Whitehurst, and Michael Rubin have been enthusiastic supporters from this project's inception. SURJ's Danielle Ring's skills in canvassing and attention to detail helped make the Acorn Park event successful. I could not have begun to understand Silver Spring's complicated and contested racial history without the help from such longtime Lyttonsville residents Charlotte Coffield and Patricia Tyson. I am truly indebted to them for sharing their time and their memories of a difficult time in our community's history and their candid observations on how history and historic preservation are produced in Silver Spring. This essay is dedicated to them and to Lyttonsville.

Notes

1   James W. Loewen, *Sundown Towns: A Hidden Dimension of American Racism* (New York: New Press : Distributed in the United States by Norton, 2005).

2   David S. Rotenstein, "Gentrification Hits Small Cities Too: Unsustainable Policies in Decatur, Georgia," *Tikkun Daily Blog*, March 26, 2013, http://www.tikkun. org/tikkundaily/2013/02/26/gentrification-hits-small-cities-too-unsustainable-policies-in-decatur-georgia/; David S. Rotenstein, "Historic Preservation Shines a Light on a Dark Past," in *Preserving Places: Reflections on the National Historic Preservation Act at Fifty from The Public Historian*, ed. Tamara Gaskell (National Council on Public History, 2016), 18–19, http://ncph.org/wp-content/uploads/2009/12/Preserving_Places.pdf.

3   Darlene Roth, "City of Decatur Historic Resources Survey," Report Prepared for the City of Decatur. (Decatur, GA: Darlene Roth and Associates, Inc., 1990); Darlene Roth, "South Decatur Historical and Architectural Survey" (Decatur, GA: City of Decatur, 1987).

4   Keystone Preservation Associates, LLC and Morrison Design, LLC, "Historic Resource Survey Final Report" (Decatur, GA: City of Decatur, September 1, 2009), http://www.decaturga.com/Modules/ShowDocument.aspx?documentid=2105.

5   "Silver Spring Historical Society - About," microblog, *Facebook*, accessed July 21, 2017, https://www.facebook.com/pg/sshistory/about/?ref=page_internal.

6   As a consultant to land use attorneys and developers I have participated in several undertakings reviewed by the Montgomery County Planning Department and County Council where the Silver Spring Historical Society has been the leading proponent for designating properties under the county's historic preservation ordinance that my clients opposed. My consulting practice has not included such work since 2013.

7   Bruce Richard Johansen, "Imagined Pasts, Imagined Futures: Race, Politics, Memory, and the Revitalization of Downtown Silver Spring, Maryland" (Dissertation, University of Maryland, 2005), http://drum.lib.umd.edu/handle/1903/3210.

8   Gwen Marcus Wright to David Rotenstein, "RE: Silver Spring CBD African American Sites," August 4, 2016.

9   United States Census, 1860 Slave Schedules, District 5, Montgomery County, Maryland.

10 Manisha Sinha, *The Slave's Cause: A History of Abolition* (New Haven, CT: Yale University Press, 2016).

11 "News of the Capital's Suburbs," *The Washington Post (1923–1954)*, April 26, 1925.

12 "The Heart of Washington Development," *The Washington Post*, September 18, 1927.

13 "Limits of 'Silver Spring' Defined," Montgomery County Code § 1-17 (1955), https://babel.hathitrust.org/cgi/pt?id=mdp.39015070559045;view=1up;seq=1.

14 Sean Emerson, "Around The Corners : Where Is 'Silver Spring'?," *Around Four Corners*, March 14, 2014, http://www.aroundfourcorners.com/2014/03/where-is-silver-spring.html; Dan Reed, "Just up the Pike: How Did Silver Spring Get Its Boundaries? And How Would You Define Them?," *Just Up the Pike*, August 26, 2014, http://www.justupthepike.com/2014/08/how-did-silver-spring-get-its.html.

15 Using Sechrist's thesis, Montgomery County real estate atlases, and Montgomery County Planning Department GIS data I have created a spatial database with 77 entries corresponding to residential subdivisions recorded in Montgomery County. Within that population, 47 had racial restrictive covenants recorded by the subdividers, developers, or individual property owners. Census data analyzed by historian Bruce Johansen revealed that even by 1960 only 1.1 percent of Silver Spring and Wheaton's population was African American. Johansen, "Imagined Pasts, Imagined Futures: Race, Politics, Memory, and the Revitalization of Downtown Silver Spring, Maryland," 86.

16 Karen Dunaway, "E. Brooke Lee, MSA SC 3520-1576," *Archives of Mary-land*, 2001, http://msa.maryland.gov/megafile/msa/speccol/sc3500/sc3520/001500/001576/html/1576bio.html; Royce Hanson, *Suburb: Planning Politics and the Public Interest* (Ithaca: Cornell University Press, 2017), 15–20; Richard Jaeggi, "The King of Silver Spring," *Takoma-Silver Spring Voice*, August 2002; Johansen, "Imagined Pasts, Imagined Futures: Race, Politics, Memory, and the Revitalization of Downtown Silver Spring, Maryland," 55–56.

17 John W. Anderson, "E. Brooke Lee Outlasts His Political Machine," *The Washington Post*, April 2, 1958; Marie Macaulay Garber, "E. Brooke Lee vs. Charter: The Fight to Modernize Montgomery County Government, 1938–1950" (Thesis, George Washington University, 1964).

18 E. Brooke Lee, "Should Washington Welfare Families Be 'Imported' Here?," *Bethesda-Chavy Chase Tribune*, February 16, 1967; E. Brooke Lee, "Impending Racial Laws Deemed to Be Inequity," *Bethesda-Chevy Chase Advertiser*, March 29, 1967.

19 Lee, "Impending Racial Laws Deemed to Be Inequity."

20 Steven Lubar, "Trolley Lines, Land Speculation and Community-Building: The Early History of Woodside Park, Silver Spring, Maryland," *Maryland Historical Magazine* 81, no. 4 (1986): 316–329; Stephanie Ann Sechrist, "Silver Spring, MD: Residential Development of a Washington Suburb, 1920 to 1955" (Thesis, George Washington University, 1994).

21 Richard R. W. Brooks, *Saving the Neighborhood*, Kindle edition (Harvard University Press, 2013); Robert Fishman, *Bourgeois Utopias: The Rise and Fall of Suburbia* (New York: Basic Books, 1987); Robert M. Fogelson, *Bourgeois Nightmares: Suburbia, 1870–1930* (New Haven, CT: Yale University Press, 2005); Kevin Fox Gotham, "Urban Space, Restrictive Covenants and the Origins of Racial Residential Segregation in a US City, 1900–50," *International Journal of Urban and Regional Research* 24, no. 3 (September 1, 2000): 616–633, doi:10.1111/1468-2427.00268.

22 Map of Building Sites for Sale at Silver Spring Lying Near the Depot of the Baltimore and Ohio Railroad. Montgomery County Land Records, Plat No. 54.

23 Deed from R. Holt Easley to William and Hannah Jouvenal, May 19, 1904. Montgomery County Land Records, Liber JLB 178, folio 89.

24 Shelley v. Kraemer, 334 U.S. 1 (United States Supreme Court 1948).271 U. S. 323, distinguished. Pp. 334 U. S. 8-23.

25 "Other Devices Being Studied As Substitutes for Covenants: Realty Men Expect Rule to Have Little Effect on Prices," *The Washington Post*, May 5, 1948.

26 Judith Viorst, "Q. Is There a Silver Spring, and If so, Why?," *Washingtonian*, July 1967, 68.

27 Dennis E. Gale, *Washington, D.C.: Inner-City Revitalization and Minority Suburbanization*, Comparative American Cities (Philadelphia: Temple University Press, 1987); Howard Gillette, *Between Justice and Beauty: Race, Planning, and the Failure of Urban Policy in Washington, D.C* (Baltimore: Johns Hopkins University Press, 1995), 212–213.

28 Historian Bruce Johansen analyzed the Silver Spring Historical Society's articles, public presentations, and walking tours in his 2006 University of Maryland dissertation. Johansen, "Imagined Pasts, Imagined Futures: Race, Politics, Memory, and the Revitalization of Downtown Silver Spring, Maryland."

29 Jerry A. McCoy and Silver Spring Historical Society (Silver Spring, MD), *Historic Silver Spring*, Images of America (Charleston, SC: Arcadia, 2005).

30 Richard C. Jaffeson, *Silver Spring Success: An Interactive History of Silver Spring, Maryland* (Silver Spring, MD: The Author, 2000); Potomac-Hudson Engineering, Inc., "Historic Sites Survey Report," Report prepared for the Maryland-National Capital Park and Planning Commission (Silver Spring, MD: Potomac-Hudson Engineering, Inc., December 2002).

31 David Brack, "Twenty Years of Civil Rights Progress" (Rockville, MD: Montgomery County Human Relations Commission, n.d.), https://www.montgomery-countymd.gov/humanrights/resources/files/civil_right_progress.pdf; "25 Negroes Stage Sit-in At Restaurant," *The Washington Post, Times Herald (1959–1973)*,

June 18, 1962, sec. City Life; "In Te Matter of Minnie L. Blair and Crivella's Way-side Restaurant," *Race Relations Law Reporter* 10, no. 3 (1965): 1403–1404.

32 Andrew Barnes, Washington Post Staff Writer, "Pickets Hit Apartment Firm Again," *The Washington Post, Times Herald (1959–1973)*, March 20, 1966, sec. City Life; "75 Pickets Protest Apartment Policies," *The Washington Post, Times Herald (1959–1973)*, March 13, 1966; "Apartment Pickets Shift To Hyattsville," *The Washington Post, Times Herald (1959–1973)*, March 14, 1966, sec. City Life; "ACCESS Pickets March On 2d Apartment Builder," *The Washington Post, Times Herald (1959–1973)*, March 28, 1966, sec. Business & Finance.

33 Richard Longstreth, "The Neighborhood Shopping Center in Washington, D. C., 1930–1941," *Journal of the Society of Architectural Historians* 51, no. 1 (March 1992): 5–34; Richard Longstreth, "Silver Spring: Georgia Avenue, Colesville Road and the Creation of an Alternative 'Downtown' for Metropolitan Washing-ton," in *Streets: Critical Perspectives on Public Space*, eds. Zeynep Çelik, Diane Favro, and Richard Ingersoll (Berkeley: University of California Press, 1994), 247–258, 294; Richard Longstreth, "The Mixed Blessings of Success: The Hecht Company and Department Store Branch Development after World War II," *Perspectives in Vernacular Architecture* 6 (1997): 244–262.

34 "At the heart of Lee's effort lay an altruistic desire to see Silver Spring emerge as the leading Maryland community in the metropolitan area," Longstreth wrote in one book chapter. "Silver Spring would, in effect, become the core of a new kind of urban realm, better than the traditional city." Longstreth, "Silver Spring: Georgia Avenue, Colesville Road and the Creation of an Alternative 'Downtown' for Met-ropolitan Washington," 252.

35 Stephanie Ann Sechrist, "Silver Spring, Maryland."

36 Derald Wing Sue et al., "Racial Microaggressions in Everyday Life," *American Psy-chologist* 62, no. 4 (2007).

37 Garance Burke, "A Little Taste of History in Silver Spring; Nostalgists Hope To Save Tavern," *The Washington Post*, June 27, 2003; Jerry A. McCoy, "Historic— Warts and All," *The Washington Post*, August 2, 2003.

38 "The Burger King," Silver Spring Heritage Tour sign, 8200 block Georgia Avenue, Silver Spring. Emphasis added.

39 Jean Jones Staff Reporter, "Negro Eating Ban Is Checked," *The Washington Post and Times Herald (1954–1959)*, August 26, 1957, sec. Sports.

40 Records of the Montgomery County Human Relations Commission, Public Ac-commodations, 1957–1975. Montgomery County Archives.

41 Margaret E. Farrar, *Building the Body Politic: Power and Urban Space in Washington,*

D.C. (Urbana: University of Illinois Press, 2008), 52–57; Henri Lefebvre, *The Production of Space* (Oxford: Blackwell, 1991), 217–226; Steve Pile, *The Body and the City: Psychoanalysis, Space, and Subjectivity* (London: Routledge, 1996), 211–221.

42 Montgomery County Planning Board, "Opinion: Project Plan No. 9-94001, Caldor Store," June 9, 1994, 4.

43 Louis Aguilar, "Caldor Coming to Silver Spring," *The Washington Post*, March 17, 1994, https://www.washingtonpost.com/archive/business/1994/03/17/caldor-coming-to-silver-spring/2de4d794-76f5-4bb1-ac2e-4f7d786c9b8c/?utm_term=.f15c76edd1c5.

44 M-NCPPC Development Review Division Staff to Montgomery County Planning Board, "Site Plan Review #8-94030," Memorandum, (n.d.), 7.

45 Deed of Easement, Caldor-Silver Spring, L.L.C. to Maryland-National Capital Park and Planning Commission, April 24, 1995. Montgomery County Land Records, Liber 13370, folio 154–161.

46 Marilyn Clemens to Calvin Nelson, "RE: Silver Spring Art Panel Review of the Caldor Store Memory Wall by Artist Mame Cohalan," Memorandum, (July 20, 1994).

47 Mame Cohalan, Interview, interview by David S. Rotenstein, April 26, 2017.

48 Elizabeth Chang, "Where to Find Washington's New Chinatown, Little Ethiopia, Etc.," *The Washington Post*, February 17, 2016.

49 Mitti Hicks, "Parks Petition Asks Officials to Acknowledge Racism in Public ... ," *Montgomery Community Media*, July 11, 2017, http://www.mymcmedia.org/parks-petition-asks-officials-to-acknowledge-racism-in-public-displays-video/.

50 Dell Upton, *What Can and Can't Be Said: Race, Uplift, and Monument Building in the Contemporary South* (New Haven, CT: Yale University Press, 2015).

51 Ibid., 75–76.

52 Civil rights actions in Silver Spring include efforts to desegregate local eateries after Montgomery County enacted an open accommodations law in 1962 and demonstrations against local builders and apartment community managers who refused to rent to African Americans. Some of these actions are summarized in a publication commemorating the twentieth anniversary of Montgomery County's Human Relations Commission. Bruce Johansen also deftly covers this period in his dissertation on nostalgia and historic preservation in Silver Spring. Brack, "Twenty Years of Civil Rights Progress"; Johansen, "Imagined Pasts, Imagined Futures: Race, Politics, Memory, and the Revitalization of Downtown Silver Spring, Maryland."

53 Mike Riley to David S. Rotenstein, "RE: Acorn Urban Park Petition Letter & Comments," July 11, 2017. The agency's reliance on the Silver Spring Historical Society as an authority is an area the Protesting Invisibility partners have identified as problematic considering the society's established record of producing racialized histories (See Johansen, "Imagined Pasts, Imagined Futures: Race, Politics, Memory, and the Revitalization of Downtown Silver Spring, Maryland.").

54 Derek S. Hyra, *Race, Class, and Politics in the Cappuccino City* (Chicago: The University of Chicago Press, 2017); Sylvie Tissot, "Of Dogs and Men: The Making of Spatial Boundaries in a Gentrifying Neighborhood," *City & Community* 10, no. 3 (2011): 265–284, doi:10.1111/j.1540-6040.2011.01377.x; Sylvie Tissot, *Good Neighbors: Gentrifying Diversity in Boston's South End* (London: Verso, 2015).

IV

JOBS AND THE ENVIRONMENT: MOVING BEYOND THE HERRENVOLK DEMOCRACY OF COAL

ENERGY AND THE TRUMP ADMINISTRATION: PIPELINES, PROMISES, AND THE THIRD ENERGY SHIFT

Tom Foley
Georgetown University

As Americans, we love our history, and in that sense, President Trump is no different. Oftentimes, however, his idea of American history is not rooted in evidence or reality, and his passion for his idea of America's past makes it difficult for him to convey his vision for an American future. This stems, in part, from his misunderstanding, or ignorance, of aspects of our history that lack the heat of battle or the thrill of victory, but were nevertheless critical to our national military, economic, and democratic successes. Take for example, his policies on energy and climate science.

Forward, to the Past

A major feature of candidate Trump's campaign rhetoric on energy policy was a promise to bring back coal.[1] Since taking office on January 20, President Trump has continued to embrace a fossil-fueled vision for the American future simultaneous with a denial of anthropogenic—human-influenced—climate change. He has signed executive orders accelerating the construction of the Dakota Access Pipeline in North Dakota and inviting a new application for the Keystone XL Pipeline which would connect tar sands in Canada to American Gulf Coast refineries from which it could then be exported. Trump's EPA administrator Scott Pruitt (who, as Oklahoma Attorney General sued the EPA 13 times) has begun to roll back Obama-era restrictions on greenhouse gas emissions from power plants and undo the extension of federal protection over 60 percent of the nation's lakes, rivers, streams, and wetlands under the Waters of the United States Rule (issued under the authority of the Clean Water Act of 1972).[2] The Secretary of the Interior, Ryan Zinke, is currently reviewing the boundaries of the National Parks and national monuments and is widely expected to permit new oil, gas, and coal exploration on public lands. Finally, the President's decision to withdraw the United States from the Paris Climate Agreement may become his most lasting—and most damaging—foreign policy.

Rhetorically, the Trump Administration is committed to a resurgence of coal. In action, the administration's energy policy combines a strong desire to undo Obama-era programs—regardless of efficacy and evidence—with missed opportunities. Take, for example, the President's choice to exit the Paris Climate Accord, a seminal achievement for the Obama administration and the international community in the form of a framework for addressing global threats with broad participation from industrialized, rapidly industrializing, and developed countries alike. President Trump justified his decision to exit the Paris Climate Accord by stating that the United States faced unfair requirements on energy production and usage that countries like China and India did not. In actuality, the Paris agreement is entirely voluntary (which has led some to argue that the United States out of the agreement is better than the United States *in* but not abiding by its commitments under the agreement). Meanwhile, although the president issued a series of executive orders designed to speed the construction of petroleum pipelines using only American steel, for six months he failed to first nominate and then have confirmed commissioners sufficient for a quorum on the Federal Energy Regulatory Commission (FERC), the agency that must approve all energy infrastructure projects—pipelines, most notable. This has meant that $15 billion in construction projects have been delayed and threatened with cancelation since February.[3] No policy or political justification for this delay exists.

The administration's support for the coal industry coincides with an uptick in coal production and prices as well as a boost in morale (though, importantly, not one in demand) by encouraging coal extraction on federal lands.[4] This, however, occurs as broader economic and technological trends have contributed to the long-term decline of coal production. Earlier this year, coal production declined to levels not seen since 1978 as coal-fired power plants continue to close at home and abroad.[5] Developing countries are increasingly abandoning coal plants—built, under construction, and still in the planning stages—as they realize the limitations of fossil-fuels on independence and economic growth. What was once mainly an economic problem—how to keep trucks and ships carrying products moving to stores frequented by customers travelling by bus and automobile—is now an existential challenge, too. As analyses of climate change based on current mitigation efforts and energy consumption patterns grow more ominous and perilous to economic growth, national security, and human health, the need for a rapid implementation of new energy systems and a swift retirement of oil and coal regimes is pressing. And yet, the Trump administration continues to doubt the very existence of anthropogenic climate change and, so far, has prioritized a return to a mythical American energy Eden. Some lessons from previous global energy transitions elucidate the peril of this ignorance on energy policy and how the administration's doubling down on fossil fuels threatens to imperil the economic future and wellbeing of all Americans.

The world has undergone two previous energy transitions on a global scale: from wood to coal, and from coal to oil. Neither has occurred quickly or without significant economic and social dislocation and profound environmental and health devastation. The ecological and environmental devastation wrought by previous energy transitions stems, in large part, from the fact that coal and oil found widespread use in the Industrial Revolution of the nineteenth century and the transportation revolution of the twentieth century. Rather than simply replacing an old source of energy used for a particular purpose (in the case of wood, heating, cooking, and metallurgy), the exploitation of fossil fuels led to the utilization of these fuels for more purposes. Coal initially replaced wood in home heating, then iron production, then became the motive power of railroads and the fuel for mechanization and illumination throughout American homes and factories. Petroleum replaced coal oil as an illuminant, but quickly found application as a lubricant, a paint additive, a stock for chemical processes, home heating, and most significantly, as a motive fuel for automobiles, ships, tanks, submarines, and airplanes. The more that was extracted, the more that was burned.

With the transitions to both coal and oil, the "legacy" fuel remained widely used for decades (in the case of coal, centuries). In these previous shifts, governments have been slow to realize the economic benefits of new energy regimes. But once they realize the pathway to prosperity is paved by scientific and technological innovation, states have been quick and substantial in their work to support new energy systems.

Pennsylvania, for example, has been at the forefront of energy transitions. The first shift, from wood to coal, was boosted by anthracite mining in northeastern Pennsylvania in the 1820s. But getting the coal to market in Philadelphia required state-sponsorship and financial support to construct the canals and railroads necessary to fuel Philadelphia's and the world's industrial revolution. Early Americans were familiar with bituminous coal and its variations. Bituminous coal from mines around Richmond, Virginia as well as imported coal from Nova Scotia and Britain fueled iron forges and sometimes hearths when wood and charcoal were in short supply. However, these coals were relatively easy to light but generated heavy smoke. Anthracite was hard to ignite but, thanks to its high-energy density and low levels of impurities, generated little smoke. Eager to encourage use of a fuel uniquely found in the Commonwealth, Pennsylvania legislators encouraged the exploitation of anthracite by providing corporate charters for canal and coal companies. By the late 1820s, the legislature stepped in to support a statewide system of canals to connect the state commercially and to facilitate the flow of coal from the geographically isolated interiors of the state to its markets and metropoles. The state also encouraged the use of coal for industrial purposes without providing direct financial assistance, having encountered severe budgetary issues after investing in infrastructure projects (including the Pennsylvania Canal) and banks. At a time when the legislature strictly controlled who obtained a corporate charter and for what purpose, the state passed a law in 1836 providing corporate privileges and protections to any iron producer who burned anthracite coal rather than charcoal.[6] Where there was a will, there was a way. Anthracite proved the vital fuel for the industrialization of the United States, facilitated by the state's interest in promoting its own economic privilege.

Historian Christopher Jones writes that the shift from wood to coal for heating needs was not inevitable, but that remaining stubbornly within the old energy system "would have required difficult trade-offs."[7] In 1860, residents of Pennsylvania's largest city, Philadelphia, could have remained dependent solely on wood for their heating needs, but it would have required 850,000 cords of wood annually—excluding industrial needs.[8] To produce that amount of firewood would require 885 square miles of dedicated woodland—approximately 2 percent of the entire state.[9] Americans could have remained in an organic energy economy, but doing so would have required an incredible amount of central planning and maintenance of resources, a strict prioritization of fuel uses and conservation, and the sacrifice of industrial growth to ensure the population remained sufficiently fed and heated.

The second energy shift began in northwestern Pennsylvania, when in 1859 Edwin Drake successfully drilled the first well for petroleum. The subsequent abundance of the diverse hydrocarbon illuminated cities and farmhouses and eventually revolutionized our entire way of life, from where we travel to how we shop to what we do on Sundays. Again, the transition from coal to oil was facilitated by state and federal construction of roads and highways and safety regulations for automobiles on roads. The military was at the forefront of the transition. In 1911, the navy decided to switch from coal to oil for ships, thereby increasing range and speed—the British Navy switched in the same year. In 1919, Captain Dwight D. Eisenhower led a coast-to-coast caravan of military vehicles to demonstrate both the utility of automobiles to the services and the profound need for well-maintained roads.[10] That trip from Washington, D.C. to San Francisco took two months, and its memory remained with General Eisenhower when as Supreme Allied Commander victorious over Nazi Germany he surveyed the Autobahn and when as President he advocated for the interstate highway system.

In the case of both coal and oil, government assumed a decisive position in ushering in the age of a new energy system. The financing, creation of a favorable regulatory climate, and actual construction of infrastructure to transport coal and oil from hinterland production sites to metropolitan markets depended on the foresight and initiative of elected officials at state and national levels. Government commitment to new energy systems helped signal confidence, ongoing support, and product effectiveness. In Pennsylvania, this commitment came in the form of canal construction and tax incentives for iron producers who used anthracite coal. At the federal level, the decisions to shift naval motive power from coal to oil signaled a sea change that cemented petroleum's place in the emerging global military, commercial, and social systems.

A Long Time Coming: A Third Energy Shift

The third shift has been ongoing for several decades, arguably since the oil crises of the 1970s and President Jimmy Carter's installation of solar panels on the White House in 1977 (they were removed in 1981 by the Reagan administration). It incorporates multiple streams of energy production—wind, solar, nuclear, tidal, and natural gas. The Reagan administration dealt the third transition a devastating blow by reversing Carter's policies and funding initiatives, but in the last 8 years, renewable energy appears to have crossed important price point and consumer thresholds.[11] Over half a million fully electric cars roam American roads already, while the number of hybrid vehicles is far higher.[12] In April, Tesla, the car company that makes only electric vehicles, briefly overtook general motors (GM) as the most valuable automobile company in the United States.[13] While Tesla has only a fraction of the market share of GM, its focus on all-electric vehicles daily appears more prescient, particularly as the number of countries that have set an end date for gasoline-powered car sales rises.[14] Even oil-rich Texas has invested billions in renewable energy. Texas connected its windy western plains to its cities through a program called Competitive Renewable Energy Zones which has helped make it the nation's leader in wind energy production.[15] Texas is not alone, either. Twenty-nine states and the District of Columbia have established requirements that a percentage of their overall electricity generation come from renewable sources.[16] California, a leader in renewable energy investment and infrastructure innovation, is considering modifying its clean-energy production goals from 50 percent of all electricity by 2035 to 100 percent by 2045.[17]

Supporters of fossil fuels often resist renewable energy commitments by citing the choice between economic growth or environmental protections. This, however, is a false choice. Solar energy, in particular, is a job creator and a job maintainer. According to the Department of Energy, the solar industry employs more workers (43 percent) in the Electric Power Generation sector than fossil fuels combined.[18] While more workers are currently employed in the extraction of fossil fuels (1.1 million), future jobs will, undoubtedly, be found in renewables and natural gas. In 2016 alone, employment in the solar sector increased by 25 percent in 2016 and wind power saw a 32 percent increase. After all, those sectors are where the electricity is coming from. Over the last 10 years, electricity production from natural gas has risen 33 percent, while electricity from solar increased a whopping 5,000 percent.

Supporters of pipelines, and particularly the Keystone XL pipeline, often cite its economic benefits in terms of construction jobs. The President claims 28,000 jobs will be created by the pipeline, but most experts estimate the number of temporary construction positions to be around 4,000 full-time jobs for 1 year.[19] To this argument, consider the construction potential in building a renewable energy infrastructure. We will need new long-distance transmission lines to carry solar energy from areas of mass production (like the Southwest) to areas of mass consumption (like the Northeast), similar to Texas's Competitive Renewable Energy Zones program. We will need to convert some (not all at once) gas pumps to electric charging stations. The assembly and installation of home- and industrial-scaled batteries and solar panels will continue to boost small business and manufacturing jobs nationally. Companies like Tesla are already transforming corporate and individual thinking about energy, but national public leadership is also essential. A renewable energy infrastructure portends economy-wide modernization and construction projects that will create hundreds of thousands of new jobs.

Energy and Democracy

Scholars of energy, transitions, and politics have observed that the nature of a fuel source and its related technological systems often have political repercussions. Both Timothy Mitchell in his study of the relationship between coal, oil, and democracy and Bruce Podobnik's study of global energy shifts conclude that the nature of coal mining, heavily reliant on manpower in the nineteenth century, lent itself to broader political participation and labor power.[20] Oil naturally flowed (and often gushed from wells under high pressure, eliminating the need for pumping machinery) and thus required less work by human muscle, negating much of the worker's opportunity to leverage his labor to political ends. By typically keeping the sites of extraction and refining geographically separate, the oil industry further limited its vulnerability to strikes and nationalization (in international oil fields, that is).

The social and political differences between coal and oil extraction are profound. Whereas coal mines typically begot towns in which workers and their families resided for as long as work was available in the mine, oil field work appears to have been much more masculine and transient. This was particularly true after workers successfully established a well and connected it to a pipeline (developed first in the mid-1860s for short distance transportation near Pithole, Pennsylvania), when the work required changed dramatically. Oil flows; coal does not. While coal and oil in the nineteenth century shared similar destinations—engines, lamps, and furnaces, the laboring societies they created were strikingly different.

This third major energy transition, like the previous two, portends significant social, political, and environmental changes, some by design and some inevitably unexpected. As solar panels cover houses, factories, and fields, the means of electricity production will be dramatically dispersed. The modes of energy production will continue to be diversified—solar, wind, hydroelectric, tidal, and natural gas will overlap at both large-scale public utility electricity generation sites and at homes and offices. New dependencies between sunny and windswept states and dark and calm ones may emerge. And, as business historian Alfred Chandler tied the rise of the modern corporation to the emergence of coal, railroads, and later oil, we might also ask whether the multinational corporate model will evolve with the transition to decentralized energy production. Many more questions remain, but we can only begin to answer them if we acknowledge the reality and inevitability of change.

When governments support energy transitions, the benefits are widely enjoyed, for labor and industry and for consumers and producers. The Trump administration has the opportunity to advance the revolution in how we power our way of life. Silencing climate and energy scientists and threatening future funding for innovation are not the ways to do this. Wishful thinking cannot change the evidence.

If history teaches us only one thing, it is that we cannot return to it, only learn from it and move forward. Change is the only constant. Previous shifts in energy have produced incredible economic transformations—coal and the Industrial Revolution, oil and the modern interconnected global economy. By ignoring the potential and inevitability of renewable fuels, by threatening federal research funding, and by shirking the opportunity to build the energy infrastructure of the future, President Trump makes our past a prison of complacency.

Notes

1   Thomas Fitzgerald, "In Pa. Coal Country, Trump is King," *Philly.com*, September 18, 2016, http://www.philly.com/philly/news/politics/presidential/20160918_In_Pa__coal_country__Trump_is_king.html; Colin Deppen, "Trump Promised to Bring Back Pennsylvania's Coal, Steel, and Energy Jobs. But Can He?," *PennLive.com*, November 17, 2016, http://www.pennlive.com/news/2016/11/trump_promised_to_make_pennsyl.html; Ashley Parker and Coral Davenport, "Donald Trump's Energy Plan: More Fossil Fuels and Fewer Rules," *New York Times*, May 26, 2016, https://www.nytimes.com/2016/05/27/us/politics/donald-trump-global-warming-energy-policy.html?_r=0.

2   Juliet Eilperin and Steven Mufson, "Trump to Roll Back Obama's Climate, Water Rules Through Executive Action," *Washington Post*, February 20, 2017, https://www.washingtonpost.com/news/energy-environment/wp/2017/02/20/trump-

to-roll-back-obamas-climate-water-rules-through-executive-action/?utm_term=.
e5c589f4b55f.

3   Samantha Page, "Trump's 'Order' That All Pipelines Be made with U.S. Steel
    is a Classic Fake-Out," *ThinkProgress*, March 7, 2017. https://thinkprogress.
    org/trumps-order-that-all-pipelines-be-made-with-u-s-steel-is-a-classic-fake-
    out-8bdf843ffece/; David Blackmon, "Trump's Pipeline Executive Orders:
    Proceed with Caution," *Forbes*, January 25, 2017, https://www.forbes.com/sites/
    davidblackmon/2017/01/25/trump-executive-orders-on-dapl-and-keystone-
    proceed-with-caution/ - 182dab083ef4h; Lori Ann LaRocco, "Energy CEOs say
    Investor Money and Jobs at Risk Because FERC isn't Functional," *CNBC.com*,
    July 10, 2017, https://www.cnbc.com/2017/07/10/energy-ceos-threaten-to-
    withdraw-investments-if-ferc-isnt-functional.html.

4   Eric Lipton and Barry Meier, "Under Trump, Coal Mining Gets New Life on U.S.
    Lands," *New York Times*, August 6, 2017, https://www.nytimes.com/2017/08/06/
    us/politics/under-trump-coal-mining-gets-new-life-on-us-lands.html?_r=0h.

5   "Short-Term Outlook: Coal," Energy Information Agency, February 7, 2017,
    https://www.eia.gov/outlooks/steo/report/coal.cfm; Benjamin Storrow, "Coal
    Plants Keep Closing on Trump's Watch," *E&E News*, February 21, 2017, http://
    www.eenews.net/stories/1060050333.

6   Sean Patrick Adams, *Old Dominion, Industrial Commonwealth* (Baltimore: Johns
    Hopkins University Press, 2004), 78.

7   Christopher Jones, *Routes of Power: Energy and Modern America* (Cambridge, MA:
    Harvard University Press, 2014), 63.

8   Jones, *Routes of Power*, 63.

9   Jones, *Routes of Power*, 63.

10 Daniel Yergin, *The Prize: The Epic Quest for Oil, Money & Power* (New York: Free
    Press, 1991), 207–208.

11 Tom Randall, "World Energy Hits a Turning Point: Solar That's Cheaper than
    Wind," *Bloomberg*, December 15, 2016, https://www.bloomberg.com/news/
    articles/2016-12-15/world-energy-hits-a-turning-point-solar-that-s-cheaper-
    than-wind; Jamie Condliffe, "Clean Energy is About to Become Cheaper than
    Coal," *MIT Technology Review*, Jun 15, 2017, https://www.technologyreview.
    com/s/608114/clean-energy-prices-are-about-to-become-cheaper-than-coal/.

12 Anthony Cuthbertson, "Electric Car Sales Pass Half a Million in U.S.," *News-
    week*, December 26, 2016, http://www.newsweek.com/electric-car-sales-pass-
    half-million-us-536331.

13 Noel Randewich, "Tesla Becomes Most Valuable U.S. Car Maker, Edges Out GM," *Reuters*, April 10, 2017, http://www.reuters.com/article/us-usa-stocks-tesla-idUS KBN17C1XF.

14 France joins Norway (2025) and India (2030) in setting deadlines for gasoline car sales. Car manufacturer Volvo will not introduce any new gasoline-powered models after 2019. The German government initially planned to have 1 million electric cars on its roads by 2020, but it has provided insufficient incentives to meet that goal. Jack Ewing, "France Plans to End Sales of Gas and Diesel Cars by 2040," *New York Times*, July 6, 2017, https://www.nytimes.com/2017/07/06/business/ energy-environment/france-cars-ban-gas-diesel.html.

15 Robert Fares, "Texas Sets New All Time Wind Energy Record," *Scientific American*, January 14, 2016, https://blogs.scientificamerican.com/plugged-in/texas-sets-new-all-time-wind-energy-record/.

16 Jocelyn Durkay, "State Renewable Portfolio Standards and Goals," *NCSL*, December 28, 2016, http://www.ncsl.org/research/energy/renewable-portfolio-standards .aspx.

17 Chris Megerian, "California Senate Leader Puts 100% Renewable Energy on the Table in New Legislation," *Los Angeles Times*, February 21, 2017, http://www. latimes.com/politics/essential/la-pol-ca-essential-politics-updates-california-senate-leader-puts-100-1487714001-htmlstory.html.

18 Niall McCarthy, "Solar Employs More People In U.S. Electricity Generation Than Oil, Coal and Gas Combined," *Forbes*, January 25, 2017, http://www.forbes.com/ sites/niallmccarthy/2017/01/25/u-s-solar-energy-employs-more-people-than-oil-coal-and-gas-combined-infographic/#3d4c16b7d27f.

19 Glenn Kessler, "President Trump's Inflated Estimate of Keystone XL Construction Jobs," *Washington Post*, January 25, 2017, https://www.washingtonpost.com/ news/fact-checker/wp/2017/01/25/president-trumps-inflated-estimate-for-keystone-xl-construction-jobs/.

20 Timothy Mitchell, *Carbon Democracy: Political Power in the Age of Oil* (New York: Verso Books, 2011); Bruce Podobnik, *Global Energy Shifts: Fostering Sustainability in a Turbulent Age* (Philadelphia: Temple University Press, 2005).

BRING BACK OUR JOBS:
WORK, MEMORY, AND ENERGY INFRASTRUCTURE

William Horne
The George Washington University

Sometime in the late 1930s, Irene Robertson interviewed Mary Teel about her memory of slavery and her life since. Some of Robertson's questions clearly made the formerly enslaved Teel feel uncomfortable, like when she asked about the Klan, education, and voting. Nonetheless, Teel's account of slavery and its aftermath repeated a theme common among her peers: years of hard work that still left her "hard up." She recalled picking cotton for, at most, a dollar per day after emancipation. Then she "cooked ten years 'fore I stopped." Her reason: "I cain't hold up at it." Years of grueling agricultural and domestic labor had taken a toll on her body and limited her ability to work. But it was not her body that ultimately removed her from the workforce; it was the washing machine. She explained that she "washed and ironed till the washing machines ruined that work for all of us black folks." In her old age, Teel reflected that her life had been marked by two key forms of capitalist exploitation: racism and the labor-saving machine.[1]

Though spoken roughly 80 years ago, Teel's frustrations with her working life might, with a few adjustments, fit neatly with those of Trump supporters who want the president to bring back coal, steel, and manufacturing jobs. They also evoke the contemporary complaints and demands of service industry and hourly workers involved in the Fight for Fifteen. Indeed, part of the problem facing working people today—automation stretching from coal mines to restaurant counters—spelled underemployment and poverty for Teel and her peers generations ago.[2]

Teel and other former slaves had lived through dramatic changes in technology and infrastructure that radically altered their working lives. Their early experiences as enslaved children were shaped substantially by revolutions in the application of steam power. The widespread use of steam-powered boats, railroads, cotton mills, sugar refineries, etc. made slavery more profitable, and allowed it to expand more quickly, than anyone could have foreseen in 1800. The end of their lives, in the 1930s, was characterized by the wear and tear of years of manual labor, coupled with a declining need for that labor through automation. In many ways, Teel's narrative illustrates Michael Denning's famous observation that "under capitalism, the only thing worse than being exploited is not being exploited." Like Denning, she critiqued the injustice of capitalism's tendency to discard the working people on which it purportedly relies. As she put it, "washin' machines ruint the black folks." They took the only work many former slaves and their children could obtain and left them to fend for themselves in a wage economy without wages.[3]

Image 1: An unidentified Mississippi woman washing clothes by hand in the late 1930s. Here, she scrubs each article one at a time, likely on a washboard, before rinsing them in a separate basin of water and hanging them to dry on the line at the top right. African American women performed this difficult, repetitive, and time-consuming labor almost exclusively in the southern U.S. before the advent of the washing machine. "Rear view of woman washing clothes," LC-USZ62-125152, Portraits of African American ex-slaves from the U.S. Works Progress Administration, Library of Congress, Washington, D.C.

Tom Foley's essay in this volume, "Energy and the Trump Administration: Pipelines, Promises, and the Third Energy Shift," fittingly reminds us that energy policy has been shaped historically by sometimes competing desires for cleanliness, efficiency, profit, and production. To that end, Foley observes that relying on oil for energy "required less work by human muscle" than coal, which disempowered working people. Here, Foley points to the impact of energy on labor, not just in industries like coal or renewables, but even for manual laborers like Teel. The poverty she expressed in her interview, compounded by racism and sexism, grew from the lost demand for her energy, replaced by the washing machine.[4]

Although proponents of the "free market" insist that capitalism is an equal opportunity exploiter, a wealth of scholarship demonstrates the opposite: poverty is a pre-existing condition uncovered by the benefits of capitalism. Men and women like Teel felt the sting of capitalist advances in energy and technology that—compounded by racism, sexism, and geography—eliminated their ability to work. Members of historically disadvantaged or exploited groups—people of color, women, LGBTQ, and working-class folk—are subject to historic and social processes that limit their access to existing sources of wealth. As a formerly enslaved woman, Teel had no family savings or inheritance upon which to draw. When changes in energy production, distribution, and application undercut the need for her muscular energy, she and those like her were left without recourse. This is their story. Depending on how we choose to address energy and equity as a society, it could easily be ours.[5]

"Hard Up"

When 76-year-old Mose Evans met his WPA interviewer, Mary B. Hudgins, he was carrying a bucket of charcoal in one hand, and supported himself with the help of a cane in the other. He told her that he was carrying the bucket of coal for his wife, a washerwoman, who used it to heat her iron. He explained that he could not work anymore, and his wife was able to get only two or three days' worth of washing per week. "My wife has to work awful hard," Mose said, "to earn enough to buy enough coal and wood," which fueled her washing business. She must have worked hard in uncomfortable conditions for this scant income. The energy she expended washing and ironing was transformed into cash that Mose used to purchase charcoal to heat her iron and boil her water so that she could continue to work. Increasingly, washing and ironing simply did not pay. It offered only a few days of pay per week for Evans and had all but disappeared for Teel.[6]

The washing machines that replaced the labor of Teel and Mrs. Evans required labor of their own to create and disseminate the machinery of the modern household. Because of the racialized and gendered division of labor in early twentieth-century America, however, these jobs went almost exclusively to white men at the expense of African American women. And these changes in work depended on a host of others—coal-fired power plants connected by rail to coal towns across Appalachia; an electrical grid that powered factories and the homes of consumers; oil wells, pipelines, refineries, and pumps. Each of these was necessary to automate the manual labor of washerwomen and at each point in this web of work, white male industrial workers replaced the black domestic labor of women like Teel.[7]

Image 2: In this 1941 photo of an electrical workers' strike, the apparently all-white workforce is juxtaposed with the gas pumps, street lights, and electrical lines that converged to facilitate the automation of domestic jobs. New forms of energy production, along with the infrastructure that supplied oil and electricity to towns and cities across the U.S., relied almost exclusively on white male workers. Though the energy revolution of the early twentieth century improved the lives of many working people, its benefits were spread unevenly. Al Ravenna, "Men milling around street across from the Brooklyn Navy Yard during an electrical workers strike," LC-USZ62-124542, Prints and Photographs Division, Library of Congress.

The link between automation and the elimination of jobs was clear to contemporaries, as historian Ruth Cowan argues that "many people purchased appliances precisely so that they could dispense with servants." In these "modern" households, the expense of black labor could be avoided along with the social discomfort of associating with African Americans, even in a rigorously hierarchical setting like domestic labor. In many ways, when we use "working class" as a euphemism for white working folk, we echo this same shift of work and wealth away from people of color and towards white men and women with machines.[8]

Cowan's research on household labor and consumerism finds a reliance on what she terms "fuel-supply systems" that supplanted the need for worker-produced energy. Then, as now, revolutions in the distribution and application of energy brought about corresponding changes in the nature, location, and availability of work. In Teel's day, jobs moved to sites of industrial labor—the factory and the mine—and to their products—the washing machine and the automobile—in the home. As Foley observes, many of these jobs are shifting to the renewable energy sector, and perhaps further investment there would produce significant growth and additional work that we may be unable to see from our present vantage point. Still, what economists often call the decoupling of growth and productivity, or what Mark Muro and Sifan Liu more recently identify as the low- and high-output America, suggest that, if innovation produces new jobs, there is no reason to think that it cannot do so asymmetrically. This should come as no surprise to students of underdevelopment and colonial history. There is a geographical component to development through which the "underdeveloped" areas facilitate the wealth and growth of the "developed" areas. Environmental historians, scholars, and activists often refer to these areas—sites of industrial pollution and energy production—as "sacrifice zones" where the wellbeing of inhabitants is sacrificed to the consumers in more "developed" areas. We, too, can be "sacrificed," perhaps not to pollution, but certainly to chronic joblessness meant to subsidize the wealth of the elite.[9]

Automation was hardly new in the first quarter of the nineteenth-century. Roy Redfield recalled an early form of automated torture in the "whippin' machine" to his WPA interviewer. If enslaved men and women failed to expend enough energy in their labors, their enslavers would, in the words of Redfield, "wind the whippin' machine and beat you" as a way of more perfectly extracting the working energy of African Americans. American slavery was replete with automation and mechanization schemes that merged steam and human power to increase profits of southern enslavers and northern "capitalists" alike. In fact, the mechanization of clothing production in England and the northeast U.S. facilitated the massive expansion of American slavery that culminated in the Civil War. Teel's unemployment was no unfortunate accident of new processes of energy application; it was integral to the development of American slavery, and with it, American capitalism.[10]

Image 3: The white male workforce of the Maytag Washing Machine Company making the washing machines that would replace the work of black washerwomen like Teel. Theodor Horydczak, "Maytag Washing Machine Company, Pouring a one-piece aluminum washer," ca. 1920–1950, LC-H814-T-0482, Horydczak Collection, Prints and Photographs Division, Library of Congress.

Image 4: Horydczak, "Maytag Washing Machine Company, Grinding and polishing," ca. 1920–1950, LC-H814-T-0482, Horydcazk Collection.

Mechanization and automation often worked in tandem to help employers and enslavers extract more labor from workers. In fact, Redfield and Teel's experiences merge here in an important way. Redfield and his fellow slaves were beaten to incentivize greater output because their bodies and labor were owned. After emancipation, however, Teel received a wage until she could be replaced by a machine. The underlying desire to eliminate the expense of waged work that characterized the experiences of both is easily grasped. If we are concerned with the plight of poor and working people, the solution does not lie in a world without machines, or in one powered only by fossil fuels. These worlds had racial, labor, and gender hierarchies of their own that patterned exploitation and unemployment. Many of them are probably not even too foreign to us. Indeed, these patterns of exploitation have, in some respects, expanded through the proliferation of biometric monitoring at corporations large and small. Though these technologies are changing the ways that many of us work, the processes of exploitation they embody would likely have been all too familiar to former slaves like Teel.[11]

"A Time of Worry"

Roy Redfield's tale of the "whippin' machine" provides an obvious example of coerced labor that most of us find objectionable. Perhaps a less obvious example lay in some of the WPA respondents' understanding of a jobless future. Eighty-year-old Isom Roberts, for example, worried that "slavery time was better for de average" black worker "than what they is gittin' now." To be clear, he also felt that, for many African Americans, slavery was the "worse thing dat has ever come upon them." It is likely that Roberts, who rented a one-room apartment in virulently racist Jim Crow Columbia, South Carolina, was trying to speak carefully about a time for which many of his white contemporaries were deeply nostalgic. However, he was also fiercely critical of white northerners and southerners, both of whom he correctly accused of having profited from slavery, while black workers "never got no money." A close reading of Roberts' tale reveals a "frail" man who supported himself through intermittent yardwork and who may have felt hopeless at his inability to obtain a regular wage or income. Perhaps fittingly, "I is so hungry" were the final words Roberts' spoke as he ended his interview.[12]

If Roberts' story of his life since slavery revealed certain frustrations with the past and the present, it also conveyed a deep concern with the future that was common among formerly enslaved workers interviewed by WPA. As he told it, "flopin' 'bout in dese automobiles, a drinkin' and carryin' on" was an "abomination in de sight of a decent person, much less dat One up yonder." While he may have simply been very religious, his critique of what were essentially expressions of excess capital and leisure time, when paired with his own poverty, suggests additional motives for his observations. Roberts had been left behind by the growth that his contemporaries, black and white, flouted when they displayed their wealth so conspicuously. So while it might be hard to imagine why he would view "slavery time" as positive, it is easy to see how being excluded from the asymmetrical growth of modernization made him bitter about what he was "gittin' now."[13]

For many formerly enslaved people, the connection was more explicit. Mary Harris saw the massive changes in work and lifestyle facilitated by the expansion of the electrical grid and automotive infrastructure as inaugurating "a time of worry." Harris had been "washin' and ironin'" for her adult life and "did sewing before machines come to this town." By the time of her interview, however, machines had taken her ability to earn a wage through either occupation. Harris claimed that these changes, the cause of her worry, were "told about in the scripture," an allusion to the apocalypse.[14]

Mittie Freeman, interviewed in Little Rock Arkansas, also felt that something was deeply wrong with modernity. As she put it, "people makes more money than in old days, but the way they makes it ain't honest." She argued that the only honest work was to "bend the back and bear down on the hoe." For Freeman, the electricity and mechanization that afforded her granddaughter a sewing machine, while it allowed her to make a dress over the course of a single day, amounted to Biblical "days of tribulations." Freeman and Harris had been pushed out of the labor force. Their energy no longer brought a wage, while those around them reaped the benefits of new systems of distributing and applying energy that—due to race, class, age, gender, and geography—they could not access.[15]

While it may be easy to chuckle at their sense that mechanization might mean the end of the world, Freeman and Harris were certainly not amused. Their testimony reveals a world so hopeless that it belied all but supernatural explanation. Andrew Nikiforuk characterizes this world as one powered by "energy slaves"—the productive service performed by enslaved African Americans as well as the petrocarbons which substantially displaced black labor. Imagining enslaved energy and its successors in carbon as existing on a continuum, as Nikiforuk does, emphasizes the ways that American capitalism is averse to autonomous workers and wages. We must also concede that our current political environment has been ruptured by similar forces and ideas to those of Freeman and Harris. Harris' "time of worry" over increasingly scarce jobs and poor wages fits neatly with an irrational Trump administration energy policy masquerading as a jobs program. In many respects, her fears express a timeless concern among American working folk that the benefits and burdens of capitalism are borne unevenly.[16]

Conclusion

Beneath Nikiforuk's "energy slaves," the rise of renewable energy, and the generations of displaced workers preceding our time lies Michael Denning's famous observation that the tendency of capitalism to generate joblessness represents its most significant mechanism of exploitation. The inability to find regular work might seem like the end of the world, and to many men and women who had survived slavery, I feel sure that it did. The growth of automation and mechanization that accompanied massive changes in energy infrastructure certainly foreclosed the only sectors of employment open to many African Americans in the first quarter of the twentieth century. Broadly speaking, these changes have disproportionately impacted those doing the most exploitative work: yesterday's washerwomen and agricultural laborers, today's coal miners, factory workers, and service-sector employees, and perhaps tomorrow's truck drivers.[17]

So where does this leave us, as participants in the system?

Like Foley, I believe that a third energy shift brings with it significant potential to rework our economy into a more equitable, livable space. However, as Foley's work also implies, the present system may belie a technological fix to problems of inequality that tend to generate capital for wealthy elites at the expense of "sacrificed" workers and communities. The elites of Teel's day had an opportunity to distribute the fruits of technological advances more equitably. They chose instead to hoard it for themselves. Innovation does not necessarily bring equity.

As our consumer–capitalist society continues to demand that each of us work even as firms automate and outsource available jobs, members of working-class and minority groups are especially vulnerable to joblessness and poverty. This is both tragic and unnecessary. These changes in the nature and availability of labor suggest that it may be time to reevaluate the place of work in society.[18]

We might use these technological changes as an opportunity to examine how and why we work. Rather than simply trumpeting the value of a day's labor, perhaps we ought to ask what values our work should reflect. If we labor simply to generate wealth, as automation and renewable energy replace human labor, perhaps our collective relationship to work needs to change. Work might no longer be necessary, or even possible, on its historically individual basis. Maybe its future lies in a universal basic income; maybe a shorter work week; or perhaps in some sort of federal job guarantee program. Whatever we decide, likely when making a choice becomes unavoidable, I hope it is something that working men and women like Roberts and Teel would not see as the end of the world.[19]

Notes

1 Narrative of Mary Teel, Holly Grove, Arkansas, 1–3, Federal Writers' Project: Slave Narrative Project, Vol. 2, Arkansas, Part 6, Quinn-Tuttle, Library of Congress (LOC), https://www.loc.gov/resource/mesn.026/?sp=287. The WPA Ex-Slave Narratives are notorious for interviewer instructions to record former slaves' dialect, which leave the narratives themselves full of misspellings and odd turns of phrase. Many historians use these spellings and grammatical errors because they represent the best record we have of how the interviewees relayed their experiences. I have chosen to do the same here. Saidya V. Hartman, *Scenes of Subjection: Terror, Slavery, and Self-Making in Nineteenth-Century America* (New York: Oxford University Press, 1997), 12; Lynda Hill, "Ex-Slave Narratives: The WPA Federal Writers' Project Reappraised," *Oral History* (Spring, 1998): 68–70; "'I Talk More of the French': Creole Folklore and the Federal Writers' Project," *Callaloo* (Spring, 2016): 441–444.

2 Justin Worland, "Donald Trump Says He'll Bring Back Coal. Here's Why He Can't," *Time*, November 14, 2016; Kimberly Adams, "Can Trump Keep His Big Promises on Steel Jobs?" *Marketplace*, October 16, 2016, http://ti.me/2fcKHjU; http://bit.ly/2fA4agG; Jim Zarroli, "Bringing Back Manufacturing Jobs Would Be Harder Than It Sounds," *NPR*, August 18, 2016, http://n.pr/2aY5B8B; "About Us," Fight for $15, http://fightfor15.org/about-us/ (accessed September 18, 2017); Mark Munro, "Manufacturing Jobs Aren't Coming Back," *MIT Technology Review*, November 18, 2016, http://bit.ly/2fmNXJq.

3 Michael Denning, "Wageless Life," *New Left Review* (November–December 2010): 79; Daniel Walker Howe, *What Hath God Wrought: The Transformation of America, 1815–1848* (New York: Oxford University Press, 2007), 214–215, 563–569; Walter Johnson, *River of Dark Dreams: Slavery and Empire in the Cotton Kingdom* (Cambridge, MA: Harvard University Press, 2013), 73–96, especially pages 85–87; Beverly Silver, *Forces of Labor: Workers' Movements and Globalization since 1870* (New York: Cambridge University Press, 2003), 41–49.

4 Tom Foley, "Energy and the Trump Administration: Pipelines, Promises, and the Third Energy Shift," essay page 10.

5 Thavolia Glymph, *Out of the House of Bondage: The Transformation of the Plantation Household* (New York: Cambridge University Press, 2008); Tera Hunter, *To Joy My Freedom: Southern Black Women's Lives and Labors after the Civil War* (Cambridge, MA: Harvard University Press, 1997); Hartman, *Scenes of Subjection*, especially chapter four.

6 Narrative of Mose Evans, Arkansas, 4, Federal Writers' Project: Slave Narrative Project, Vol. 2, Arkansas, Part 2, Cannon-Evans, LOC, https://www.loc.gov/resource/mesn.022/?q=%22work+no+more%22&sp=256. Hunter, *To Joy My Freedom*, 74–97.

7 Lizabeth Cohen, *A Consumers' Republic: The Politics of Mass Consumption in Postwar America* (New York: Knopf, 2003), 22–28.

8 Ruth Schwarts Cowan, *More Work for Mother: The Ironies of Household Technology from the Open Hearth to the Microwave* (New York: Basic Books, 1983), 97–99.

9 Cowan, *More Work for Mother*, 98; Amy Bernstein and Anand Raman, "The Great Decoupling: An Interview with Erik Brynjolfsson and Andrew McAfee," *The Harvard Business Review*, June, 2015, https://hbr.org/2015/06/the-great-decoupling (accessed September 7, 2017); Erik Brynjolfsson and Andrew McAfee, "Jobs, Productivity and the Great Decoupling," *The New York Times*, December 11, 2012, http://nyti.ms/1fjVZu3; Mark Muro and Sifan Liu, "Another Clinton-Trump Divide: High-Output America vs Low-Output America," *The Avenue*, The Brookings Institution, https://www.brookings.edu/blog/the-avenue/2016/11/29/another-clinton-trump-divide-high-output-america-vs-low-output-america/ (accessed September 7, 2017); Kari Polanyi Levitt, *Reclaiming Development: Independent Thought and Caribbean Community* (Kingston, Jamaica: Ian Randle Publishers, 2005), esp. 46–53; Andre Gunder Frank, *Latin America: Underdevelopment or Revolution* (New York: Modern Reader, 1969), esp. 3–6; George Beckford, *Persistent Poverty: Underdevelopment in Plantation Economies of the Third World* (Kingston, Jamaica: University of West Indies Press, 1999), esp. xxvii–xxix, 9–11, 24–26, 44–51.

10 Compilation, Richmond County and Augusta, Georgia, 13, Federal Writers'

Project: Slave Narrative Project, Vol. 4, Georgia, Part 4, Telfair-Young, LOC, https://www.loc.gov/resource/mesn.044/?q=machine&sp=308; Edward Baptist, *The Half Has Never Been Told: Slavery and the Making of American Capitalism* (New York: Basic Books, 2014), 126–130, 141–142; Richard Follett, *The Sugar Masters: Planters and Slaves in Louisiana's Cane World, 1820–1860* (Baton Rouge, LA: LSU Press, 2005), 4–5.

11 "Amazon Not Only Company Using Data To Manage Workers," *Chicago Tribune*, August 17, 2015, http://www.chicagotribune.com/business/ct-amazon-ceo-response-new-york-times-20150817-story.html (accessed September 7, 2017); "Wisconsin Company To Implant Microchips In Employees," *Chicago Tribune*, July 25, 2017, http://www.chicagotribune.com/business/ct-wisconsin-company-microchips-three-square-market-20170724-story.html (accessed September 7, 2017).

12 Narrative of Isom Roberts, Isom Roberts, Columbia, South Carolina, 1–4 Federal Writers' Project: Slave Narrative Project, Vol. 14, South Carolina, Part 4, Raines-Young, LOC, https://www.loc.gov/resource/mesn.144/?q=automobile&sp=30.

13 Narrative of Isom Roberts, 3.

14 Narrative of Mary Harris, 1938, Pine Bluff, Arkansas, 1–2, Federal Writers' Project: Slave Narrative Project, Vol. 2, Arkansas, Part 3, Gadson-Isom, LOC, https://www.loc.gov/resource/mesn.023/?q=machine&sp=178.

15 Narrative of Mittie Freeman, August 27, 1937, Little Rock, Arkansas, 6–7, Federal Writers' Project: Slave Narrative Project, Vol. 2, Arkansas, Part 2, Cannon-Evans, LOC, https://www.loc.gov/resource/mesn.022/?sp=356&q=machine.

16 Andrew Nikiforuk, *The Energy of Slaves: Oil and the New Servitude* (Berkeley, CA: Greystone Books, 2012), 1–3, 12, 20–23.

17 Michael Denning, "Wageless Life," 79; Brad Plumer, "Trump is Making Promises on Coal Mining Jobs He Can't Possibly Keep," *Vox*, February 21, 2017, http://bit.ly/2xhSdUn; Wolfgang Lehmacher, "Don't Blame China For Taking U.S. Jobs," *Fortune*, November 8, 2016, http://for.tn/2eUyHTU; Mira Rojanasakul and Peter Coy, "More Robots, Fewer Jobs," *Bloomberg*, May 8, 2017, https://bloom.bg/2pW6cOO; Darrell M. West, *What Happens if Robots Take the Jobs? The Impact of Emerging Technologies on Employment and Public Policy*, The Brookings Institution (October 2015), http://brook.gs/2oOWFIs; Natalie Kitroeff, "Robots Could Replace 1.7 Million American Truckers in the Next Decade," *Los Angeles Times*, September 25, 2016, http://lat.ms/2dtJnvF.

18 David Rotman, "How Technology Is Destroying Jobs," *MIT Technology Review*, June 12, 2013, http://bit.ly/21VXp7l; Derek Thompson, "A World Without Work," *The Atlantic*, July/August, 2015, http://theatln.tc/2kCryhc.

19 Keri Leigh Merritt, "Why We Need a Universal Basic Income," *billmoyers.com*, September 15, 2017, http://bit.ly/2xpdFcg; Dylan Matthews, "This Kenyan Village is a Laboratory for the Biggest Basic Income Experiment Ever," *Vox*, http://bit.ly/2pC7I9q; Aaron Taube, "6 Arguments For A Shorter Workweek," *Business Insider*, September 1, 2014, http://read.bi/1CTJ3L2; William Darity Jr., "A Guaranteed Federal Jobs Program Is Needed," *The New York Times*, July 11, 2016, http://nyti.ms/2fB58sU.

V

INSURING MENTAL HEALTH:
TREATMENT AND ACCESS FOR THE MENTALLY ILL

TREATING MENTAL ILLNESS IN VICTORIAN BRITAIN

Jade Shepherd
University of Lincoln, UK

In 1884, four years after his release from Broadmoor Criminal Lunatic Asylum,[1] and following the death of his sister, George Longmore re-admitted himself into the asylum. Afterward, he wrote to his brother:

> Dear brother me coming to Broadmoor I know has been a sad blow to your feelings. I am sorry for causing you so much pain ... I must make the best of it for a time now. I do wish it had never happened on account of my dear wife and my dear mother.
>
> I shall be made as comfortable as can be while here. Dear brother ... I must conclude sending my kind love to you which I am sorry for causing so much pain. I hope you will forgive me and please do remember me to dear mother with many kisses and sister Betsy and John and all my friends, so goodbye for the present.
>
> I remain
> Your affectionate brother
> George Longmore[2]

Longmore appears to have been torn between two communities: one familial and one at Broadmoor. With his family unable to offer him the care he needed, Longmore seemingly viewed the asylum as a sanctuary within which he would receive the necessary treatment and support. The asylum provided not only medical care but also a strong social community. Longmore was free to talk, work, and partake in leisure pursuits alongside other male patients.

It cannot be denied that there was a lot wrong with how insanity was conceptualized and treated in the nineteenth century. Scholars have shown that treatment was sometimes cruel, isolating, and degrading. Some asylums were poorly maintained, and there were institutions within which care and compassion were considered lacking.[3] However, cases such as Longmore's alert us to the benefits of specialized institutions for the care and treatment of those living with mental illness, and the importance of the sense of community that these institutions created.

Since the old asylum system was dismantled—a process that began in Britain in the 1960s—the communities, both medical and social, that some individuals living with mental illness relied on in the nineteenth and twentieth centuries have all but disappeared. Care in the Community was designed to replace the old asylums, but amounted to nothing more than "an attractive slogan."[4] Writing in the 1970s, author PD James described it as "the absence of care in a community still largely resentful or frightened of mental illness."[5] Since James wrote this, little has changed. The apparent (albeit unintentional) current criminalization of mental illness—with the prison system seemingly replacing psychiatric hospitals—constitutes an avoidable regression to the seventeenth and early eighteenth centuries. As historian Andrew Scull has noted, "[t]he confinement of the mad in prisons shocked the consciences of nineteenth-century reformers, and helped to prompt the age of asylumdom. The closure of these nineteenth-century establishments has, it would seem, brought us full circle."[6] This essay draws upon Broadmoor patients' letters, and accounts of institutionalization in twentieth-century Britain, to highlight the benefits of, and need for, specialized institutions within which the mentally ill can seek the support, care, and community that is not always readily available to them today.

When the Broadmoor archive opened in 2008, it unleashed a vast and incredibly rich collection of patients' letters to and from their families, friends, fellow patients, and the asylum's staff, providing a rare opportunity to examine the subjective experiences of Victorian asylum patients. The existence of these documents allows historians to answer Roy Porter's call for a history of madness from below,[7] while simultaneously enabling us to qualify historians' previous suggestions that asylum patients experienced institutionalization negatively.[8] The Broadmoor patients' letters are unusual because they highlight positive as well as negative aspects of institutionalized care, allowing researchers to see which aspects of asylum life were deemed necessary and helpful to patients, by patients. Patients' letters are invaluable because they allow us to hear directly from the patient rather than through doctors' descriptions,[9] but they do have limitations and we must be aware of certain methodological issues. Marjorie Levine-Clark noted, "the thorny question of how we hear a patient's voice is especially difficult with the insane, whose rational ability to represent themselves

142

is an issue,"[10] but patients' letters should not be dismissed as meaningless ramblings.

Broadmoor patients' letters are often intelligible and articulate accounts of asylum life. There were patients in Broadmoor who, according to medical testimony, had lost all reason, but there were also two other types of patients who wrote letters: those who were deemed only partially insane and those who were sane, but refused discharge because they did not have anyone willing or able to care for them, or because their crime was so heinous that the authorities were waiting for a period of time to pass before they sanctioned their discharge.[11] Of course, even if they were deemed insane and were articulate, patients might have reported positively upon the asylum regime because they believed it might help gain them release. In addition, asylum officials might have archived positive correspondence for use in annual reports in order to promote the institution, and we may, therefore, be left with a skewed representation of asylum life.

Institutionalized Care: A Brief History

The philosophy of treatment for insanity before the nineteenth century is infamous: chains, bloodletting, and purging were used to treat and control the mad, who were hidden from view in madhouses and represented in popular and medical discourse as bestial and inherently irrational.[12] From the mid-eighteenth century, ideas about insanity began to change, and there was an increasing desire to adopt a new philosophy and treat insanity with so-called moral treatment. In Britain, this new approach began at the (private) York Retreat (1796), a purpose-built home surrounded by woodland. Its superintendent was Samuel Tuke, a lay preacher from the local Quaker community. Patients were treated via a combination of useful occupations and religion, and they lived and worked alongside the asylum's staff. In the place of restraint and seclusion, the importance of kind and patient asylum staff was emphasized, with the superintendent acting as a father figure to patients; "the bonds of family replaced the hierarchy of control."[13] Historians have referred to this change as the domestication of insanity.[14]

The Asylums Act of 1845 stipulated that each county must have an asylum to cater to its pauper insane. These asylums were designed to resemble large country houses with landscaped gardens, and had ornamental drives, parkland, farms, cricket fields and estate walls, and the airing courts attached to each accommodation block were designed so patients could view the vast landscape (fresh air and exercise also being part of treatment), and moral treatment was implemented. Recreations and amusements were promoted as important elements of treatment that would help to divert and heal (give "nerve and vigour" to) patients' "shattered" minds.[15] These amusements included reading, painting, writing, and playing games. Patients were also given religious and secular instruction as part of their treatment, and because moral value was ascribed to work to relieve idleness and prevent patients from dwelling upon their condition, they were encouraged to practice their trade (or learn one).[16]

Contemporaries viewed moral treatment in terms of progress, but some twentieth and twenty-first century scholars have criticized it. French philosopher Michel Foucault argued that asylums were institutions of social control within which physical chains were replaced with surveillance and coercion,[17] and Scull suggested that moral treatment was designed "to transform the lunatic" into "the bourgeois ideal of the rational individual." Since then, other historians have shown that some asylum patients were expected to display "normative standards of behavior," which were usually gendered (along bourgeois lines) before they could be discharged.[18] It is argued that moral treatment was designed to encourage traits such as temperance, industry, self-control, rationality, and decorum in patients. Current and ongoing scholarly research suggests that this was not the case in all asylums, though, and that some patients were discharged even though they did not possess these attributes.[19]

Historians (and contemporaries) agree that moral treatment failed. Asylums had limited resources with which to implement their claims of a cure and, from the 1860s, the existence of long-term chronic patients led to a rapid growth in the county asylum population. This meant that moral treatment—which relied on small patient numbers to be successful—was difficult to implement. Increasing patient numbers also led to the belief that insanity was incurable.[20] This so-called psychiatric pessimism led to the reintroduction of mechanical restraint and seclusion in some asylums, although some asylum medical officers did manage to "find a compromise between sifting out and treating a minority, while managing large numbers of the chronically disordered."[21]

Those deemed mentally ill could expect a long stay in these large Victorian asylums into the 1960s. In the 1950s, these institutions housed approximately 150,000 patients a day, but deinstitutionalization—or decarceration—was just around the corner.[22] The Mental Health Act of 1959 high-lighted the Conservative government's plans, under Prime Minister Harold Macmillan, to phase out asylums and integrate mental health wards into hospitals; care in the local community was now the preferred option.[23] In 1961, Enoch Powell, Minister of Health, spoke at the National Association for Mental Health. He declared asylums "doomed institutions," and stated his—the government's—intention "to set the torch to the [asylum's] funeral pyre."[24] Decarceration was driven by financial concerns; the State deemed the cost of running these vast hospitals too great. Following Powell's speech, the government stopped funding mental hospitals, and one by one they were declared unfit for purpose and shut down.

The failings of Care in the Community have been well documented for at least the last thirty years.[25] Despite the intention for care to move from the asylum to the community, there was no real plan in place, nor was there adequate funding. Community Care was, as Scull states, "a shell game with no pea."[26] One of the problems was—and remains—where were people living with mental illness to go? For individuals who could function in the world because their illness was receptive to medication, and for those who could be sent back to welcoming and supportive families, decarceration was manageable. For some others, though, decarceration brought home-lessness, poverty, crime, and loneliness. Families could not—or would not—care for their sick relative, and over-stretched hospital wards meant the only place they could be confined was a prison cell. Such difficulties remain today. Moreover, the social communities that institutionalization offered, and which helped patients survive, have all but disappeared.

Experiences of Institutionalization

Despite the shortcomings and failings of institutionalized care, some asylum patients viewed their institutionalization positively. The asylum was a place within which they would receive the care they needed; it was a place of refuge and respite for individuals struggling to survive in the world. Feeling alone and neglected by his family, one nineteenth-century patient told another: "I am very glad and cheered when I hear the flute."[27] Passages from the Broadmoor letters are reminiscent of scholar Barbara Taylor's account of her time at Friern hospital (formerly Colney Hatch Asylum) in the 1980s. Taylor viewed Friern as a "sanctuary": "I entered on my knees. I could no longer do ordinary life, and giving up the struggle was an incalculable relief."[28]

Broadmoor patients' accounts of asylum life and Taylor's recollections are, in some instances, more than one hundred years apart, and yet the similarities are striking. Broadmoor features in some patients' letters as a safe space for patients; they could work without fearing the repercussions of unemployment, or without the added pressure of knowing they had to provide for their families. Some patients' friends and families also viewed Broadmoor as a place in which patients were restored to health. The friend of one patient wrote to the superintendent: "[you] have solved the problem of how to help and relieve [patients] without ... destroying their self-respect."[29]

Institutions were deemed not only places of recovery and respite but also spaces within which patients could forge friendships and close relationships with other individuals, both staff and patients. Hospitalization features positively in those cases where patients' mental health issues fractured or destroyed their relationships with friends and families, or where patients seemingly felt that their families could not understand their plight. Taylor recalled how, in the 1980s, "the friendship of other patients ... made my days tolerable." She concluded that while institutional care was flawed, it "nurtured communities" crucial for patients' wellbeing.[30] We see this at Victorian Broadmoor, too, where, as scholars have shown was also the case at other institutions, the development and maintenance of friendship (and survival) networks was crucial for some patients.[31]

Patients looked to the asylum's staff and their fellow patients for support and companionship. The superintendent was sometimes drawn into family networks—he delivered bad news to patients on behalf of their families, he acted as a mediator between warring relatives, and he kept family secrets—but he was also there for patients when no family network existed, or when it had broken down. Some patients looked to him as a father, a brother, or a friend. Warmark, a patient in the 1920s, recalled that the superintendent "stands out in a tragic period of my life as the best friend I ever had."[32] Some of Broadmoor's Victorian patients shared this assessment, writing to the superintendent as though he were a friend. Following his transfer to the Berkshire County Asylum, former patient Robert Newport wrote to superintendent Orange: "[I] cannot find words to express ... [the] gratitude he ows [sic] [you] for all past indulgences ... which will never be forgotten."[33] Following his discharge, another patient wrote "to say how well I am ... I have a very good home indeed ... I wish to return my best thanks for being sent home and pray that you and your good lady may enjoy many, very many happy years to come."[34] While at Broadmoor, patients asked the superintendent for his advice and help in matters including visiting their fellow patients, relations with their families and the acquisition of stamps. Some patients also formed close bonds with the attendants; Henry Dodwell wrote to attendant Bailey regarding personal matters.[35] It is not surprising that such bonds were formed. Attendants spent many hours a day with patients: they washed and shaved them; distributed journals and newspapers; fed patients who were unable to feed themselves; walked with patients who needed help getting around; and introduced games and other leisure activities in the dayrooms.[36]

The recreational activities that were provided as part of treatment in Victorian asylums encouraged patients to interact with one another. Some male patients played—and by their own accounts enjoyed—team sports such as cricket, and female patients would take group rides and walks around the asylum's grounds.[37] The asylum's blocks all had dayrooms where patients could play a variety of games, and where they could write, paint, sew, and read alongside each other while in conversation, as depicted by the *Illustrated London News* [Image 1]. Here, male patients are portrayed partaking in some of the activities medical men deemed vital for diverting and thus healing the mind (reading, writing, and playing games). The patients are represented as calm and orderly, perhaps suggesting the success of such activities. Some of the men are simply talking with one another, and this social interaction was beneficial to—and valued by—some patients.

Figure 1. Male Dayroom, Broadmoor, *Illustrated London News* (1867)

Patient Anthony Owston spent time talking to William Minor about "his soul" and Henry Dodwell wrote letters to another patient detailing his grievances and describing his sadness.[38] After receiving no correspondence from his family, Philip Dawe presumed they had given up on him: "to them I am probably long sensed lapsed [sic] into too hopeless imbecility or insanity to maintain a correspondence."[39] He asked the superintendent if he could visit another patient in a different part of the asylum, presumably after meeting him at work or in the chapel. As with Longmore, whose letter began this essay, Dawe exemplifies being torn between his family and friends outside the asylum, and the doctors and patients inside the asylum. What is different, though, is the gulf that seemingly arose between Dawe and his family as a result of his mental illness; he perceived that they did not understand the reality of his condition. This was certainly one of the potential downsides of institutionalization. The rupture between Dawe and his loved ones did, however, seemingly encourage and strengthen his bonds with other patients. His case was not unusual.

While some familial relationships remained strong, for some patients their insanity and absence from home created a chasm between themselves and their loved ones.[40] Patients were sent to Broadmoor for an indefinite period of time, and this distressed both patients and their families. Having a relative committed into the asylum was also burdensome. Visiting a relative at the asylum disrupted families' day-to-day lives and imposed travel costs that were often difficult to bear.[41] As a result, while some continued to write to their detained relatives, offering words of advice and comfort, and sometimes admonishment, some never saw them again. In addition, some friends and relatives did not wish to visit because they did not wish to burden patients with their troubles, or because of the hardship a patient's crime and insanity had caused. Joseph Redding's wife told the superintendent she was unable to visit for "two reasons. I have not had the means as I was left with six children and myself to provide for. I have also been suffering with change of life. There as been many obsticles [sic] in my way which I have not wanted to trouble him with."[42] Illiterate patient John Cooper had not heard from his wife and children for many years when he asked a fellow patient ("a friend") to write to the superintendent on his behalf inquiring after their whereabouts, and to ask him to "send my love to my wife and family."[43] The superintendent contacted Cooper's wife, who wrote the following emotionally driven letter to her husband in which she made explicit the suffering she had endured as a result of his confinement:

I was surprised that you will continue writing as I wish you would not as it upsets me very much and I hope you won't do so any more ... I ... trust you will never write to me again nor any one else as it makes me ill from all the sorrow I have gone through ... please don't write no more.

And ask God to forgive you as I have had a struggling time of it these last 25 years it has brought me down to a poor old woman and your children have quite forgot you and never think anything of you and no one never mentions your name.[44]

In such cases, friendships with other patients and close bonds with the asylum's staff provided comfort to patients. In addition to receiving no visitors, some patients also had no written contact with friends or relatives, either because they received no correspondence, or because they were illiterate and had no one to write on their behalf. When patients had little-to-no contact with the outside world, being in Broadmoor could be overwhelming, lonely, and frightening. Some patients felt that they had been abandoned in the asylum, which, as historian Roy Porter observed, negated all that a family was supposed to be.[45]

Perhaps unlike their families, their fellow patients could understand what it was like to live with mental illness and the isolation of being institutionalized.[46] Some friendships lasted beyond institutionalization. Two years following her release, one patient continued to think about a friend she had made in Broadmoor for whom she "had a sisterly regard."[47] She wrote to the superintendent:

I am conscious to know if Lucy Thompson is still under your care, if so, will you give me some hope of her liberty. I have long neglected her, but now I have a home of my own and most freely will I share it with her, it is my husband's wish that I should send to you about it, for he is most anxious that we should do our best for her, if such a thing were possible, she would have every opportunity of getting on, as I am well known in the town, and have plenty of work.[48]

Such cases suggest the importance of friendships and familial-like relationships forged within institutions. Indeed, friendship ensured survival, and for some, happiness and contentment at the asylum. As Taylor wrote of her time at Friern, "friendship trumped madness—and this in itself could be a form of healing."[49]

Today, there are no such institutions to care for the mentally ill; they have been replaced with day centers, overstretched hospital wards or prison cells, and—in some areas—cognitive behavioral therapy (CBT) delivered over the telephone. Of course, individuals are free to pay for their own private care, and can, in theory, receive support from family members willing to act as their caretakers, but in reality these are options only the privileged few can afford. A lack of funding and thus resources means the treatment of mental illness is not good enough. Of course, the demise of the asylum is not necessarily a bad thing, but the services designed to replace institutionalized care in Britain do not always provide a sense of sanctuary to those living with mental illness. Unlike when the mentally ill were removed to the asylum or hospital, individuals today are not always removed from the environment that has caused or exacerbated their health issues, unless of course they have the means to pay for private care and/or a supportive family who can offer alternative surroundings. Moreover, the loneliness that often accompanies ill mental health in the twenty-first century can be terrible.[50]

Some nineteenth and twentieth-century asylum patients managed to relieve feelings of isolation and despondency through their interactions with other patients. Thus, the benefit of, and need for, community in the treatment of mental illness is clear. It is a tragedy that the social activities that encouraged friendships and communities to develop between patients in the past are not as plentiful today. Despite well-meaning campaigns[51] designed to reduce the shame associated with mental illness, some stigma still exists, but without the community or specialized institutional care that seemingly benefitted patients such as George Longmore or Philip Dawe in the nineteenth century, and Barbara Taylor in the twentieth century. These new campaigns are to be applauded, as are mental health charities. However, accessing the support and information they provide requires not only awareness of their existence and sometimes technological savvy, but also courage and tenacity. These attributes can be exhausted or denied by mental illness.

Conclusion

One of the things we can learn from patients' accounts of institutionalized care in the nineteenth and twentieth centuries is this: a sense of community and friendship can make a world of difference to the lives of people living with mental illness. The friendships some patients forged in asylums and hospitals were vital in providing them with a sense of belonging. Friendships could relieve feelings of hopelessness that sometimes followed institutionalization, and could help to reduce the amount of time patients spent dwelling on their ill health and (in some cases) indefinite institutionalization. That patients could form relationships with people who could understand and accept them was particularly important if they had no one else to turn to, as in Dawe's case. I do not want to romanticize this. We should not forget that institutionalized care was massively flawed, and that not all asylum patients made friends or adapted to being detained for an indefinite period of time away from their families and friends.[52] Nor were all patients treated with dignity or "cured." That said, the friendships formed within these institutions, and the structured treatment regime, were perceived positively by *some* patients, and made a huge difference to their lives.

Notes

1   Individuals sent to Broadmoor were treated like any other asylum patient; it did not matter that they had committed a crime. They were patients, not criminals.

2   Berkshire Record Office (BRO), D/H14/D2/2/1/1212/26.

3   For example, Andrew Scull, *Madness in Civilization: A Cultural History of Insanity from the Bible to Freud, from the Madhouse to Modern Medicine* (London: Thames and Hudson, 2015).

4   Patrick Cockburn, "Mental Health Patients are Being Treated as Criminals and Sent to Prisons Rather Than Hospitals," http://www.independent.co.uk/voices/prince-harry-mental-health-prisons-cant-be-solved-by-talking-a7695876.html (accessed July 18, 2017).

5   James quoted in Ibid.

6   Scull, *Madness in Civilization*, 378.

7   Roy Porter, "The Patient's View: Doing Medical History from Below," *Theory and Society* 14, no. 2 (1985): 175–198. The value of examining patients' experiences is demonstrated by the recent special edition of *Medical History*, "Tales from the Asylum. Patient Narratives and the (De)construction of Psychiatry," in *Medical History,*

eds. Alexandra Bacopoulos-Viau and Aude Fauvel, 60, no. 1 (2016), 1–18. See also various essays in Thomas Knowles and Serena Trowbridge (eds), *Insanity and the Lunatic Asylum in the Nineteenth Century* (London: Pickering and Chatto, 2015).

8   Scull, *Madness in Civilization*, 230; Jonathan Andrews, "Case Notes, Case Histories, and the Patients Experience of Insanity at Gartnavel Royal Asylum, Glasgow, in the Nineteenth Century," *Social History of Medicine* 11 (2) (1998): 255–281, 281. For a counter to the gloomy depictions of asylum life, Jade Shepherd, "I Am Very Glad and Cheered When I Hear the Flute: The Treatment of Criminal Lunatics in Late Victorian Broadmoor," *Medical History*, no. 4 (2016), 473–491.

9   Allan Beveridge, "Voices of the Mad: Patients' Letters from the Royal Edinburgh Asylum, 1873–1908," *Psychological Medicine* 27, no. 4 (1997), 899–908, 900.

10 Marjorie Levine-Clark, "Embarrassed Circumstances: Gender, Poverty, & Insanity in the West Riding of England in the Early Victorian Years," in *Sex and Seclusion, Class and Custody: Perspectives on Gender and Class in the History of British and Irish Psychiatry*, eds. Jonathan Andrews and Anne Digby (New York: Rodopi, 2004), 123–148, 126.

11 An individual suffering from partial insanity "suffers delusion on one point and is sane on all others". J. Russell Reynolds, *On the Scientific Value of the Legal Tests of Insanity: A Paper Read before the Metropolitan Counties Branch of the British Medical Association* (London: J & A Churchill, 1872), 46.

12 For the eighteenth century, Roy Porter, *Mind Forg'd Manacles: A History of Madness in England from the Restoration to the Regency* (Penguin Books, 1990).

13 Mike Jay, *This Way Madness Lies: The Asylum and Beyond* (London: Thames and Hudson, 2016), 94.

14 Andrew Scull, *Social Order/Mental Disorder: Anglo-American Psychiatry in Historical Perspective* (University of California Press, 1989).

15 R. Gardiner Hill, *Total Abolition of Personal Restraint in the Treatment of the Insane: A Lecture on the Management of Lunatic Asylums, and the Treatment of the Insane* (London: Simpkin & Marshall, 1839), 46. Also, W. A. F. Browne, "The Moral Treatment of the Insane: A Lecture," *Journal of Mental Science* 20 (October 1864): 309–337.

16 For occupational therapy, Ernst W. (ed) *Work Therapy, Psychiatry and Society, c. 1750–2010* (Manchester: Manchester University Press, 2016).

17 Michel Foucault, *History of Madness*, trans. By John Murphy and Jean Khalfa (London: Routledge, 2006), 485.

18 Louise Hide, *Gender and Class in English Asylums, 1890–1914* (Basingstoke: Pal-

grave Macmillan, 2014), 143; Pamela Michael, "Class, Gender and Insanity in Nineteenth-Century Wales," in *Sex and Seclusion,* eds. Andrews and Digby, 95–122, 111–115.

19 For example, Shepherd, "I Am Very Glad and Cheered When I Hear the Flute," 485–488.

20 For example, J.K. Walton, "Casting Out and Bringing Back in Victorian England: Pauper Lunatics, 1840–70," in *The Anatomy of Madness: Essays in the History of Psychiatry* 3 vols, eds. William F. Bynum, Roy Porter, and Michael Shepherd (London: Routledge, 1985–88), VII (1985), 132–146, 142; Steven Cherry, *Mental Health Care in Modern England: The Norfolk Lunatic Asylum/St Andrews Hospital 1810–1998* (Woodbridge: Boydell Press, 2003), 89–90.

21 Hide, *Gender and Class in English Asylums,* 39.

22 Scull, *Madness in Civilization,* 362.

23 Jay, *This Way Madness Lies,* 186.

24 Powell quoted in Scull, *Madness in Civilization,* 369–370.

25 For example, Scull, *Social Order/Mental Disorder,* 300–329.

26 Scull, *Madness in Civilization,* 375.

27 BRO, D/H14/D2/2/1/936c/29, letter.

28 Barbara Taylor, "The Demise of the Asylum in Late-Twentieth Century Britain: A Personal History," *Transactions of the Royal Historical Society* 21 (2011): 193–215, 212.

29 Shepherd, "I Am Very Glad and Cheered When I Hear the Flute," 481.

30 Taylor, "The Demise of the Asylum," 213. 215.

31 Hide, *Gender and Class in English Asylums,* 168–169.

32 Warmark, *Guilty but Insane: A Broadmoor Autobiography* (London: Chapman and Hall, 1939), 158.

33 BRO, D/H14/D2/2/1/729/5, letter to Orange.

34 BRO, D/H14/D2/2/1/905/34, letter to Orange.

35 BRO, D/H14/D2/2/1/936a/192, letter to Bailey.

36 *Rules for the Guidance of the Officers of Broadmoor Criminal Lunatic Asylum* (London: George E. Eyre and William Spottiswoode, 1863).

37 BRO, D/H14/D2/2/1/1116, letter from patient Matthew Jackson Hunter to his sister, 10 August 1883; patient Henry Dodwell begged Broadmoor's staff to allow the patients to play cricket after an afternoon game had been rained off, BRO, D/H14/D2/2/1/936b/46.

38 Jade Shepherd, "Victorian Madmen: Broadmoor, Masculinity and the Experiences of the Criminally Insane, 1863–1900" (unpublished PhD thesis, Queen Mary University of London, 2013), 85.

39 BRO, D/H14/D2/2/1/1069/13, letter to Nicolson.

40 My continued examination of the Broadmoor records suggests that class and gender impacted familial relationships. Husbands were more likely to support their incarcerated wives than wives were to support their incarcerated husbands. This is because as a rule husbands were not driven to financial ruin if their wife spent time way from the home. Male patients' wives found it more difficult to care for themselves and their families, and thus had no choice but to leave their husbands for another man. Middle-class wives were seemingly more likely to support their incarcerated husbands.

41 This was also the case for colonial families. Catharine Coleborne, "Challenging Institutional Hegemony: Family Visitors to Hospitals for the Insane in Australia and New Zealand, 1880s–1910s," in *Permeable Walls: Historical Perspectives on Hospital and Asylum Visiting*, eds. Graham Moody and Jonathan Reinarz (Amsterdam: Rodopi, 2009), 289–308.

42 BRO, D/H14/D2/2/1/1102/70, letter to the superintendent.

43 BRO, D/H14/D2/2/1/373/5, letter from John Cooper "written for him by a friend".

44 BRO, D/H14/D2/2/1/373/6, letter to John Cooper from his wife. Date unknown.

45 Roy Porter, *A Social History of Madness: Stories of the Insane* (London: Phoenix, 1999), 188.

46 In his exploration of the role families played in understanding and caring for insane relatives, historian Akihito Suzuki highlights the "emotional burden" they struggled with. *Madness at Home: The Psychiatrist, the Patient and the Family in England, 1820–1860* (University of California Press, 2006), 180–181.

47 BRO, D/H14/D1/2/2/107/6, letter to Orange, March 1874.

48 BRO, D/H14/D1/2/2/107/5, letter to Orange, February 1874.

49 Barbara Taylor, *The Last Asylum: A Memoir of Madness in our Times* (Penguin, 2014), 148.

50 Loneliness, https://www.mind.org.uk/information-support/tips-for-everyday-living/loneliness (accessed July 18, 2017).

51 This includes Heads Together which brings together a number of mental health charities. https://www.headstogether.org.uk/about-heads-together (accessed July 18, 2017).

52 Some asylum patients believed they were wrongfully confined, others claimed that they were mistreated and abused by asylum staff. See for example, Peter McCandless, "Liberty and Lunacy: The Victorians and Wrongful Confinement," *Journal of Social History* 11, no. 3 (1978): 366–386; Anne Shepherd, "The Female Patient Experience in Two Late-Nineteenth Century Surrey Asylums," in *Sex and Seclusion*, eds. Andrews and Digby, 223–248.

INHERITING EXPULSIONS FROM THE INSURANCE INDUSTRY

Kathleen M. Brian
Western Washington University

On Thursday, May 4, 2017, the U.S. House of Representatives voted to pass the American Health Care Act (AHCA). The exodus of major insurers, as well as states' scramble for Medicaid waivers, began immediately.[1] Meanwhile, the U.S. Senate began to work toward its own, parallel piece of legislation—ultimately dubbed the Better Care Reconciliation Act (BCRA)—within 48 hours.[2] When it became clear that the ill-fated BCRA would not become law, Senate Majority Leader Mitch McConnell offered instead the Obamacare Repeal Reconciliation Act (ORRA).[3] Of course, the AHCA, BCRA, and ORRA, as well as the "skinny repeal"[4] option subsequently offered as the Health Care Freedom Act (HCFA[5]), were intended to repeal and recast the Patient Protection and Affordable Care Act (ACA) of 2010.[6] While the failure of each piece of legislation has left some hopeful, the latest threat to the ACA is that government officials will, as President Trump dismissively advised, simply "let Obamacare implode."[7]

In each instance, mental health advocates called foul: for despite significant differences in the various plans, all would viciously undermine those aspects of the ACA most identified with significant gains in the realm of insurance equity for mental health care and substance abuse treatment.

Though far from perfect, the ACA, in conjunction with the subsequent Health Care & Education Reconciliation Act (2010), represented the culmination of a decades-long effort to secure equal coverage for mental health, substance abuse, and behavioral health treatment.[8] It established minimum policy standards for mental health care, in part, by defining it as an essential health benefit. It eliminated payment limits and exclusions based in pre-existing conditions that disproportionately targeted individuals with mental disabilities. It expanded the number of qualified individuals with access to mental health services under the rubric of Medicaid and created new possibilities for home- and community-based mental health care.[9]

Each of the legislative efforts put forward since May—the AHCA, the BCRA, the ORRA, the HCFA, and even implosion—would, in effect, nullify these successes under the guise of free market equilibrium and individual choice. Atop targeted dismantlings of the ACA, they could layer new stipulations for the creation of high-risk pools for individuals with pre-existing conditions, as well as enacting Medicaid rollbacks, not least of all through the capacious potential for state exemptions and the redefinition of essential health benefits.[10] At least one Senate version also sanctioned what have come to be known as "bare-bones policies" that would exclude coverage for mental health care.[11] Simply put, in each instance, people with mental disabilities would be poised to experience significant, disruptive, and deadly setbacks in the realm of access.

Our contemporary political landscape thus suggests a flare-up of a lethal pre-existing condition for disabled citizens: unequal access to insurance coverage.

Since the 1990s, advocates of mental health parity have worked to bring this inequity into public debate through a determined focus on policy at both the state and federal levels. Citing the extent to which, historically speaking, the healthcare requirements of people with mental disabilities have been marginalized or excluded, they have increasingly articulated their demands for equitable coverage through appeals to anti-discrimination oversight. That private insurance companies would not bear financial responsibility for mental health care, they reminded policy makers, was neither natural nor unavoidable.[12] In other words, these activists remade equal access to care as a civil rights issue. And if federal legislation is any indication, the strategy was a successful one: the ACA was preceded by, and extended key provisions in, the Mental Health Equitable Treatment Act of 2001 (MHET) and the Mental Health Parity and Substance Abuse Equity Act of 2008 (MHPSAE).

Despite this shift in framework, and despite this apparent progress, the economic interests of the insurance industry, imbricated with the economic interests of the elite, continued to set the terms of the debate. Thus, the healthcare requirements of people with mental disabilities remained unspeakable beyond the realm of profitability. Even liberal demands for mental health, that is, were (and are) yoked to an economic model of wellbeing that resulted, in no small degree, from the insatiability of the insurance industry.

I want to suggest, then, that any conversation about health care must begin with the collective acknowledgement of a simple fact: the selective incorporation of humans based on statistical predictions of vitality is the foundation upon which insurance companies assembled themselves. The very essence of the industry was (and is) the development of exclusions, based in statistical imaginings, that were (and are) intended to swell corporate profit. Until we are willing to imagine the unimaginable—namely, the provision of care without insurance as intermediary—we will remain fettered by the voracious pecuniary cravings of corporations. And a crucial first step toward imagining alternative possibilities is to remind ourselves of the remarkably recent creation of this pernicious and dangerously biopolitical model.

It was by no means inevitable that we would come to think of human well-being in financial terms, or that, within this framework, insurance companies would cast mental disabilities and substance dependency as pre-existing conditions that justified exclusion from benefits and higher premiums. Yet, this is now undeniably the case.

A handful of scholars have developed explanations for how this came to be. Insurance coverage for the healthcare needs of people with mental disabilities, the story goes, was something of an afterthought; a problem that did not present itself with any force until the second half of the twentieth century. This oversight was reasonable, by and large, because people with mental disabilities received medical care under the broad rubric of public, residential institutions, regardless of whether said institution was nominally educational, therapeutic, custodial, or carceral. The zealous insurance reformers of the 1930s, perpetuating the long-established understanding of mental health care as a state concern, emphasized state legislatures that had the power to mandate minimum benefit levels for certain psychiatric diagnoses and substance abuse disorders. It was not until the 1950s that psychiatric services were covered for the insured middle- and upper-classes. As a result of these disparate forces, the more equitable coverage of mental health care only became an urgent question in the period of deinstitutionalization, which began in earnest in the postwar period and accelerated across subsequent decades.[13]

We could pose a number of critiques in response to this standard narrative, not least of all that many people with mental disabilities were unable to access adequate care, mental or physical, under the state-run system. We might also, though, question the assumption that insurers were generally unconcerned with mental disability. We might ask instead what insurance underwriters talked about when they talked about mental disabilities, and how these conversations might have contributed to baseline exclusionary strategies within the industry.[14]

In the United States, the industrial, accident, and health insurance industries were spawned in the late-nineteenth- and early-twentieth centuries from the commercial life insurance industry, which became a significant presence only in the middle third of the nineteenth century. It took roughly a century for the insurance model to claw its way to its present central position within the healthcare system.[15] The infancy of commercial life insurance, then, exposes the economic model of wellbeing in the making, and helps to explain the exclusion of people with mental disabilities.

The notion that an individual would send regular payments to a corporation, the officers of which, according to a pre-arranged contract, would hold the money and distribute it to third-party recipients in cases of illness or death, only gained significant traction in the antebellum period.[16] Even then, it did not convince a majority. Rather, it was the purview, by and large, of the urban white middle classes. In their efforts to become and remain viable, companies partitioned humans into "good risks" and "bad risks" that mirrored, in part, bourgeois standards of morality and self-care.[17] They attended to general healthfulness and the use of certain substances—alcohol in particular. They also refused to insure individuals who held certain jobs, or who lived in—or traveled to—purportedly dangerous places. Mining and sailoring, for example, often meant automatic disqualification, while travel to the South and the Pacific Northwest—considered particularly treacherous—also meant expulsion.[18]

It was simple enough to determine whether a person lived in Alabama or worked with explosives. Sniffing out an applicant's daily doings and habits of health, though, could be trickier. The industry's initial answer to this was to expand its agency system, which allowed companies to rely on an insurance agent's local knowledge and proximate access to applicants to verify or refute a medical certification sent along by a local practitioner or the applicant himself.[19] It was not unheard of, after all, for a family doctor to fib a little, or to minimize a condition, in order to secure coverage for a friend or long-time patient. In fact, insurance companies soon decided to circumvent the intimacy of the doctor–patient relationship altogether by including doctors on their payroll. These medical examiners, financially beholden to the companies for their livelihood, were specifically tasked with excavating the "real" health status of an applicant over and against the applicant's own claims. Whether uncovered by an agent or a medical examiner, for example, an observed "habit of intemperance"—later remade as alcoholism and drug addiction—typically meant automatic rejection. Though they varied slightly from company to company, and from policy to policy, conditions of exclusion were detailed, precise, and indicated exactly who the insurance companies wanted to insure: young, temperate, non-disabled men who populated the urbanizing, industrializing northeast.

It does not take much to imagine company men imagining just how long such vital consumers would pay into the company without demanding remuneration. And as the insurance industry grew over the middle third of the nineteenth century, so too did the financial interest in elongating life and predicting death. New studious alliances among medical, legal, and insurance professionals emerged. They developed studies of mortality and disease morbidity that sometimes relied on data generated by the state, while at other times drew on the experience of the companies themselves. The formation of a discreet insurance public facilitated the circulation of this new knowledge. The contours of this public began to emerge in 1852 with the commencement of *Tuckett's Insurance Monitor*, the first periodical published in the United States to deal exclusively in news of the insurance industry and related developments.[20] In subsequent decades, such industry journals allowed insurance advocates to compare notes, strategize, and perfect exclusionary practices. They also facilitated new knowledge networks and intercompany alliances that one contemporary termed an "insurance fraternity."[21]

These novel networks culminated with the announcement, in 1878, of an intercompany registry, which held the potential to revolutionize the industry through the creation of intra-industry alliances. It contained the names of every person who had applied to participating companies for a policy of life insurance with "especial reference to those persons who are found to be unfit subjects."[22] The registry, which began as a network of twenty companies, was to be circulated each week to guard against people who, having been rejected by one insurance underwriter, "at once report to another company, who, from carelessness on the part of their medical officer or other causes, grant a policy only to find in short time that they have made a mistake."[23] The systematic development of exclusions based on pre-existing conditions, in other words, was well underway.

Two other developments of the second half of the century bore significantly on how insurance companies related to people with mental disabilities, and both were encapsulated in the industry's evolving attitude toward suicide. Most early insurance policies excluded death by suicide in order to maximize profits by minimizing risk.[24] As the decades wore on, however, insurers became increasingly concerned with connections between insanity and self-harm. They were also, at the same time, inexorably drawn to hereditary explanations of mental disabilities generally, and death by suicide specifically.

In the case of commercial life insurance, these phenomena were deeply connected. Immediately following the Civil War, insurance companies found themselves increasingly embroiled in what one termed the "suicide contests," or legal battles over whether or not a company had the right to refuse policy payouts in cases of suicide. Insurers had long worked to avoid paying beneficiaries in such cases. The majority of antebellum policies included a stipulation to the effect that, when death occurred as a result of "one's own hand," the company was not liable. These stipulations soon began to be colloquially referred to as the "suicide clause," and it became increasingly contested during the economic depression of the 1870s.[25] At its most fundamental, the story of this legal warfare is one of escalating attempts by beneficiaries and insurance companies to guarantee their own economic interests. The proliferation of suits, however, had a secondary effect, as well, not least of all because companies kept losing. Of 243 decisions between 1843 and 1900, 69 percent were decided in favor of the beneficiaries.

Some companies responded to this ominous legal cloud by adopting a policy of "liberality" in order to avoid the courts altogether. The well-established New York Life, for example, began an advertising campaign in 1866 that boasted that their policies carried no suicide clause whatsoever, though they would join the intercompany register just twelve years later.[26] Other companies developed a handful of alternative methods.[27] The Equitable Life Assurance Society, for example, adhered to a policy of temporal inclusion, assuring its clientele that "policies issued by the Society are indisputable on account of suicide after the first two years."[28] Still others mitigated liability by contracting to return only the premium, without dividend, in cases of suicide. The latter was a practice followed with slight variations by, among others, the Germania Life, the Mutual Benefit Life Insurance Company of New Jersey, and the Columbia Life Insurance Company.[29]

More important for our purposes, however, is that the industry's growing legal losses contributed to many companies' zealous pursuit of the
family history, the chronicity of certain diagnoses, and the claim that
"a suicidal tendency was eminently heritable."[30] If antebellum attempts
at exclusion depended largely upon empirical observation of individual
habits of behavior or physiological characteristics, postbellum attempts
at exclusion placed a suicided policyholder in the context of an ancestral
body of diseased family members whose various pathologies served to
foreshadow self-destruction.[31] Though insanity did not always "tend to
shorten life directly," detecting its presence in either the applicant or the
applicant's family was understood to be the first line of defense against
suicidal policyholders. In his treatise on effective examinations of policy
applicants, for example, J. Adams Allen instructed medical examiners
that its presence, even when "incipient or masked," should serve as an
automatic disqualification.[32]

While it could be assumed that no agent would "knowingly bring for examination an insane person," Allen noted that it occasionally happened
that cases were presented in which the earliest symptoms were just beginning to manifest themselves. In such cases, he wrote, it was "the duty
of the examiner to reject all in whom he may find any evidence of un-
sound mind."[33] Examiners should be on the lookout, Allen warned, for
cunning maniacs who could outwit examiners in order to "secure large
policies upon his dangerous life."[34] An even greater threat came from
families whose "dread of insanity" led to "a morbid feeling of sufficiently
strong to mislead observation, to warp the judgment, and to occasion
sins of concealment and untruthfulness toward those [medical examin-
ers] who have a right to expect, and to demand the fullest and most explicit confidence."[35] According to Allen, the transmission of insanity was
particularly insidious from mother to daughter, from father to son, and
from either parent whose physical characteristics closely resembled a
particular child. Yet the manifestation of insanity among the applicant's
siblings was even more important for "establishing the family proclivity,
than that of parents."[36] He confidently assured his readers that, in nearly
one-half of all cases of "obvious insanity, its presence in the family within three generations can be traced."[37] Examiners first imbued suicidal
individuals with the perceived pathology of parents, grandparents, and
siblings before mapping this onto relatives and descendants who might

seek coverage. Medical and actuarial studies proliferated as a way to "prove" these claims and, in turn, justify benefits exclusion.

By the final decades of the nineteenth century, then, the practice of pre-policy exclusions for a majority of people with mental disabilities—but especially those whose families carried the "taint" of suicide—had become common sense. So when asylum physician and superintendent Robert Jones wrote in 1905 that "insanity *per se* is inimical to life," few in the insurance industry would have been surprised.[38] The exclusion of people with mental disabilities was a crucial foundation upon which the insurance industry constructed itself. It was central to their business model.

This, of course, was the same historical moment in which debates about universal or compulsory health insurance became increasingly cacophonous, incorporating the voices of government officials and politicians, union leaders and labor activists, medical and legal professionals, academics and social reformers. Early demands stressed remuneration for lost wages over remuneration for medical care. It was not until the 1930s and 1940s, when confronting the rising cost of medical care that resulted from the insurance company model, that reformers reversed this emphasis and began actively to imagine insurance as a primary financial facilitator of care. It was also during these decades that the insurance model, with the dogged support of the American Medical Association (AMA), ascended to dominance and, in the scramble to prove their own efficacy, expanded general coverage.[39]

At that point, however, the insurance industry had made the systematic exclusion of people with mental disabilities an everyday doing for more than a half-century. For insurance companies, the economic model of wellbeing that allowed them to prosper was quite simple: avoid underwriting these people.

———————————

The most pressing pre-existing condition that, in our contemporary debates about health care, far too often goes unarticulated: private insurance companies become viable only through systematic exclusion. Their own longevity is dependent on their statistical imaginings of the longevity of others. Since the second half of the nineteenth century, they have worked very hard to imagine people with mental disabilities as inherently, immutably less vital.

Conversations around mental health care and substance abuse treatment, not to mention the other healthcare requirements of people with mental disabilities, must be informed by this history. Perhaps then they will be able to venture beyond—or, better yet, *before*—the economic model of wellbeing with all the irreverence of the economically indefensible. Public resistance to the AHCA, as well as the repeated failure of Republican senators to replace and/or repeal the ACA, has opened a space in which select Democrats have begun to bring the question of a single-payer system back into the arena for debate.[40] This is a crucial first step. For as Ben Feldman argues in this volume, and as so many unlikely reformers have in the past, we need to "demand the 'impossible' until it is impossible no longer."[41] It is time to grapple with that which has been designated unworkable, improbable, and unthinkable: the provision of health care for its own sake, without the parasitic presence of insurance companies.

Notes

1   Amy Goldstein, "Aetna Exiting all ACA Insurance Marketplaces in 2018," *Washington Post*, May 10, 2017, https://www.washingtonpost.com/national/health-science/aetna-exiting-all-aca-insurance-marketplaces-in-2018/2017/05/10/9dedbeea-35d4-11e7-b373-418f6849a004_story.html?utm_term=.7c81fd3eee8e; Chris Lee, "Medicaid Waiver Requests in Wisconsin and Maine Seek to Impose Work Requirements and Time Limits for Beneficiaries," *Kaiser Family Foundation*, May 10, 2017, http://kff.org/medicaid/press-release/medicaid-waiver-requests-in-wisconsin-and-maine-seek-to-impose-work-requirements-and-time-limits-for-beneficiaries/; Mary Beth Musumeci, Elizabeth Hinton, and Robin Rudowitz, "Proposed Medicaid Section 1115 Waivers in Maine and Wisconsin," *Kaiser Family Foundation*, May 10, 2017, http://kff.org/medicaid/issue-brief/proposed-medicaid-section-1115-waivers-in-maine-and-wisconsin/.The American Health Care Act (H.R. 277, 115th Cong., 2017), accessed May 10, 2017, https://www.congress.gov/115/bills/hr277/BILLS-115hr277ih.pdf.

2   Sean Sullivan, Paige Winfield Cunningham, and Kelsey Snell, "While House Passes GOP Health-Care Bill, Senate Prepares to do its Own Thing," *The Washington Post*, May 4, 2017, https://www.washingtonpost.com/powerpost/if-house-passes-gop-health-care-bill-a-steeper-climb-awaits-in-the-senate/2017/05/04/26a901da-30bd-11e7-8674-437ddb6e813e_story.html?utm_term=.787baf9ba0b4.

3   The Better Care Reconciliation Act of 2017 accessed July 17, 2017, https://www.budget.senate.gov/imo/media/doc/SENATEHEALTHCARE.pdf.

The Obamacare Repeal Reconciliation Act (H.R. 1628, 115th Cong., 19 July 2017), accessed July 29, 2017, https://www.documentcloud.org/documents/3897538-REPEAL7-19-17.html.

4   Thomas Kaplan, "Health Care Overhaul Collapses as Two Republican Senators Defect," *New York Times*, July 17, 2017, https://www.nytimes.com/2017/07/17/us/politics/health-care-overhaul-collapses-as-two-republican-senators-defect.html?_r=0; Ben Jacobs and Lauren Gambino, "Republican Healthcare Debate: What is a 'Skinny Repeal' of Obamacare?," *The Guardian*, July 27, 2017, https://www.theguardian.com/us-news/2017/jul/27/us-healthcare-bill-obamacare-skinny-repeal?utm_source=esp&utm_medium=Email&utm_campaign=GU+Today+USA+-+Collections+2017&utm_term=236864&subid=18752826&CMP=GT_US_collection.

5   The Health Care Freedom Act (H.R. 1628, 115th Cong., 27 July 2017), accessed August 1, 2017, https://www.budget.senate.gov/imo/media/doc/HealthCareFreedomAct.pdf.

6   Thomas Kaplan and Robert Pear, "House Passes Measure to Repeal and Replace the Affordable Care Act," *New York Times*, May 4, 2017, https://www.nytimes.com/2017/05/04/us/politics/health-care-bill-vote.html?_r=0; Danielle Kurtzleben, "Words You'll Hear: The Better Care Reconciliation Act," *NPR*, July 9, 2017, http://www.npr.org/2017/07/09/536328454/words-youll-hear-the-better-care-reconciliation-act. The Patient Protection and Affordability Care Act (Pub. L. No. 111-148, 124 Stat. 119 (2010)), accessed May 10, 2017, https://www.gpo.gov/fdsys/pkg/PLAW-111publ148/pdf/PLAW-111publ148.pdf.

7   Associated Press, "The Latest: Trump says 'let Obamacare Implode'," *New York Times*, July 28, 2017, https://www.nytimes.com/aponline/2017/07/28/us/politics/ap-us-congress-health-overhaul-the-latest.html?_r=0.

8   On this history, see Colleen L. Barry, Haiden A. Huskamp, and Howard Goldman, "A Political History of Federal Mental Health and Addiction Insurance Parity," *The Milbank Quarterly* 88, No. 3 (2010): 404–433; Richard G. Frank, Chris Koyanagi, and Thomas C. McGuire, "The Politics and Economics of Mental Health 'Parity' Laws," *Heath Affairs* 16, No. 4 (July/August 1997): 108–119; Gerald Grob and Howard H. Goldman, *The Dilemma of Federal Mental Health Policy: Radical Reform or Incremental Change?* (New Brunswick, NJ: Rutgers University Press, 2006); and Thomas C. McGuire, *Financing Psychotherapy: Costs, Effects, and Public Policy* (Cambridge, MA: Ballinger Pub. Co., 1981).

9   "Health Care Reform," *Judge David L. Bazelon Center for Mental Health Law*, accessed May 11, 2017, http://www.bazelon.org/Where-We-Stand/Access-to-Services/Health-Care-Reform.aspx; "Insurance Market Reforms in the Patient Protection & Affordable Care Act and the Health Care & Education Reconciliation Act," *Judge David L. Bazelon Center for Mental Health Law*, accessed May 11, 2017, http://

www.bazelon.org/LinkClick.aspx?fileticket=4SLhcBf-V7o%3D&tabid=137.

10 Rachel Garfield and Julia Zur, "Medicaid Restructuring Under the American Health Care Act and Implications for Behavioral Health Care in the US," *Kaiser Family Foundation*, March 24, 2017, http://kff.org/medicaid/issue-brief/medicaid-restructuring-under-the-american-health-care-act-and-implications-for-behavioral-health-care-in-the-us/. See especially "Title I," which rolls back the successes established in the ACA; "Title II, Sec. 232," which addresses Medicaid; and "Title III, Sec. 301, Subtitle B," and "Title III, Sec. 311," which address the creation of high-risk pools for individuals with pre-existing conditions. American Health Care Act, H.R. 277, 115th Cong. (2017), accessed May 10, 2017, https://www.congress.gov/115/bills/hr277/BILLS-115hr277ih.pdf.

11 Sean Sullivan, Juliet Eilperin, and Kelsey Snell, "Revised Senate Health-Care Bill Still Lacks the Votes to Pass," *The Washington Post*, July 13, 2017, https://www.washingtonpost.com/powerpost/mcconnell-to-release-new-gop-health-plan-allowing-bare-bones-insurance-policies/2017/07/13/8f0509c4-67bb-11e7-8eb5-cbccc2e7bfbf_story.html?utm_term=.3eb4edac881f.

12 Barry, Huskamp, and Goldman, "A Political History of Parity," 409–411.

13 See especially Barry, Huskamp, and Goldman, "A Political History of Parity," 409–411; Grob and Goldman, *The Dilemma of Federal Mental Health Policy*; and Howard H. Goldman, Steven S. Sharfstein, and Richard G. Frank, "Equity and Parity in Psychiatric Care," *Psychiatric Annals* 13, No. 6 (June 1983): 488–491. On the comparative role of psychotropic drugs and federal policy on the process of deinstitutionalization, see William Gronfein, "Psychotropic Drugs and Deinstitutionalization," *Social Problems* 32, No. 5 (June 1985): 437–454. Jonathan Metzl's research exposes the extent to which the racialized and gendered dimensions of this process were obscured by the rhetoric of "criminality". See Jonathan Metzl, *The Protest Psychosis: How Schizophrenia Became a Black Disease* (Boston: Beacon Press, 2009), especially pp. 139–44 and 175–211.

14 Most works on the insurance industry do not deal extensively with mental disabilities or with mental health care. See, for example, John E. Murray, *Origins of American Health Insurance: A History of Industrial Sickness Funds* (New Haven, CT: Yale University Press, 2007); Ronald L. Numbers, ed. *Compulsory Health Insurance: The Continuing American Debate* (London: Greenwood Press, 1982). When they do, it is typically in passing and subsumed under more general concerns. See, for example, Christy Ford Chapin, *Ensuring America's Health: The Public Creation of the Corporate Health Care System* (New York: Cambridge University Press, 2015), 11, 184, 226; Ronald L. Numbers, *Almost Persuaded: American Physicians and Compulsory Health Insurance* (Baltimore: The Johns Hopkins University Press, 1978), 76, 5, 2, 7; John Fabian Witt, *Crippled Workingmen, Destitute Widows, and the Remaking of American Law* (Cambridge, MA: Harvard University Press, 2004), esp. 76–95; and Sharon Ann Murphy, *Investing in Life: Insurance in Antebellum America* (Baltimore:

The Johns Hopkins University Press, 2010), 77–96.

15 In using this verb, I tentatively position myself in contradistinction to an argument
advanced by Christy Chapin, who sees the American Medical Association as, in
essence, forcing the hand of the commercial life insurance industry in the late
1930s. See Christy Ford Chapin, *Ensuring America's Health: The Public Creation of
the Corporate Health Care System* (New York: Cambridge University Press, 2015),
esp. 27–33.

16 The best work on industry strategies for expansion during this period can be found
in business historian Murphy, *Investing in Life*. Despite the title, Murphy deals extensively with the wartime and postbellum tactics of various companies, arguing
that the expansion of industry during the 1860s forced life insurance firms to liber-
alize policies, spend extensively on various marketing techniques, and participate
in the postbellum "speculative frenzy" in order to maintain a competitive footing in
the market. In Murphy's account, the suicide contests emerge only as a cautionary
tale of the liberalizing tactics of postbellum companies. Murphy writes into body
of scholarship that attempts to account for the historical processes by which life
insurance companies became so incredibly (and suddenly) successful in the 1840s.
Early interpretations emphasized economic factors and developments internal to
the industry, such as the development of the agency system and other marketing techniques. Particularly successful representations of this school are J. Owen
Stalson, *Marketing Life Insurance: Its History in America* (New York: McGraw Hill,
1969) and Morton Keller, *The Life Insurance Enterprise, 1885–1910* (Cambridge,
MA: Harvard University Press, 1963). In response to this, cultural historians have
emphasized ideological changes such as secularization that made the purchase of
life insurance more palatable for middle-class Anglo-Americans. See Viviana A.
Zelizer, *Morals and Markets: The Development of Life Insurance in the United States*
(New York: Columbia University Press, 1979). Like Stalson, Murphy underscores
the centrality of the agency system; but she argues that the system was important
not because it brought a greater number of policy-seekers to the firm but because
it allowed agents to evaluate candidates in person, thereby imbuing the physical
examination with greater surety and lowering the amount of risk the companies
would assume. See Sharon Ann Murphy's *Investing in Life: Insurance in Antebellum
America* (Baltimore: Johns Hopkins University Press, 2010), 22–23, 175.

17 Viviana A. Zelizer emphasizes ideological changes such as secularization that made
the purchase of life insurance more palatable for middle-class Anglo-Americans.
See Zelizer, *Morals and Markets: The Development of Life Insurance in the United
States* (New York: Columbia University Press, 1979).

18 Pennsylvania Mutual Life Insurance Company, "Insurance Policy for Walter Giles,"
28 August 1854, Vertical File 60167, H. Furlong Baldwin Library Special Collections, Maryland Historical Society, Baltimore.

19 This argument is advanced in Sharon Ann Murphy's *Investing in Life: Insurance in*

Antebellum America (Baltimore: Johns Hopkins University Press, 2010), 22–23, 175. For more on the expansion of the agency system, see J. Owen Stalson, *Marketing Life Insurance: Its History in America* (New York: McGraw Hill, 1969) and Morton Keller, *The Life Insurance Enterprise, 1885–1910* (Cambridge, MA: Harvard University Press, 1963).

20 J. Owen Stalson, *Marketing Life Insurance: Its History in America* (New York: McGraw Hill, 1969), xxxix.

21 This insurance public began with the commencement of *Tuckett's Insurance Monitor* (1852), which was followed by the *American Law Register* (1852); *Insurance Monitor* (1853); *Life Insurance Advocate* (1855); *United States Insurance Gazette* (1855); *Philadelphia Underwriter* (1857); *American Life Assurance Magazine and Journal of Actuaries* (1859); *American Exchange and Review* (1862); *Baltimore Underwriter* (1865); *American Law Review* (1866); *Day's Insurance Messenger* (1867); *Digest of Insurance Law in the United States* (1867); *Our Mutual Friend* (1867); *Aetna* (1868); *Insurance Times* (1868); *Mutual Benefit Life Insurance Advocate* (1868); *New York Newsletter* (1868); *Spectator* (1868); *Hahnemannian* (1869); *Union Central Advocate* (1869); *Journal of the Mutual Life Association of Virginia* (1870); *Minnesota Atlas* (1870); *Agent* (1870); *Oak Leaf* (1870); and the *Insurance Law Journal* (1871).

22 "A LIFE INSURANCE COMBINATION. REGISTERING REJECTED APPLICANTS," *American Life Assurance Magazine and Journal of Actuaries* 19 (1878): 91.

23 Ibid., The twenty companies involved initially were the New York Life Insurance Company; National Company (Washington); National Life (Montpelier); Northwestern (Milwaukee); Mutual Life (Philadelphia); Phoenix (Hartford); Union Central (Cincinnati); Provident (New York); Aetna (Hartford, Berkshire, Pittsfield); Brooklyn Company (New York); Mutual and General (Hartford); Germania (New York); Continental (Hartford); Globe (New York); Home (New York); Hartford Life and Accident (Hartford); Knickerbocker (New York); Manhattan (New York); Mutual (Springfield, MA); and John Hancock Life (Boston).

24 "Suicide," *Insurance Monitor Extra* 10 (December 1862): 1. The Massachusetts Hospital Life Insurance Company included a suicide clause in the first policy it issued in 1823. See Sharon Ann Murphy, *Investing in Life: Insurance in Antebellum America* (Baltimore: Johns Hopkins University Press, 2010), 92.

25 "The Suicide Risk," *New York Observer and Chronicle*, June 17, 1875, as reprinted from the Philadelphia *Observer*. The *Observer* also noted that the *Philadelphia Ledger* remarked that "the general adverse results" of the contests would "some time or other make it necessary for the underwriters to devise some new form for that clause in their policies."

26 "New York Life Insurance Compy.," *Bangor Daily Whig & Courier*, November 15,

1866. This advertisement ran almost daily for the next two months. See *the Bangor Daily Whig & Courier* for February 15–17, 19, 22, 24, 26–29 (1866); December 1, 3–8, 10–15, 18–20, 24, 27–29, 31 (1866); and the first week of January, 1867. A similar advertisement ran in the Boston *Daily Advertiser* the following October. See also "NO SUICIDE CLAUSE. New York Life Insurance Company," *North American*, 25 April 1887B.

27 "Homeopathic Mutual Life Insurance Company," *Insurance Monitor* 17 (1869): 554.

28 "Equitable Life Assurance Society," *Baltimore Underwriter* 1 (15 July 1865): 8.

29 Frey v. Germania Life Insurance Co., 56 Mich. 29; 22 N.W. 100 (1885), LexisNexis *29; Salentine v. Mutual Benefit Life Insurance Co., 24 F. 159 (1885), LexisNexis *9; Adkins v. Columbia Life Insurance Company, 70 Mo. 27 (1879), LexisNexis *1. Germania LIC's incorporation date is taken from Spectator Company, *The Insurance Yearbook* (New York: The Spectator Company, 1893), 23.

30 "Life Assurance Medical Officers Association: Insanity and Epilepsy in Relation to Life Assurance," *Lancet* (10 December 1904): 1656–1657. Quote from p. 1657.

31 Some, such as the influential actuary and reformer Elizur Wright, went so far as to agitate for separate insurance companies for teetotalers. See, for example, "Temperance Life Assurance," *Tuckett's Monthly Insurance Journal* ii Vol. 6 (June 1858): 87; "Veterans Temperance Corps," *Insurance Monitor Weekly* (March 25, 1869): p. 15. Although Wright's "temperance policy" did not become popular, traces of it remained in the temperance clause, increasingly invasive medical examinations, and the rejection of applicants based on a family history that included an insane or suicidal relative. For an excellent treatment of Wright's life, various careers, and connections to Jacksonian reform movements, see Lawrence B. Goodheart, *Abolitionist, Actuary, Atheist: Elizur Wright and the Reform Impulse*, (Kent, OH: Kent State University Press, 1990). He discusses Wrights' ideas for a temperance policy on 144–45. The family history is thereby a central tool of what Michel Foucault has termed metasomatization. Foucault also uses the term "metabody," which I use interchangeably with "ancestral body." The family history, which places the individual body in the context of a pathologized ancestral body, is a central tool of the phenomenon Michel Foucault has termed *metasomatization*. Though he had not developed the term "metasomatization," Foucault took the first steps toward a comprehensive theory of the process in *Psychiatric Power: Lectures at the Collège de France, 1973–1974*, trans. Graham Burchell (New York: Palgrave Macmillan), especially 270–72. This analysis was developed and furthered in his lecture of the following year, which focused on the emergence of "the condition" and "the abnormal" in psychiatric discourse. See Michel Foucault, *Abnormal: Lectures at the Collège de France, 1973–1974*, trans. Graham Burchell (New York: Picador), especially 311–317. While Foucault developed this concept through an analysis of psychiatric discourse and praxis, the suicide contests demonstrate that this phenomenon was also at play in federal courtrooms.

32 J. Adams Allen, *Medical Examinations for Life Insurance, Seventh Edition, Revised and Enlarged* (New York: The Spectator Company, 1880), 137.

33 Jeremiah R. Levan, *A Treatise on Medical Examination for Life Insurance* (Philadelphia: Press of Wm. F. Fell & Co., 1885), 149.

34 J. Adams Allen, *Medical Examinations for Life Insurance, Seventh Edition, Revised and Enlarged* (New York: The Spectator Company, 1880), 137.

35 J. Adams Allen, *Medical Examinations for Life Insurance, Seventh Edition, Revised and Enlarged* (New York: The Spectator Company, 1880), 139.

36 J. Adams Allen, *Medical Examinations for Life Insurance, Seventh Edition, Revised and Enlarged* (New York: The Spectator Company, 1880), 138.

37 J. Adams Allen, *Medical Examinations for Life Insurance, Seventh Edition, Revised and Enlarged* (New York: The Spectator Company, 1880), 138.

38 Robert Jones, "Remarks Upon Insanity and Epilepsy in Regard to the Duration of Life," *American Journal of Insanity* 61, No. 3 (January 1905): 467–482. Quote appears on p. 481.

39 Chapin, *Ensuring America's Health*, esp. 27–36.

40 Alexander Burns and Jennifer Medina, "The Single-Payer Party? Democrats Shift Left on Health Care," *New York Times*, June 3, 2017, https://www.nytimes.com/2017/06/03/us/democrats-universal-health-care-single-payer-party.html.

41 Ben Feldman, "Be Realistic: Demand the Impossible!," *Activist History Review*, March 31, 2017, https://activisthistory.com/2017/03/31/be-realistic-demand-the-impossible/.

VI

POVERTY AS POLICY: WAGELESSNESS AND AID

TAXING VALUES: WHAT OUR TAX CODE SAYS ABOUT US

Tessa Davis
University of South Carolina

For most Americans, election years and filing deadlines (for many, an otherwise lovely spring day in mid-April) are the few times we give much thought to the Internal Revenue Code. Lost in the minutiae of deciding whether to itemize or take the standard deduction, determining eligibility for credits, or trying to track down the statement the mortgage company sent so TurboTax can calculate one's home mortgage interest deduction, the grander aims of the tax system often fade into the background. The intricacies of the Code are not, however, simply byzantine rules meant to confuse and frustrate, but rather are the result of the best and worst impulses of how we, as citizens and human beings, treat one another.

When the Trump Administration released its "2017 Tax Reform for Economic Growth and American Jobs" one-pager, it articulated four goals: (1) "Grow the economy and create millions of jobs," (2) "Simplify our burdensome tax code," (3) "Provide tax relief to American families—especially middle-income families," and (4) "Lower the business tax rate from one of the highest in the world to one of the lowest."[1] In any tax policy course, students are taught that the system has at least two goals: raising revenue and advancing social policy. Tax policy scholars evaluate the tax regime in light of those goals and with three common questions in mind: is a given provision or set of provisions administrable, is it efficient, and is it fair? As other tax scholars have noted, the Administration's "plan" is thin on details, substance, and reform,[2] but it does offer an opportunity to examine the extent to which taxes are, ultimately, a story about how we view and treat others.

Consider the Administration's third stated goal: tax relief for middle-income families. The document suggests three means of achieving that goal: reducing the number of tax brackets, doubling the standard deduction, and providing "tax relief" for families with children or other dependents.[3] With the exception of doubling the standard deduction, these means are vague and in no way guaranteed to benefit the intended families.[4] Nevertheless, the goal of reducing the tax burden on families may seem uncontroversial. Yet the very definition of family within the Code is, in fact, the subject of a great deal of controversy.

Early in the semester of each income tax course I teach, I assign an exercise to students that I preface with the assertion that they do not know what family is, at least not for the purposes of the Code. In one moment, siblings fall within the family circle[5] and in the next, they are pushed out.[6] In 1948, due to the outcome of two important Supreme Court cases, *Lucas v. Earl* and *Poe v. Seaborn*, and the different property law regimes of common law and community property states, the United States shifted to a joint filing system for married couples, formalizing a married couple as a familial unit in the tax code. Relatedness became a means of conveying benefits, as well as one of policing bad behavior. A family's taxes might decrease after marriage (the so-called marriage bonus) or upon having a child, for example, while the kiddie tax of the late 1980s targeted revenue reducing income shifting from parents to children. Whether to provide tax reductions or to shore up the tax base, such rules that rely upon concepts of family in identifying their targets must, as a threshold matter, decide who counts as family. Until 2013, same-sex couples were excluded from the Code's concept of family per operation of the Code and the Defense of Marriage Act.[7] Unmarried couples and others lacking a legal signifier of their relationships, however much they may resemble families with legal status, still fall outside the Code's concept of family. For such families-in-substance, the tax reductions for caregiving (tax expenditures in the language of tax policy) available to many are unavailable to them. Though the specific tax consequences of falling outside the Code's definition of family turn upon a given family's particular circumstances, the social import of the exclusion is universal: *family* does not include your family.

The impulse to provide tax relief for caregiving reflects a concern for the caregiver's ability to pay tax. Those outside tax policy circles may not use the language of ability to pay, but the concept is fairly intuitive. The same income in the hands of two different individuals may provide different levels of wellbeing. Ability to pay seeks to account for that fact. For example, an annual income of $60,000 likely affords a single person with no dependents more expendable income than the same income does a family of four. In the language of tax policy then, the individual and the family have different abilities to pay tax. Our progressive tax system reflects the idea that as an individual's income increases so too should her tax rate and liability.

Tax expenditures, like the child tax credit, account for the fact that income is an imperfect metric. Stated differently, the family of four may need to keep a bit more of their income to pay for the necessities than does the single person with the same income. By asking the person without caregiving responsibilities to pay more tax than the family with the same income, we allocate the shared responsibilities of government differently in the name of fairness. Returning to the metrics of tax policy analysis, in search of a fair allocation of taxation, we frequently sacrifice simplicity.

Which families warrant tax relief in the view of the current administration? If then-candidate Trump's tax proposal is instructive, only so-called traditional families. As a candidate, President Trump released a tax proposal that included repealing the head of household filing status, a filing status that aims to reduce the tax liability of an unmarried individual with dependents as compared to her tax liability if forced to use the tax tables for an unmarried individual.[8] By effectively defining family narrowly as a married couple with children (or, in certain instances, adult dependents), the proposal would reinforce and show preference for a particular model of family, subsidizing its costs on the backs of others. Thus, a vague goal likely to have broad appeal—tax relief for middle-income families—may spur policies that reflect both compassion and bias.

An intersection of health care and tax law provides another example of how the Code, so often perceived as a body of law about nothing but revenue, economic policy, and the voraciousness of Uncle Sam, has import well beyond its assumed scope. Section 213 provides a deduction for unreimbursed medical expenses. Only available to the extent such medical expenses exceed 10% of an individual's adjusted gross income (a term of art defined in §62), §213 is meant to relieve the potential financial strain of taxes when an individual incurs extraordinary medical costs. Thus, though the general rule is that personal costs are nondeductible, §213 departs from that general rule when, through no fault of her own (it seems reasonable to most to assume that an individual does not seek out medical costs) someone must allocate her income to care rather than taxes. Compassion and a concern for one's ability to pay—expressions of a sense of fairness—once again emerge as drivers of the substance of the Code.

The definition of medical care is critical to interpreting §213 as it provides the means of sorting costs we are willing to subsidize—e.g., cancer treatments—and costs that we are not—elective plastic surgery, for example.

Accordingly, the definition of medical care also reveals the biases of the time in which it applies and the individuals who interpret it. For years, for example, elective birth control did not qualify as medical care, while elective vasectomies did. Currently, there is a quiet debate centering upon whether fertility treatments provided to or for same-sex couples satisfy the requirement of §213.[9]

In a case now pending before the Eleventh Circuit Court of Appeals, a gay male couple utilized egg donation, in vitro fertilization, and surrogacy to have a child. The couple then attempted to deduct the costs as medical care and, following the Service's denial of the deduction, brought a refund suit in the Middle District of Florida.[10] The Code defines medical care as "amounts paid for the diagnosis, cure, mitigation, treatment, or prevention of disease, or for the purpose of affecting any structure or function of the body."[11] Though the IRS has permitted deductions for fertility costs to heterosexual couples, it has taken the position that such costs are not medical care when the individuals who incurred them are homosexual. The rationale for the deduction is not as brazenly discriminatory as denying the deduction *because* the taxpayer is gay. Instead, as evidenced in the *Morrissey* case, the rationale is less openly biased, but still problematic. The Revenue Agent, who initially denied the deduction, justified his decision, in part, on the grounds that the couple did not have a "medical condition," but instead made a choice not to have children with someone of the opposite sex—i.e. their costs simply did not satisfy the statutory definition of medical care.[12] Though the Appeals Officer denounced the Revenue Agent's "outdated" view of sexuality and acknowledged that the couple is effectively infertile, she nevertheless denied the deduction, stating the current law did not permit a deduction under such circumstances.[13] The Middle District agreed with the Service, granting the Service's motion for summary judgment and therein upholding the denial of the deduction.[14]

As of this writing, the outcome of the *Morrissey* case is yet to be decided, but in it, as in the discussion of who qualifies as family in the Code, we find an example of the ways in which tax law intersects with deeply personal and culturally contingent institutions. Just as criminal law reflects hundreds of years of compromise and change in notions of morality, justice, punishment, retribution, and deterrence, so too is tax law the result of over one hundred years of grappling with what we as individuals owe one another, our notions of fairness and belonging, and our tendencies toward opportunism and harmful bias. In an article published prior to the *Morrissey* case,

I argued that the Code should be read to encompass as medical the reproductive care Professor Morrissey and his spouse utilized.[15] Doing so would, I argue, bring greater consistency to the Code and move tax law closer toward treating individuals fairly regardless of their gender, sexuality, or marital status. These flash points—family and reproduction—are important markers of how intertwined tax is with its social and cultural context, but they are not the only. The intersection of tax and notions of belonging and collective responsibility perhaps comes into greatest relief in answering the threshold question of who belongs to the taxable community.

There is a joke among tax circles that "a fair tax is one you pay and I don't." With that notion in mind, a sovereign in a democratic country might be inclined to collect tax from those with the least power to object by voting representatives out of office. President Trump's repeated assertion that Mexico will pay for a border wall built by the U.S. government strikes a similar chord. Why should Americans foot the bill for the costs of operating state and federal governments if the revenue could be collected from the French, the British, or simply anyone but us? Setting aside enforcement concerns with taxing foreign citizens, the idea that individuals with no connection to the U.S. should bear the financial responsibility of paying for the costs of its government should seem absurd.[16] But the absurdity of the idea points us to the foundational and complex issue of defining the taxable community. Perhaps bringing a non-resident, non-citizen into the U.S. taxable community clearly violates widely-held notions of representative government and fairness in taxation, but why? Is it because the individual does not live in the U.S. or because she is a non-citizen? Does our view of her obligations to the U.S. government change if our hypothetical foreign individual has never set foot in the U.S., but owns substantial property in many states? Determining the boundaries of the state's taxing power and the proper relationship between competing states' rights to tax individuals with tenable ties to multiple communities are persistent challenges of domestic and international tax policy. Such debates also bring to the fore the inextricable nature of tax and foundational (and value-laden) aspects of nation building.

Presumably, there is widespread agreement that American citizens should pay taxes to the U.S. government. Legal requirement aside, the notion of the social contract and sense that those who benefit from the federal government should share the burden of its costs underlie the citizen's responsibility to pay tax. Stated differently, American citizens seem a natural taxable community for the U.S. government. This assertion may appear so self-evident as to seem useless. But the value of articulating a rationale for why American citizens belong within the taxable community enables us to test the margins of that rationale as we decide who else may belong within that community. Should an American citizen living abroad pay U.S. tax or may her country of residence assert some claim to her tax dollars?[17]

Immigration rhetoric provides an opportunity to examine contemporary politics and tax policy. Many persist in believing the myth that immigrants, documented or undocumented, do not pay taxes while benefitting from social programs.[18] Others stop short of perpetuating the myth but argue that, while immigrants do pay some state and federal taxes, they systematically exploit the tax system by fraudulently claiming refunds or simply by generally being a drain on state and federal budgets.[19] At the core of this debate is disagreement over who belongs to the American community. Bound up within that discussion are questions that are fundamental in tax policy such as who bears the collective responsibility of paying for our government and what constitutes a "fair share" of taxes paid. When should immigrants be included in the taxable community and how does one's immigration status impact determining what constitutes a fair share of taxes?

Delving into the details of tax law's definition of the taxable community reveals a deep substantive connection between tax and immigration law. American citizens are, of course, taxable and remain so even when living and working overseas.[20] Yet the Code does not stop at taxing U.S. citizens. In addition to U.S. citizens, anyone classified as what the Code terms a *resident alien* is taxable in the same manner and by the same laws as U.S. citizens. Even noncitizens are taxable on U.S. source income. Importantly, tax looks to immigration to define the concept of resident alien, expressly pulling lawful permanent residents (colloquially known as green card holders) into the taxable community as U.S. persons. Just as tax draws upon immigration law categories to define the taxable community, immigration law uses tax to police the boundaries of formal membership in the U.S. community. The ways in which tax and immigration law draw upon the other to shape their own doctrine and achieve policy ends creates an important set of connections that I have labeled the *tax-immigration nexus*. Examining those connections—the substance of the *tax-immigration nexus*—allows us to see the ways in which tax and immigration law both reflect and shape notions of citizenship and belonging.

Using the concept of a lawful permanent resident, let us again consider the question of how we draw the boundaries of the taxable community. Consider the example of an LPR and U.S. citizen who are neighbors. Both work at the regional hospital in their hometown and their lives are largely indistinguishable. They drive the same roads and send their children to the same schools. To not tax the LPR would likely strike the U.S. citizen as unfair. Should membership in the taxable community be so rigid as to turn on formal immigration or citizenship status when two individuals are in many ways indistinguishable? The tax-immigration nexus illustrates that performative citizenship—living and working as a member of a community—is enough to justify taxation even if an individual lacks formal immigration or citizenship status. Quite simply, an LPR is a taxable resident alien under tax law. Indeed, the concept of performative citizenship imbedded in the concept of tax residence is one reason why even undocumented immigrants are required to pay tax on substantially the same terms as resident U.S. citizens and documented immigrants. And as immigration law requires tax compliance before an individual can become a naturalized citizen, it bolsters the idea that paying taxes—sharing the responsibility of government—is a core requirement of being a citizen.

Tax is often held out as the exclusive realm of policy wonks, economists, and accountants. Among tax scholars, the error of this view is summed up in the sentiment of the famed Oliver Wendell Holmes: "I like to pay taxes. With them, I buy civilization."[21] Tax intersects with topics as seemingly disparate as the boundaries of family, the definition of medical care, and what it means to be a citizen because civilization does not come cheap. Roads, a healthy environment, education, and health care—such public goods require public support. Allocating the responsibilities of such support through taxation necessitates defining what is a fair tax burden. But fairness itself is hard to define and the temptation (and political expedience) to charge "the other" with not pulling their collective weight may be great. For many, the Trump Administration's one-pager may appeal to an extent; tax relief, simplification, and assisting middle-class families seem to be laudable goals. The difficulty comes in cutting through the buzzwords in order to determine the substance of the proposal. In tax, the devil truly is in the details and those details may be hard to decipher without technical knowledge. Yet if we are to have an open and honest debate over how to share the collective responsibilities of government, over the extent to which we want to care for each other as citizens and residents, getting into the weeds of tax reform is essential. And as the debate over tax reform moves forward, we, as citizens, should ensure that the laws we support elevate our best values.

Notes

1   "2017 Tax Reform for Economic Growth and American Jobs," accessed August 22, 2017, https://www.documentcloud.org/documents/3678871-Donald-Trump-s-tax-proposal.html#document/p1.

2   Neil Buchanan, "Saturation Coverage of Non-News About Tax Policy," April 2017, http://www.dorfonlaw.org/2017/04/saturation-coverage-of-non-news-about.html.

3   "2017 Tax Reform."

4   For a wonderful analysis of then candidate Trump's tax plan, see Lily L. Batchelder., "Families Facing Tax Increases Under Trump's Tax Plan (October 28, 2016)," Urban-Brookings Tax Policy Center Research Report, Oct. 28, 2016, https://ssrn.com/abstract=2842802. For an analysis of the recent tax announcement, see Chuck Marr, "Commentary: New Trump Tax Plan Has Specific Costly Tax Cuts at the Top, Fuzzy Promises for Everyone Else," April 2017, http://www.cbpp.org/federal-tax/commentary-new-trump-tax-plan-has-specific-costly-tax-cuts-at-the-top-fuzzy-promises-for.

5   IRC §267.

6   IRC §318.

7   *U.S. v. Windsor* 133 U.S. 2675 (2013), *U.S. v. Windsor,* 570 U.S. ___ (2013); IRS Rev. Rul. 2013-17 (2013).

8   Batchelder. Note that the proposal is no longer readily available. IRC §1-2.

9   Tessa Davis, "Reproducing Value: How Tax Law Differentially Values Fertility, Sexuality & Marriage," *19 CARDOZO J. OF LAW & GENDER* 1 (2012); Katherine T. Pratt, "Deducting the Costs of Fertility Treatment: Implications of *Magdalin v. Commissioner* For Opposite-Sex Couples, Gay and Lesbian Same-Sex Couples, and Single Women and Men," *2009 Wis. L. Rev.* 1283 (2009); Katherine T. Pratt, "Inconceivable? Deducting the Costs of Fertility Treatment," *89 Cornell L. Rev.* 1121, 1142–43 (2004).

10 *Morrissey v. United States,* No. 8:15-CV-2736-T-26AEP, 2016 WL 8198717 (M.D. Fla. Dec. 22, 2016).

11 IRC §213.

12 Brief for the appellant, at 5, *Morrissey v. U.S.,* No. 17-10685 (11th Cir. 2017).

13 Brief for the appellant at 5–6.

14 *Morrissey.* IRC § 213.

15 "Reproducing Value."

16 Allison Christians, "Drawing the Boundaries of Tax Justice," in *Quest for tax reform continues: The royal commission on taxation 50 years later 53,* 53 (Kim Brooks ed., 2013).

17 There is a rich literature on taxation and both immigration and emigration. Tessa Davis, "The Tax-Immigration Nexus," *94 Den. L. Rev.* 195 (2017); Reuven S. Avi-Yonah, "The Case Against Taxing Citizens," Tax Notes Int'l, May 2010, at 680; Cynthia Blum and Paula N. Singer, "A Coherent Policy Proposal for U.S. Residence-Based Taxation of Individuals," *41 Vand. J. of Trasnat'l L.* 705 (2008); Mark S. Hoose, "Trading One Danger for Another: Creating U.S. Tax Residency While Fleeing Violence at Home," *12 Fla. Tax Rev.* 827 (2012); Michael S. Kirsch, "Revisiting the Tax Treatment of Citizens Abroad: Reconciling Principle and Practice," *16 Fla. Tax Rev.* 117 (2014); Michael S. Kirsch, "Taxing Citizens in a Global Economy," *82 N.Y.U L. Rev.* 443 (2007); Francine J. Lipman, "The Taxation of Undocumented Immigrants: Separate, Unequal, and Without Representation," *9 Harv. Latino L. Rev.* 1 (2006); Ruth Mason, "Citizenship Taxation," *89 S. Cal. L. Rev.* 169 (2016); Philip F. Postlewaite and Gregory E. Stern, "Innocents Abroad? The 1978 Foreign Earned Income Act and the Case for Its Repeal," *65 Virginia L. Rev.* 1093 (1979); Renée Judith Sobel, "United States Taxation of Its Citizens Abroad: Incentive or Equity," *38 Vand. L. Rev.* 101 (1985); Edward A. Zelinsky, "Citizenship and Worldwide Taxation: Citizenship as an Administrable Proxy for Domicile," *96 Iowa L. Rev.* 1289 (2011); Almaz Zelleke, "Basic Income in the United States: Redefining Citizenship in the Liberal State," *63 Rev. Soc. Econ.* 633 (2005).

18 Researching the question of whether immigrants pay taxes brings a great deal of correct information to the fore. The misinformation requires delving into fringe sources, such as Breitbart or The Daily Caller, or fora that are not fact-checked, such as Reddit threads. As an example, see Brendan Bordelon, "'The Five': Why do liberals hate Bundy for dodging taxes when illegal immigrants do the same?," *The Daily Caller,* accessed August 21, 2017, http://dailycaller.com/2014/04/15/the-five-why-do-liberals-hate-bundy-for-dodging-taxes-when-illegal-immigrants-do-the-same/.

19 As an example, see Tom Tancredo, "IRS Corruption Fuels Billions in Fraudulent Payments to Illegal Aliens," *Breitbart,* http://www.breitbart.com/big-government/2016/04/16/irs-corruption-fuels-billions-fraudulent-payments-illegal-aliens/ (accessed August 21, 2017).

20 The fact that an American living abroad is taxable does not necessarily mean she will owe U.S. tax. Due to international law norms, treaties, and substantive tax law in the form of credits and an exemption, an American citizen living abroad may have no positive tax liability in the U.S. though she does face significant filing requirements. IRC §§ 901, 911, and 7701.

21 There are different versions of this quote, the most common being "Taxes are what we pay for civilized society."

FROM MORAL TO POLITICAL ECONOMY: THE ORIGINS OF MODERN PHILANTHROPY'S CHARITABLE FEEDBACK LOOP

Thomas Barber
Louisiana State University

Today, American philanthropy and inequality exist in a feedback loop of sorts. Philanthropic organizations such as the United Way and the Red Cross transform donations, or labor, into research or humanitarian activities intended to benefit humankind in general, but not to alleviate individual hardships. In fact, careful reporting has revealed that the Red Cross misused assets and misled the public while going to extraordinary lengths to maintain their image as serving those in need.[1] Meanwhile, experts continue to note rising poverty and inequality throughout the globe. While it is easy to blame stagnant wages and undemocratic policies for these shortcomings, it is clear that there is a significant disconnect between how we imagine our systems of wealth and relief and their actual impact.[2]

This essay traces philanthropy's shortcomings to an interrelated cluster of religious and economic ideas. By the eighteenth century, Protestant theologians understood good works as visible evidence of individual salvation, a formulation that many benefactors thought legitimized their temporal wealth and status. At the same time, economic theorists from Benjamin Franklin to Adam Smith emphasized how philanthropy empowered the state while it enriched benefactors. Together these ideas replaced charity's traditional emphasis on almsgiving, which benefitted the poor, with an emphasis on institutional aid (education, rehabilitation, and imprisonment) meant to strengthen the nation's economy while promoting indifference to the beneficiary. Confidence in these theories resulted in a new charitable paradigm whose intellectual foundations are responsible for today's charitable feedback loop, which perpetuates poverty while claiming to alleviate it.

Change Comes to Philanthropy

Before the sixteenth century, Europeans considered philanthropy an entirely religious act. After England left the Catholic Church in 1534, however, the country's theologians worked to distinguish their charitable assumptions and actions from their Catholic counterparts. Dissident Protestant clergy and officials reinterpreted charity along strict theological lines defined by notions of stewardship and austerity. Their faith in religious predestination led many of England's Protestants to accept that God made the rich and the poor. As a consequence of this divine distribution of wealth, theologians advised the wealthy to act as stewards of God's temporal wealth, a duty that involved caring for the unfortunate. These strict Calvinists also derided Catholic philanthropists for a patronage of the arts instead of charity to the poor. As biblical literalists, early Protestants committed themselves to radical altruism that emphasized individual poor relief by giving alms, or goods, rather than institutional care committed to abstract causes such as education and rehabilitation.

Protestantism's growth among Great Britain's gentry and aristocracy undermined its commitments to individualized care, cultural austerity, and religious character. Wealthy Protestant philanthropists donated liberally as a way to promote the Protestant cause, express personal piety, and seize divine rewards. Commitments to these objectives put wealthy philanthropists at odds with ministers who insisted that no good works, regardless of magnitude, could influence individual salvation. The conflict between clergy and benefactors resolved only after moderate minister William Perkins (1558–1602) offered a centrist position. Perkins insisted that good works were evidence of an individual's salvation, not the means to obtain salvation. Perkins' formulation helped decouple religion from philanthropy and undermined the benefactor's relationship to the beneficiary. His preaching transformed charity into a separate, virtuous action, regardless of the benefactor's ideology. Perkins' stance led one writer to conclude, "Charity thinketh no evil."[3] By the late seventeenth century, the combination of charity as an unquestionable good and the charity-for-reward mentality had unintentionally promoted indifference to the poor. Simply fulfilling God's command to give mattered more than what actually happened to charity's beneficiaries. Sir Thomas Browne (1605–1682), a seventeenth century philanthropist quipped "I give no almes to satisfie the hunger of my brother, but to fulfill and accomplish the Will and command of my God."[4] A century after the English Reformation, notions of reward and personal salvation, not austerity, encouraged Protestant indifference to the poor.

Philanthropy on the Fringe of Empire:
Charity in British North America

Britain's North American colonies, many of which would eventually form the United States, partially mirrored these changes in the metropolis. Waves of Protestant settlers, including both Boston's Puritans and Philadelphia's Quakers, for example, valued charitable acts as evidence of salvation, not steps toward it. Even highly conservative Puritan ministers like Cotton Mather (1663–1728) argued that charitable acts brought material rewards. In *Bonifacius: An Essay upon the Good* (1710), Mather promised his readers that those who dedicated themselves to charity could expect "surprising prosperity of their affairs." For Mather, the benefits of charity explained how "small mechanics, or husbandmen, have risen to estates, which once they never durst have dreamed of."[5] Although Mather accepted that good works might bring material wealth, he remained a committed advocate of the poor unlike many London philanthropists at the turn of the eighteenth century. Mather admonished audiences to "Remember the Poor" by distributing poor relief in money or goods, not merely access to education, employment, and medical services in times of financial need.

Benjamin Franklin's (1706–1790) philanthropic efforts in Philadelphia brought the colony and metropolis into alignment by liberally borrowing London's charitable assumptions about material rewards and indifference to the poor. Franklin was not only a voracious reader of European thought, but was also a frequent traveler. As a major consumer of British print culture, he encountered writings like Daniel Defoe's (1660–1731) *Essay on Projects* (1697), which suggested that well-organized, private philanthropic projects might generate positive economic returns to the larger community. As a colonial diplomat stationed in London, Franklin also encountered leading authorities who sought to reform the nation's prisons, schools, asylums, and hospitals. These thinkers expected that marshalling the nation's labor through educational ventures and public works would serve the common good and alleviate the suffering of poor and working folk.

Franklin's role in the creation of Philadelphia's first hospital underscores his connection to, and appreciation of, charitable principles that imagined an expanded economic role for philanthropic action. The hospital's promotional pamphlets argued that both material and spiritual benefits would follow its construction. Franklin's account of the institution's founding drew upon what had by then become familiar expectations of Protestant charity. In his initial petition to the state legislature, Franklin promised that the hospital "will be a good Work, acceptable to GOD" because "Relief of the Sick Poor is not only an Act of Humanity, but a religious Duty."[6] Likewise, his newspaper's campaign for the hospital drew heavily on the parable of the Good Samaritan. Franklin advised his readers that they should "hear the Voice of this Samaritan," who extolled the material benefits of charity, "as if it were the Voice of GOD sounding in our Ear."[7] The hospital's design also promoted widespread donations to exhibit public piety. Small donations of £10 bought a voice in Britain's growing benevolent empire by giving these patrons a chance to "elect by Ballot."[8] Donors, according to Franklin, would also be able to gain public recognition as benevolent and involved members of the community.

Franklin argued that the hospital served as a "work of Publick Service."[9] He viewed this service not only as an act of charity, but also as a path toward sustained economic growth that rested on marshalling a nation's productive powers. Franklin was a frequent public advocate, even before the hospital campaign, of harnessing the Empire's changing demographics to cement its strength. In *The Nature and Necessity of a Paper Currency* (1729), he equated Britain's national power with its productive capacity. Paper currency, he then argued, unlocked these productive energies because it would enable farmers to buy land and artisans to secure small loans. Almost twenty-five years later, he characterized the hospital as an efficient means to harness the state's productive power. By curing the sick, Franklin hoped the hospital would restore "the useful and laborious Members to a community."[10] Effective management of labor, Franklin claimed, would bring a variety of financial rewards that included elevating Philadelphia's status, increasing its trade, and educating its doctors.

Franklin's dual appeal to rewards, both religious and secular, helped secure the campaign's success. The Pennsylvania Assembly and the governor approved the hospital's charter in 1756 in no small part thanks to Franklin's philanthropic efforts. In fusing philanthropy and economic principles, mainstream philanthropy became synonymous with economic growth. It was under an ideology that was equal parts humanitarian and economic that an important segment of the early republic's reformers shaped their efforts.[11] Prisons and workhouses disciplined their wards not only to punish the guilty or idle, but also to protect formal commerce carried on by merchants from the type of petty retailing poor and working-class folk that political leaders considered detrimental to imperial, and later, national wealth.

The Moral Economy Remains:
The Rise and Fall of the United Society for Manufacturers

Unlike in Pennsylvania, religious tradition, not institutional disruption, maintained Massachusetts's moral economy before and throughout the Revolutionary era. New Englanders still measured their charitable efforts against the religious notions that idealized the universal altruism embodied by the Good Samaritan story far into the eighteenth century. As late as 1720, Reverend Thomas Foxcroft of Boston pleaded with his congregation to practice charitable habits which "must reach unto all, whether our own Country, Acquaintances and Relatives, or Strangers, Aliens and Foreigners."[12] Though dominant, Foxcroft's position was not unassailable. By the mid-eighteenth century, prominent intellectuals Thomas Hobbes and Bernard Mandeville challenged the relevance of disinterested charity on the premise that greed formed the basis of all human conduct.[13] These ideological extremes yielded tangible results in colonial New England, where some philanthropists sought to remake economic self-interest into the region's moral economy.

The most notable attempt at reframing charitable assumptions involved Boston's first experiment in female factory labor. The pauperism crisis began after King George's War when returning veterans, widows, and orphaned children suddenly ballooned the taxes that subsidized public welfare. Confronted by an ever-growing poor rate and unable to convince the state to revise its tax laws, Boston's political and financial leaders turned to institutional philanthropy, popular in London, to halt rising poor tax rates. Christened by its founders as the United Society for Manufacturers (USM) in 1748, the charity advertised that it would eliminate tax hikes for public welfare by employing widows and children in cloth manufacturing.[14]

In a city where the majority still understood charity as a religious duty, the USM's founders immediately encountered problems. The new philanthropic venture, with its promises to unite economic principles and charitable zeal, initially attracted few subscribers among a citizenry determined to maintain all things orthodox. The charity's intended beneficiaries also avoided the institutions. The employment-as-welfare offered by the institution likely attracted few participants because its design so closely resembled that of the public workhouses erected throughout the 1720s, while its labor required looming skills that even many urban New Englanders lacked.[15] In making production its main objective, the USM's design encroached on charitable traditions that associated relief with the alleviation of individual suffering, rather than the material wellbeing of its advocates.

The society's unorthodox goals proved unappealing to Boston's broader community and frightened away both benefactors and beneficiaries from the project during its first two years of operation. Backers revived the failing project when they leased a new building and dropped their former name in 1750. As the more benevolent sounding Society for Encouraging Industry and the Employment of the Poor, the organizers offered free spinning schools and began production in 1751. The work, however, did not last long. A smallpox epidemic among Boston's lower classes "completely destroyed the linen manufacture," the *Boston Post-Boy* reported in 1752.[16]

Disinterest and disease failed to curb the promoters' enthusiasm for private institutional charity, which sought to realign charity along economic, rather than entirely religious principles. One USM promoter, Reverend Samuel Cooper, candidly admitted that the charitable "Temper" he and his colleagues recommended "does in the most effectual Manner advance our own private Interest." Still, he couched these profit motives with scriptural appeals. Cooper asserted that "Charity seeketh not her own, yet she always *finds it*."[17] In doing so, he suggested that self-interest, or "Self-Love" as he phrased it, was a desire that might be domesticated and brought to serve virtue, a claim that would have sat well with Hobbes or Mandeville. The theology of self-interest, for Cooper, intertwined with religious duty. The USM's fitful existence disturbs conventional narratives of American philanthropy that charitable intentions and economic interests are not naturally aligned, but follow cultural conventions. In Boston's case, the altruism, exemplified by Foxcroft's rhetoric and embedded in everyday practice, prevented serious consideration of the benevolence offered by the USM's promoters.

Just six years after Cooper's sermon, the United Society for Manufacturers closed its doors in 1758. Even in times of economic hardship brought on by war, Bostonians rejected charitable vision offered by the Society for Encouraging Industry and the Employment of the Poor. The society's few subscribers and its attempt at rebranding itself demonstrate the durability of the old charitable calculus. Locals maintained a healthy skepticism of efforts to institutionalize care that smacked of self-interest and rejected anything less than universal benevolence. The region could not revive its efforts to unite charity with either individual or state economic interests until the 1820s.

The Elitist Origins of Charitable Reform

Attempts to realign charity with economic principles resulted from the hardships that visited New York City in the years before and after the War of 1812. Thomas Jefferson's decision to confront British impressment of Americans with an embargo caused considerable job losses in New York and drastically increased the city's commitment to poor relief. The conflict's conclusion, which ended wartime production and Europe's need for American goods, unleashed another period of joblessness and indigence on the city. These episodes once again renewed discussions about charity's function in New York, and eventually throughout the nation.[18]

Convinced that New York's economic hardships required more than immediate relief, a close-knit group of municipal officials, bankers, merchants, and other professionals formed the Society for the Prevention of Pauperism (SPP) in 1817. The group's notables included DeWitt Clinton, Cadwallader D. Colden, Stephen Allen, Thomas Eddy, John Griscom, and John Murray Jr. Together Clinton, Colden, and Allen's mayoral terms represented more than two decades in the office from 1803 to 1824. In addition to their political careers, Colden worked as a lawyer and Allen retired as a successful merchant. Quaker, businessman, and philanthropist Thomas Eddy obtained his wealth through speculating on public funds and selling insurance. Eddy's lifelong friend John Murray Jr. gained his fortune as a banker. John Griscom worked as a teacher and education advocate before joining the SPP. These men embodied New York's elite, which made their alliance in SPP particularly powerful.[19]

Their past charitable work and public service also made some of these men respected philanthropists before their work in the SPP. Clinton shaped some of the city's most important cultural institutions. Under his guidance, and with his political support and patronage, Clinton served as an officer in the Free School Society, the American Academy of Fine Arts, the New York Historical Society, the Humane Society, and many others. John Griscom gained Clinton's attention for his experience with, and support of, the Lancasterian educational system, a British innovation that promoted peer tutoring, which enabled far greater numbers of students to be taught by a single instructor. Fluent in the leading theorists on prison reform, Eddy successfully convinced New York's legislature to establish the state's first penitentiary. Prison advocacy led Eddy to broader attempts at criminal reform, a campaign that gained Colden's attention in 1800. Their influence, then, derived not only from their wealth and power, but also from their longstanding roots in, and understanding of, charitable work.

When they approached the problem of pauperism, these men did not look to the past, but to the most current theories regarding education, economics, and prison reform. At Columbia University, Alexander Hamilton exposed Clinton to the fundamentals of political economy.[20] Thomas Eddy maintained correspondence with Patrick Colquhoun, a leading British political economist who considered the poor an untapped reservoir of national wealth.[21] John Griscom toured Europe after the group's earliest discussions about pauperism in order to obtain information from the region's most recognized philanthropists. Their common interest, intellectually as well as fiscally, lay in restructuring charity as philanthropy.[22]

When these men did look to the past, they consulted those efforts, not of the mutual aid societies or religious charitable efforts, but rather those earlier attempts that merged economic interest with humanitarian desire. To this end, they praised the New York Society for the Promotion of Industry, formed in 1814 which, like Boston's United Society for Manufacturers, sought to provide textile factory work for female laborers.[23] Benjamin Franklin also remained a charitable reference point for Thomas Eddy, who urged listeners to follow the printer's economic precepts and philanthropic example.[24] The ideas of this group of reformers shows that influential philanthropists of the 1810s and 1820s had little desire to recreate the rural, static, social order that came before them or the charitable practices that had held that order together. Instead, the unprecedented scope of pauperism after 1815 inspired a renewed surge of philanthropic thinking from urban leaders and activists who feared that conventional philanthropy, with its altruistic bent, might weaken the national economy and ultimately destroy the nation.

Charity Remade—New York Society for the Prevention of Pauperism and the Remaking of American Philanthropy

In its inaugural report, the SPP identified pauperism, and the public alms it relied upon, as a national problem that could be solved only through "judicious management." They conceived of traditional Christian benevolence, which made few distinctions among its beneficiaries and provided immediate relief rather than job training, as wholly inadequate. Failure to reform charitable practice, the society prophesied, would collapse "some of the pillars of social order." The SPP imported these visions of destruction from Britain where the "greatest efforts ... to provide for the sufferings of the poor" caused "enormous taxation." For the society, such problems represented the most "perplexing ... and imposing departments of political economy." As an issue of both moral and economic concern, pauperism's solution required "radical change" to remedy the "evil [that] lies deep in the foundation of our social and moral institutions."[25]

The society found that radical change came by redefining both the nature of poverty and society's role in fighting pauperism. Borrowing extensively from British political economist Patrick Colquhoun, SPP's committee on idleness and employment reminded audiences that poverty was simply a condition where the "individual has no surplus labour ... and consequently no property, but what is derived from the constant exercise of industry." Poverty (subsistence labor), therefore, was an "indispensable ingredient in society" because without it, there would be no incentive to keep or acquire wealth. As the foundation of wealth, poverty was "inseparable from society." Without it, there would be "no riches, no refinement," and "no benefit" to those "who may be possessed of wealth." For SPP, poverty benefitted society by encouraging individuals to accumulate wealth.[26]

Indigence remained the real evil for Colquhoun. If poverty denoted "adequate ability, and no more," indigence signified the absence of the ability to labor. People became indigent when their labor could not provide for their subsistence. Using these distinctions, Colquhoun concluded that civil society's "great object is ... to call forth and to render profitable, the greatest possible amount of industry" by "wise regulations," which prevented the "poor from descending to a state of indigence."[27] Colquhoun's distinctions between poverty and indigence suggest that correct charitable action must improve labor and exert control through state-sanctioned regulations and expanded control through groups such as the SPP. This construct also made it clear that the nation's wealth and civilization were the rewards for a state that successfully extracted labor from indigence.[28]

To defeat the pauperism created by indigence, the SPP promoted two institutions that fused charity and economic interest: the savings banks and the House of Refuge for Juvenile delinquents. The banks required deposits of only a dollar, which reform advocates explained would enable the "laboring classes to make the most of their earnings."[29] Account holders could more easily deposit money and accumulate wealth to help prevent pauperism. If the savings bank assisted those Colquhoun and the SPP deemed poor, then the House of Refuge targeted the indigent. By institutionalizing minors twenty-one and under, the Refuge hoped to prevent indigence through the occupational and moral training of the city's criminal and abandoned youth.

Both ideas fused humanitarian impulses and economic principles. Individual savings, the SPP thought, safeguarded workers during their periods of scarcity, while the House of Refuge realized the importance of separating juvenile offenders from their adult counterparts. Yet, both innovations promised to enhance the nation's wealth in a variety of ways. Early nineteenth-century Americans worried that the country would remain beholden to foreigners, especially the British, if they continued to rely upon them for their cheap goods. Philanthropy became a critical ally in forging an independent national economy rooted in domestic consumption and production. The fiscal discipline, symbolized by the bank, promised to undermine pawn brokers and the many petty vendors who derived their livelihood from selling and buying imported goods. The value of benevolence remained embedded in juvenile detention. Institutionalizing the youth provided occupational training that the SPP hoped would increase the nation's agricultural and manufacturing power by transforming delinquent and abandoned children into farmers and artisans. In promoting individual savings and juvenile detention, SPP members hoped to advance a national economy grounded in wealth.

Unlike Franklin's efforts or those of the USM in colonial Boston, the SPP's work attracted attention and inspired action at the local and state levels. New York's legislature chartered the state's first savings bank in 1819 soon after the SPP's second report.[30] Until 1860, state legislatures authorized and, for the most part, funded juvenile asylums that copied New York's model.[31] As systems of labor extraction founded to enrich the state and its elites, these institutions legitimized only charitable designs that contained a demonstrable labor component. In doing so, these reformers embedded the principles of political economy within institutions of charitable relief. Wealth, rather than wellbeing, became the established motive that guided municipal and state interaction with vulnerable populations.

The wide adoption of savings banks and juvenile asylums represented the beginning of the charitable feedback loop in the United States. Combating poverty and pauperism with economic principle, SPP reformers' emphasis on charity's value to the state and society created an altruism deficit responsible for exacerbating inequality. Long after the SPP's chief institutions came under scrutiny by antebellum populists, philanthropically-minded policymakers, employers, and middle-class Americans continued to calculate how charitable action might be used to compel work and enrich elites.

Our current, neoliberal fetishization of economic growth continues to influence thinking about inequality and, more importantly, our response to these inequalities. Philanthropic efforts often remain largely indifferent to the needs of the poorest Americans and, as a consequence, confront inequality with institutions or programs aimed at providing basic job skills and building our future workforce. For example, in a 2005 speech at the National Education Summit on High Schools, Bill Gates attributed his interest in public education to fears that the nation's workforce would lose its competitive edge in world markets.[32] The Baltimore protests over the police shooting death of Freddie Gray sparked prolonged national discussion not only about police use of force, but also about its connections to inequality. Presidential candidate Jeb Bush pointed to a failed public education system that was unable to give students the skills needed to traverse the occupational ladder as an underlying cause for the inequality that fueled the 2015 protests.[33] While ostensibly hoping to end inequality through institutionally organized economic growth, Gates' and Bush's opinions harken directly back to Franklin's efforts to employ philanthropy as means to secure the state's wealth and create public order.

Conclusion—Trusting the Beneficiary, Ending the Feedback Loop

The philanthropic paradigm created by Protestant dissenters, remade by Benjamin Franklin, and recently channeled by policymakers and philanthropists today, carries significant benefits. Twentieth-century philanthropy, and the ideology that organized it, established the research institutions necessary to improve public health and provide greater access to education. These victories, however, should not be allowed to obscure the fact that our long-standing commitment to uplift-oriented charity wrongly blames the poor for their plight and denies more effective means to fight inequality.

Brazil's recent efforts against poverty demonstrate the kind of reforms needed to make philanthropic aid more effective. Mired in political instability and hyperinflation that trapped a third of its population below the international poverty line (surviving on $2 a day), Brazillian President Luiz Inácio Lula da Silva decided to radically change how the country fought inequality. Lula started the Family Grant initiative which, instead of offering the poor only institutional solutions such as education, rehabilitation, and incarceration, provided needy folk with cash. As *Foreign Affairs* writer Jonathan Tepperman notes, the plan made officials throughout the country nervous. However, the program's success soon showed these fears to be grossly misplaced. What Lula understood, and what more academic studies suggest, is that "the people who best understood what the poor really needed were the poor themselves," according to Tepperman.[34]

The needs of our country's poor and working folk demand better than a philanthropy of self-interest to escape today's charitable feedback loop. They deserve our compassion, respect, and the meaningful, systematic aid that accompanies it. It is ultimately our intellectual commitment to a consumerism that fetishizes the individual which condemns poor Americans to a charitable feedback that perpetuates inequality. This system, tied to eighteenth and early nineteenth-century charitable values that celebrate accumulation while refusing to acknowledge its ties to scarcity, prevents meaningful solutions to this chronic problem. As inequality, unemployment, and underemployment continue to expand, American leaders can no longer speak condescendingly about the benefits of training and hard work. As Donald Trump's racist populism demonstrates, the problem can no longer be ignored. Our moment requires nothing less than true Samaritans.

Notes

1   Laura Sullivan, "In Search Of The Red Cross' $500 Million in Haiti Relief," National Public Radio, June 3, 2015, http://www.npr.org/2015/06/03/411524156/in-search-of-the-red-cross-500-million-in-haiti-relief.

2   Gideon Rose, "Inequality," *Foreign Affairs*, January/February 2016, https://www.foreignaffairs.com/articles/world/2015-12-08/inequality.

3   Thomas Fuller, *History of the Worthies of England*, quoted in Mordechai Feingold, "Philanthropy, Pomp, and Patronage: Historical Reflections upon the Endowment of Culture," *Daedalus* 116, No. 1 (Winter 1987): 162.

4   Thomas Browne, quoted in Feingold, "Philanthropy, Pomp, and Patronage," 163.

5   Cotton Mather, *Bonifacius: An Essay upon the Good,* originally published in 1710 (Cambridge: Harvard University Press, 1966), 111.

6   Benjamin Franklin, "'To the Honourable House of Representative of the Province of Pennsylvania: The Petition of Sundry Inhabitants of the Said Province," (January 1750-1) in *Some Account of the Pennsylvania Hospital* (1754); reprint: Baltimore: Johns Hopkins Press, 1954, 4.

7   Benjamin Franklin, *Pennsylvania Gazette,* (8-15-1751) in *Some Account of the Pennsylvania Hospital* (1754); reprint: Baltimore: Johns Hopkins Press, 1954, 22.

8   Benjamin Franklin, *Some Account of the Pennsylvania Hospital; From its first Rise, to the Beginning of the Fifth Month, called May, 1754* (Philadelphia: B. Franklin and D. Hall, 1754), Papers of Benjamin Franklin, American Philosophical Society and Yale University, http://franklinpapers.org/franklin//framedVolumes.jsp;jsessionid=FB9AD5977B3A8C3AE4CBFA74196E798D.

9   Benjamin Franklin, "An Act to Encourage the Establishing of an Hospital for the Relief of the Sick Poor of this Province, and for the Reception and Cure of Lunaticks," in *Some Account of the Pennsylvania Hospital* (1754); reprint (Baltimore: Johns Hopkins Press, 1954), 5.

10 Benjamin Franklin, "Paper Currency," in *The Papers of Benjamin Franklin,* vol. 1. http://franklinpapers.org/franklin//framedVolumes.jsp.

11 G.J. Barker-Benfield, "The Origins of Anglo-American Sensibility," in *Charity, Philanthropy, and Civility in American History* (Cambridge: Cambridge University Press, 2002), 73, 83.

12 Quoted from Conrad Edick Wright, *The Transformation of Charity in Postrevolutionary New England* (Boston: Northeastern University Press, 1992), 20.

13 Ibid., 21.

14 Gary B. Nash, *The Urban Crucible: The Northern Seaports and the Origins of the Americans Revolution* (Cambridge: Harvard University Press, 1986), 118.

15 Ibid.

16 Quoted from Gary B. Nash, *The Urban Crucible,* 118.

17 Samuel Cooper, *A Sermon Preached in Boston ... August 8, 1753* (Boston: Draper for Henchman, 1753), 21.

18 Raymond A. Mohl, "Humanitarianism in the Preindustrial City: The New York Society for the Prevention of Pauperism, 1817–1823," *The Journal of American History* 57, No. 3 (Dec 1970): 577.

19 "John Griscom," *Dictionary of American Biography* (New York: Charles Scribner's Sons, 1936), *Biography in Context*, http://link.galegroup.com.libezp.lib.lsu.edu/apps/doc/BT2310012277/BIC1?u=lln_alsu&xid=d9fecbda; Clinton and Eddy's role as political and economic elites see Brian Phillips Murphy, *Building the Empire State: Political Economy in the Early Republic* (Philadelphia: University of Pennsylvania Press, 2015), 170, 184.

20 James Renwick, *Life of Dewitt Clinton* (New York: Harper and Brothers, 1840), 29.

21 Samuel Lorenzo Knapp, *Life of Thomas Eddy: Comprising an Extensive Correspondence with many of the most Distinguished Philosophers and Philanthropists of this and other Countries* (New York: Conner and Cooke, 1834), 181.

22 John H. Griscom, "John Griscom, LL.D.: Late Professor of Chemistry and Natural Philosophy; With an Account of the New York High School; the Society for the Prevention of Pauperism; the House of Refuge; and other Institutions," 164.

23 Raymond A. Mohl, "Humanitarianism in the Preindustrial City: The New York Society for the Prevention of Pauperism, 1817–1823," 586.

24 Samuel Lorenzo Knapp, *Life of Thomas Eddy*, 32.

25 John Griscom, *Report to the Managers of the Society for the Prevention of Pauperism in New York; By their Committee on Idleness and Sources of Employment* (New York: Clayton and Kingsland 1819), 3–4.

26 Ibid.

27 Ibid., 5

28 G.J. Barker-Benfield's "The Origins of Anglo-American Sensibility," in *Charity, Philanthropy, and Civility in American History*, 84, 86.

29 John Griscom, *Report of A Committee on the Subject of Pauperism* (New York: Samuel Wood and Sons, 1819), Ibid., 13.

30 John Griscom, *Memoir of John Griscom*, 162.

31 B.K. Pierce, *A Half Century with Juvenile Delinquents; Or The New York House of Refuge and its Times* (New York: D. Appleton and Company, 1869), 248.

32 Bill Gates, "Remarks at National Education Summit on High Schools," accessed April 13, 2017, http://www.gatesfoundation.org/media-center/speeches/2005/02/bill-gates-2005-national-education-summit.

33 Jeb Bush, "Commentary: Jeb Bush's War on Poverty revamp," *Chicago Tribune*, May 6, 2015, http://www.chicagotribune.com/news/opinion/commentary/ct-jeb-bush-

war-poverty-poor-educaton-reform-opportunity-perspec-0506-jm-20150506-story.html.

34 Jonathan Tepperman, "Inequality," *Foreign Affairs*, January/February 2016, https://www.foreignaffairs.com/articles/brazil/2015-12-14/brazils-antipoverty-breakthrough.

CONCLUSION: POLICING PATRIOTISM AND THE RESPONSIBILITIES OF ACTIVIST HISTORY

Cory James Young
Georgetown University

Abraham Lincoln used the occasion of his First Inaugural Address on March 4, 1861 to attempt to calm the fears of his political opponents. "While the people retain their virtue and vigilance," Lincoln reminded a sundered nation, "no Administration by any extreme of wickedness or folly can very seriously injure the Government in the short space of four years."[1] Secessionists in South Carolina disregarded his plea for level-headedness and commenced the Civil War five weeks later. Indeed, the Confederates— in what is surely one of history's most incredible ironies—managed to destroy their own government in the short space four years. Contemporary Americans must learn from the Confederate failure: now more than ever, when there seems to be no shortage of wickedness and folly emanating from the administration of President Donald Trump, the people must retain their virtue and vigilance.

Demand the Impossible is an experiment in doing activist history. While the twelve essays in this volume each approach the task somewhat differently, the end result is a collection of histories that speak deliberately to the present moment. Some, like Sarah Senette's biography of Pompeyo (and black masculinity) on trial, examine the deep foundations of contemporary phenomena. Others, like Kyla Sommers' elegant and unyielding compilation of anti-black federal policy toward D.C., showcase more direct continuities between past and present. Kathleen Brian's essay on the fundamentally exclusionary nature of the U.S. insurance industry and Tessa Davis' study of the cultural import of U.S. tax policy are perhaps this volume's clearest cases of history as activism—instances where comprehending the history itself is essential to fighting for change. And a few, including Ben Feldman's opening essay (from which this book takes its title) and David Rotenstein's piece on racism and public space in Silver Spring, call us to action as scholars and activists. All four "types"—foundations, continuities, histories for activists, and calls to action—constitute activist history.

The questions that historians ask about the past have always been asked from the present; this is not what makes activist history unique. Instead, activist history asserts that scholars are themselves historical actors. It recognizes that historians use the past to make arguments, implicitly or explicitly, about their own present—and encourages them to do so. This does not mean that the essays in this collection are somehow more subjective than other forms of historical writing. Rather, these pieces not only acknowledge that contemporary events shape the types of questions we ask, but also that the answers we find might help us to better society. As Douglas McRae watched the debates over Confederate statue removal from São Paulo, for instance, he realized that Brazil's own history of valorizing conquerors could both speak to the U.S. experience and point to the necessity of removal in the twenty-first century. Tom Foley worried about the human and financial costs of the Trump administration's failure to embrace the third energy shift and so examined the history of successful government investment in coal and oil. Jade Shepherd lamented the shortcomings of modern mental health care and sought wisdom in the lessons learned from dismantling the British asylum system. These modern concerns invite historical questions, and the answers historians find must help guide us toward innovative and effective policy.

The opening paragraph of the American Historical Association's 2016 statement on the nature and goals of the discipline declares that history "requires empathy for historical actors." The AHA statement then asserts that a learning outcome of practicing the historical method is to develop "empathy toward people in the context of their distinct historical moments."[2] *Demand the Impossible* contends that active engagement with the past should stoke compassion not just for "historical actors" but also for their descendants living in the present moment. By organizing activist scholarship into thematic couplets, this volume highlights the value of thinking comparatively about time periods, regions, and topics. Although reading outside one's research field can reveal useful methods and insightful questions, it is perhaps most important as an exercise in empathy. Activist history brings together scholars who might not otherwise remember to converse with one another. History is, of course, replete with examples of the value of bringing together disparate voices to struggle for a shared goal.

In January 1817, 200 years before the inauguration of Donald Trump, some 3000 free black Philadelphians assembled at the Mother Bethel African Methodist Episcopal Church to discuss their response to the recently formed American Colonization Society (ACS). The goal of the ACS was essentially to deport free blacks to Africa. Then as now, proponents of the "go home to Africa" movement did not especially care that the targets of their derision had been born in the United States (and in some cases had families who had been in the Americas for longer than they had); that was irrelevant. Prominent black leaders like Richard Allen, James Forten, and Absalom Jones all spoke in favor of colonization. The movement did have some black support, especially from well-to-do folks who were tired of staring through the stained glass ceiling that separated white and black America. It appeared possible that colonization would create leadership opportunities for frustrated African American professionals as well as insulate black progress from white racism.[3] The arrangement seemed promising. Yet when Forten called for supporters to come forward, not a single one of the 3000 attendees raised their hand. The rank-and-file representatives of black Philadelphia rejected colonization in a unanimous voice. Forten later reflected that "there was not a soul that was in favor of going to Africa" and that the force of their dissent seemed liable to "bring down the walls of the building."[4] This was a profound victory for democracy in an age where the United States did not recognize the legitimacy of most of its residents' political voices. In Philadelphia, the people were piloting the ship, and they elected to keep it anchored to American shores.

After much deliberation, the assembly voted on several resolutions rejecting colonization. Here is a brief overview of the language they employed: as the direct descendants of "the first cultivators of the wilds of America," black Philadelphians claimed a right to "the blessings of her luxuriant soil, which their blood and sweat manured." They expressed particular disdain for the "unmerited stigma" that free people of color posed a threat to the safety of a republic founded on principles of liberty for all. They associated military service with citizenship and suffrage, reminding advocates of colonization that, despite lacking the vote, black Patriots had "rallied around the standard of their country" to defeat the British during the Revolution. Most incredibly, however, the 3000 attendees of the Mother Bethel anti-colonization meeting vowed never to "separate voluntarily from the slave population in this country; they are our brethren by the ties of consanguinity, of suffering, and of wrongs; and we feel that there is more virtue in suffering privations with them, than fancied advantages for a season."[5]

In a remarkable act of democratic dissent, thousands of former slaves and their children announced that they would not be moved. They asserted their kinship with southern slaves and denounced all efforts to strip them of their northern allies. They firmly disavowed Jefferson's hypothesis in his *Notes on the State of Virginia* that "if a slave can have a country in this world, it must be any other in preference to that in which he is born to live and labour for another." Sensitive to the demands of his fellow countrymen, James Forten worked to oppose colonization and gradual abolition throughout the 1820s, sustaining the abolition movement in the face of white apathy, or what one historian has called the "perishability of revolutionary time."[6] The Philadelphia leadership continued to disavow colonization at the behest of their constituents. Within two years, the activists had explicitly tied colonization to the propagation of slavery in the United States. They recognized that colonizationists had no intention to "interfere with a species of property which they hold sacred" and that "any plan of colonization without the American continent or islands, will completely and permanently fix slavery in our common country." Note that the protesters expressed concern for their "common country," thereby asserting their right to a place in the nation they helped to build. Black Philadelphia came out against "every measure that may have a tendency to convey an idea that they give the project a single particle of countenance or encouragement."[7] It was due to the continued agitation of black men and women that U.S. abolitionism rejected colonization in favor of a racially integrated politics.

This is an inspiring lesson for those of us striving today for a more just and tolerant society. The movement to oppose deportation was headed by a grassroots coalition who understood that skin color should not form the basis of American citizenship. They forcefully reminded their opponents that black and unfree Americans had toiled, sweat, bled, fought, and died for the United States, which was their country. They fought for the principle of inclusion by refusing to abandon their homes—by demanding to be seen. This is a provocative lesson for those of us fighting for our own causes in the twenty-first century. So too must we refuse to be moved.

In his 2014 book *The Half Has Never Been Told*, Edward Baptist argues that violence was the essential technology by which antebellum cotton planters coerced from their enslaved cotton pickers the massive amounts of labor increasingly required to sustain the mechanized textile industry. Baptist states correctly in his introduction that dismissing the centrality of the enslaved to this nineteenth-century boom functions as a means of denying that "the massive quantities of wealth and treasure piled by that economic growth is owed to African Americans."[8] In their now-withdrawn review of his work, *The Economist* declared: "This is not history; it is advocacy."[9] Yet this is a false distinction: historians, by our very nature, are advocates for increasing public awareness of the topics we study. This is why we research, teach, and publish. This is why we educate and advise. Activist historians differ only in our assertion that the topics we study might help us steer toward justice. So of course we celebrate the abolitionists. Of course we stand with the slaves and the freedpeople.

In 1852 Frederick Douglass delivered his now famous "What to the Slave is the Fourth of July" address before the Rochester Ladies Anti-Slavery Society, not far from the town where I grew up in Western New York. He condemned slavery with fiery rhetoric and despaired the failures of the revolutionary freedom movement. Yet he knew then that the slave's history was American history, and that this shared experience provided a way forward: "We have to do with the past only as we can make it useful to the present and future."[10] Douglass concluded his speech that day by reciting William Lloyd Garrison's poem, "God Speed the Year of Jubilee." It seems fitting to conclude this work with that poem's final stanza, which calls for vigilance in the face of staggering adversity and for action in the name of a more equitable future:

> Until that year, day, hour, arrive,
> With head, and heart, and hand I'll strive,
> To break the rod, and rend the gyve,
> The spoiler of his prey deprive—
> So witness Heaven!
> And never from my chosen post,
> Whate'er the peril or the cost,
> Be driven.

Notes

1   "First Inaugural Address of Abraham Lincoln," The Avalon Project: Documents in Law, History, and Diplomacy, 2008, http://avalon.law.yale.edu/19th_century/lincoln1.asp.

2   Thanks to Katie Benton-Cohen for bringing this to my attention. See "AHA History Tuning Project: 2016 History Discipline Core," American Historical Association, https://www.historians.org/teaching-and-learning/tuning-the-history-discipline/2016-history-discipline-core (accessed September 7, 2017).

3   Gary Nash, *Forging Freedom: The Formation of Philadelphia's Free Black Community, 1720–1840* (Cambridge, MA: Harvard University Press, 1988), 235–237.

4   Quoted in Nash, *Forging Freedom*, 238.

5   "Colonization," *American Watchman* (Wilmington, DE), September 20, 1817, 4 cited in Gary J. Kornblith, ed. *Slavery and Sectional Strife in the Early American Republic, 1776–1821* (New York: Rowman and Littlefield, 2009), 137–138.

6   David Brion Davis, *The Problem of Slavery in the Age of Revolution, 1770–1823* (New York: Oxford University Press, 1975), 306.

7   "Protest and Remonstrance of the People of Colour," *American Watchman* (Wilmington, DE), November 24, 1819, 3.

8   Edward Baptist, *The Half Has Never Been Told: Slavery and the Making of American Capitalism* (New York: Basic Books, 2014), xix.

9   "Our withdrawn review 'Blood cotton'," *The Economist*, https://www.economist.com/news/books/21615864-how-slaves-built-american-capitalism-blood-cotton (accessed September 7, 2017).

10 David Zirin, "'What to the Slave Is the Fourth of July' by Frederick Douglass," *The Nation*. July 24, 2012, https://www.thenation.com/article/what-slave-fourth-july-frederick-douglass/ (accessed September 7, 2017).

CPSIA information can be obtained
at www.ICGtesting.com
Printed in the USA
LVHW05s2313240718
584848LV00009B/327/P